INTRODUCING LYOTARD

The surge of interest in Jean-François Lyotard's writings has pushed him into the centre of debate on the postmodern. His willingness to question the political and to investigate the intersection of art and politics undermines the charge that deconstruction has abdicated its political responsibility. This introduction, by discussing the entire range of Lyotard's writing, situates his interest in the postmodern in terms of a larger project of rethinking the politics of representation.

Bill Readings traces Lyotard's attacks on structuralism, Marxism and semiotics, contrasts his work with the literary deconstruction of Paul de Man and draws out the implications of post-structuralism's attention to *difference* in reading. The art of reading and the reading of art, as the evocation of the difference of events, displace both consumer culture and Romantic nostalgia.

This book performs an introduction of Lyotard's work to current debates in Anglophone critical theory. All with an interest in those debates will benefit from the first truly introductory text on Lyotard. In addition, students with an interest in art, philosophy, and literature will find the discussion of Lyotard's writings on these subjects a useful point of departure for critical thought.

Bill Readings is Assistant Professor of English at Syracuse University, New York.

D0024396

CRITICS OF THE TWENTIETH CENTURY

General Editor: Christopher Norris,
University of Wales,
College of Cardiff

A. J. GREIMAS AND THE NATURE OF MEANING
Ronald Schleifer

CHRISTOPHER CAUDWELL
Robert Sullivan

FIGURING LACAN
CRITICISM AND THE CULTURAL UNCONSCIOUS
Juliet Flower MacCannell

HAROLD BLOOM
TOWARDS HISTORICAL RHETORICS
Peter de Bolla

F. R. LEAVIS
Michael Bell

POSTMODERN BRECHT
A RE-PRESENTATION
Elizabeth Wright

DELEUZE AND GUATTARI
Ronald Bogue

ECSTASIES OF ROLAND BARTHES
Mary Wiseman

JULIA KRISTEVA
John Lechte

GEOFFREY HARTMAN
CRITICISM AS ANSWERABLE STYLE
G. Douglas Atkins

EZRA POUND AS LITERARY CRITIC
K. K. Ruthven

PAUL RICOEUR
S. H. Clark

INTRODUCING LYOTARD

Art and Politics

Bill Readings

London and New York

First published 1991
by Routledge
11 New Fetter Lane, London EC4P 4EE

Simultaneously published in the USA and Canada
by Routledge
a division of Routledge, Chapman and Hall, Inc.
29 West 35th Street, New York, NY 10001

© 1991 Bill Readings

Typeset in 10/12pt Baskerville by
Redwood Press Ltd, Melksham, Wiltshire
Printed in Great Britain by
Redwood Press Ltd

All rights reserved. No part of this book may be reprinted or
reproduced or utilized in any form or by any electronic,
mechanical, or other means, now known or hereafter invented,
including photocopying and recording, or in any information
storage or retrieval system, without permission in writing from
the publishers.

British Library Cataloguing in Publication Data
Readings, Bill
Introducing Lyotard: art and politics – (Critics of the
twentieth century).
1. French philosophy. Lyotard, Jean François
I. Title II. Series
194

ISBN 0–415–02196–0
ISBN 0–415–05536–9 pbk

Library of Congress Cataloging-in-Publication Data
Readings, Bill
Introducing Lyotard: art and politics / Bill Readings.
p. cm. – (Critics of the twentieth century)
Includes bibliographical references.
ISBN 0–415–02196–0. – ISBN 0–415–05536–9 (pbk.)
1. Lyotard, Jean-François. 2. Deconstruction. 3. Postmodernism.
I. Title. II. Series: Critics of the twentieth century (London,
England)
B2430.L964R42 1991   90–32992
194—dc20   CIP

Contents

v

Editor's foreword

The twentieth century has produced a remarkable number of gifted and innovative literary critics. Indeed it could be argued that some of the finest literary minds of the age have turned to criticism as the medium best adapted to their complex and speculative range of interests. This has sometimes given rise to regret among those who insist on a clear demarcation between 'creative' (primary) writing on the one hand, and 'critical' (secondary) texts on the other. Yet this distinction is far from self-evident. It is coming under strain at the moment as novelists and poets grow increasingly aware of the conventions that govern their writing and the challenge of consciously exploiting and subverting those conventions. And the critics for their part – some of them at least – are beginning to question their traditional role as humble servants of the literary text with no further claim upon the reader's interest or attention. Quite simply, there are texts of literary criticism and theory that, for various reasons – stylistic complexity, historical influence, range of intellectual command – cannot be counted a mere appendage to those other 'primary' texts.

Of course, there is a logical puzzle here, since (it will be argued) 'literary criticism' would never have come into being, and could hardly exist as such, were it not for the body of creative writings that provide its *raison d'être*. But this is not quite the kind of knock-down argument that it might appear at first glance. For one thing, it conflates some very different orders of priority, assuming that literature always comes first (in the sense that Greek tragedy had to exist before Aristotle could formulate its rules), so that literary texts are for that very reason possessed of superior value. And this argument would seem to find commonsense support in the difficulty of thinking what 'literary criticism' could *be* if it seriously renounced all sense of

vii

the distinction between literary and critical texts. Would it not then find itself in the unfortunate position of a discipline that had willed its own demise by declaring its subject non-existent?

But these objections would only hit their mark if there were indeed a special kind of writing called 'literature' whose difference from other kinds of writing was enough to put criticism firmly in its place. Otherwise there is nothing in the least self-defeating or paradoxical about a discourse, nominally that of literary criticism, that accrues such interest on its own account as to force some fairly drastic rethinking of its proper powers and limits. The act of crossing over from commentary to literature – or of simply denying the difference between them – becomes quite explicit in the writing of a critic like Geoffrey Hartman. But the signs are already there in such classics as William Empson's *Seven Types of Ambiguity* (1928), a text whose trans-formative influence on our habits of reading must surely be ranked with the great creative moments of literary modernism. Only on the most dogmatic view of the difference between 'literature' and 'criti-cism' could a work like *Seven Types* be counted generically an inferior, sub-literary species of production. And the same can be said for many of the critics whose writings and influence this series sets out to explore.

Some, like Empson, are conspicuous individuals who belong to no particular school or larger movement. Others, like the Russian Formalists, were part of a communal enterprise and are therefore best understood as representative figures in a complex and evolving dia-logue. Then again there are cases of collective identity (like the so-called 'Yale deconstructors') where a mythical group image is invented for largely polemical purposes. (The volumes in this series on Hartman and Bloom should help to dispel the idea that 'Yale deconstruction' is anything more than a handy device for collapsing differences and avoiding serious debate.) So there is no question of a series format or house-style that would seek to reduce these differ-ences to a blandly homogeneous treatment. One consequence of recent critical theory is the realization that literary texts have no self-sufficient or autonomous meaning, no existence apart from their after-life of changing interpretations and values. And the same ap-plies to those *critical* texts whose meaning and significance are subject to constant shifts and realignments of interest. This is not to say that trends in criticism are just a matter of intellectual fashion or the merry-go-round of rising and falling reputations. But it is important to grasp how complex are the forces – the conjunctions of historical and cultural motive – that affect the first reception and the subsequent fortunes of a critical text. This point has been raised into a systematic programme by critics like Hans-Robert Jauss, practitioners of so-called 'reception theory' as a form of historical hermeneutics. The volumes in this series will therefore be concerned not only to expound what is of lasting significance but also to set these critics in the context of present-day argument and debate. In some cases (as with Walter Benjamin) this debate takes the form of a struggle for interpretative power among disciplines with sharply opposed ideological viewpoints. Such controversies cannot simply be ignored in the interests of achieving a clear and balanced account. They point to unresolved tensions and problems which are there in the critic's work as well as in the rival appropriative readings. In the end there is no way of drawing a neat methodological line between 'intrinsic' questions (what the critic really thought) and those other, supposedly 'extrinsic' concerns that have to do with influence and reception history.

The volumes will vary accordingly in their focus and range of coverage. They will also reflect the ways in which a speculative approach to questions of literary theory has proved to have striking consequences for the human sciences at large. This breaking-down of disciplinary bounds is among the most significant developments in recent critical thinking. As philosophers and historians, among others, come to recognize the rhetorical complexity of the texts they deal with, so literary theory takes on a new dimension of interest and relevance. It is scarcely appropriate to think of a writer like Derrida as practising in any conventional sense of the term. For one thing, he is as much concerned with 'philosophical' as with 'literary' texts, and has indeed actively sought to subvert (or deconstruct) such tidy distinctions. A principal object in planning this series was to take full stock of these shifts in the wider intellectual terrain (including the frequent boundary disputes) brought about by critical theory. And, of course, such changes are by no means confined to literary studies, philosophy and the so-called 'sciences of man'. It is equally the case in (say) nuclear physics and molecular biology that advances in the one field have decisive implications for the other, so that specialized research often tends (paradoxically) to break down existing divisions of intellectual labour. Such work is typically many years ahead of the academic disciplines and teaching institutions that have obvious reasons of their own for adopting a business-as-usual attitude. One important aspect of modern critical theory is the challenge it presents to these traditional ideas. And lest it be thought that this is merely a one-sided takeover bid by literary critics, the series will include a number of volumes by authors in those other disciplines, including, for instance, a study of Roland Barthes by an American analytical philosopher.

We shall not, however, cleave to theory as a matter of polemical or principled stance. The series will extend to figures like F. R. Leavis, whose widespread influence went along with an express aversion to literary theory; scholars like Erich Auerbach in the mainstream European tradition; and others who resist assimilation to any clear-cut line of descent. There will also be authoritative volumes on critics such as Northrop Frye and Lionel Trilling, figures who, for various reasons, occupy an ambivalent or essentially contested place in modern critical tradition. Above all the series will strive to resist that current polarization of attitudes that sees no common ground on interest between 'literary criticism' and 'critical theory'.

CHRISTOPHER NORRIS

Preface

Deconstruction's first impact was in literary theory, where it now teeters on the edge of an entropic state, the embers stirred only by the de Man controversy. This is in part an effect of the market: there are only so many 'applications' of Derrida possible before it becomes generally recognized that deconstruction problematizes interpretative method in ways that make it unattractive to those attempting to produce dissertations and books-for-tenure. It is paradoxical that the assault on deconstruction, fuelled though it may be by the structural necessities of the academic institution, is carried on in the name of the anti-institutional radicalism of the Left. The constant accusation against deconstruction in America is that it lacks political responsibility. Instances of this fill journals such as *Critical Inquiry*; the furore of the de Man affair is perhaps even more emblematic of the historico-political 'incorrectness' of which deconstruction stands accused. Figures such as Jon Wiener have greeted the revelation of de Man's juvenile publication of anti-Semitic material as 'historical proof' of the irresponsibility of deconstruction's problematization of such categories as 'historical proof'.

It is in the light of these conditions that the importance of Lyotard in the current American academic scene can hardly be underestimated. Lyotard's abiding concern with the intersection of art and politics, his willingness to question the political, has made him one of the most urgently discussed figures on the 'theoretical scene' of literary and cultural studies. His work seems most directly to address the kinds of criticism being levelled against post-structuralism on the grounds of political relevance, even if only by virtue of his direct interrogation of precisely what is at stake in the criterion of 'political relevance'. The fact that this struggle has involved a contesting of the terrain of the postmodern has lent added impact to Lyotard's intervention.

Ironically, this book sets out to show that Lyotard's interest in the postmodern is not a matter of trend-spotting, though it is certainly an historical accident that he has become best known in the USA for having participated in this particular national obsession in cultural punditry. More significantly, taking on the term 'postmodernity' has led Lyotard's writing to be taken up across a number of disciplines: literature, philosophy, legal studies, political science, art history, intellectual history and cultural studies are some. Indeed, the name of Lyotard is one of the more cross-disciplinary sites of theoretical discussion in the American academy today (in a manner interestingly distinct from that of Derrida, who tends to be asked what 'deconstruction' can do for various fields). Lyotard's willingness to engage with the Frankfurt school, for example, has made his writing more urgent for American philosophy and political science departments than that of Derrida (for whom the British Left constructed a peculiarly post-Althusserian genealogy which had little purchase).

The effect of this in publishing has been a flow of translations, and the recent appearance of *The Differend*, along with the forthcoming *Discours, figure* should stimulate further interest, not least as they correct the understanding of Lyotard as primarily a theorist of the postmodern. Special issues of *Diacritics* and *SubStance* indicate the extent to which Lyotard has become, on the basis of the relatively small amount of material available in translation, a dominant figure on the theory circuit. And this in spite of the fact that he spends much of his time attacking the hegemony of theoretical metalanguages.

But if Lyotard's significance is certain, what is extremely debatable is the way in which his work will be linked to current debates in the Anglophone academic world: the belated or *nachträglich* nature of his arrival in English holds out the hope that his work may escape the institutional language game of master and disciple by which the work of Derrida and de Man have been so bedevilled. One of the reasons for Lyotard's escaping the fate of de Man and Derrida has to do with the fact that his work appears as of less than apocalyptic import. Without wishing to descend too far into punditry, one may hope that Lyotard's work will provide us with a way to re-read post-structuralism without having to rush towards slogans or banners, that it may allow us to realize that deconstruction is not simply the end of all hitherto existing theories and histories of art and philosophy.

The question of what happens to the name of Lyotard is a significant one. One may hope that rather than being the latest best hope of post-structuralism, or being the site of post-structuralism's engagement with that which it was (erroneously) believed to ignore or dismiss, a reading of Lyotard may offer the possibility for post-structuralism to throw off the cloak of 'theoretical metalanguage' under which it has been smuggled into the United States and get to work. Here, the cross-disciplinary aspect of Lyotard's work seems particularly crucial and relevant to the growing dispersion of the American academy.

Bill Readings
USA, August 1989

Acknowledgements

'History has a stutter. It says wh-wh-whoo- watch out'
The Mekons, 'Sympathy for the Mekons', *Honkytonkin'*
(Minnesota, Twin Tone Records, 1988)

The debts incurred in the writing of this book are immense. Diane Elam's contribution is too complex and extensive to admit of specification. I began to understand both its and the book's necessity in taking a seminar led by Hillis Miller. Stephen Melville gave the manuscript a careful and subtle reading that gave rise to many material changes. Among others who engaged me in the discussions to which it is addressed are Steve Cohan, Peter de Bolla, Wlad Godzich, Tom Huhn, Martin Jay, Veronica Kelly, Steve Mailloux, Bruce Robbins, Nick Royle, Bennet Schaber (who actually wrote three sentences of it), and Ann Wordsworth. One should also mention the lively articulation of differences amongst my colleagues and successive classes of graduate students at Syracuse. I am grateful to the Office of the Vice President for Research and Graduate Affairs at Syracuse University for helping to fund the research and to Eloise Knowlton for help with the index.

Syracuse, 1989

Abbreviations used for Works by Lyotard

DF	*Discours, figure*
DPMF	*Dérive à partir de Marx et Freud*
DP	*Des Dispositifs pulsionnels (2nd ed.)*
EL	*Economie libidinale*
IP	*Instructions païennes*
RP	*Rudiments païens: genre dissertatif*
TD	*Les Transformateurs Duchamp*
JG	*Just Gaming*
PMC	*The Postmodern Condition*
LD	*The Differend: Phrases in Dispute*
AEP	*L'Assassinat de l'expérience par la peinture: Monory*
TI	*Tombeau de l'intellectuel et autres papiers*
PMEAE	*Le Postmoderne expliqué aux enfants*
QP	*Que Peindre?: Adam Arakawa Buren*
P	*Peregrinations: Law, Form, Event*
HJ	*Heidegger et 'les Juifs'*
LI	*L'Inhumain: causeries sur le temps*

Works are listed in rough order of first publication. A fuller bibliography is provided at the end of the book. Translations from texts available only in French are my own.

Introduction

A LONG INTRODUCTION

The genre of this text is that of the short introduction. This book on Lyotard should be a more or less critical paraphrase and summary, packaging the ideas of its subject in a handy and accessible form, responding to the twin demands of concision and clarity. It should offer enlightenment as to the critical or theoretical project of its subject in the shortest time possible. Jean-François Lyotard's work may be understood as a thoroughgoing rejection of the place of theory or critique, of the project of enlightenment, of the commodification of knowledge. This book is impossible.

And yet, it is possible. It is possible because a book may not have to justify itself in the terms of the modernist demands of clarity and historical coherence, or the market's demands of commodification and exchangeability. This would make the book something in the order of a postmodern aesthetic experiment, a testament to an irreducible alterity, like Derrida's postmodern book as post card, *La Carte postale*. Lyotard's own generic experiments have offered the book as conversation (*Just Gaming*), as collection of various kinds of epistle (*Le Postmoderne expliqué aux enfants*), as philosophical note- and sketchbook (*The Differend*) and, less happily, as violent affirmation of purely ephemeral desire (*Economie libidinale*).[1] With these generic experiments as a subject, it would seem only fitting that the strategy of this book parallel one of these experiments. This book aims to share the goal of *Discours, figure* by providing a survey that results only in the demand that we return to a reading which is stripped of the illusion of mastery or exhaustiveness. This is perhaps the most honest way of circumventing the usual agonies of introductions that are anxious lest they may come to stand in for reading their objects. Another way of saying this is that this book may permit the reader to approach Lyotard's *Peregrinations*, in which he offers an introduction to his own intellectual career which is concise, fascinating, and yet perhaps incomprehensible to those not already familiar with that career. If I issue this injunction to 'read Lyotard', it is because he more than anyone has made me aware of the risk implied in the packaging of knowledge, the danger of introductions. This is the threat that introductions, of any sort, may be descriptive rather than performative. By this I mean that their function as introductions may cover over the particularity of their subject-matter by offering a too easily accessible representation of it.

THE PROBLEM OF PARAPHRASE I: READING AND THE EVENT

Let us begin again, with the question of introduction. The introductory 'Reading Dossier' attached to Lyotard's *The Differend* suggests the extent to which his writings must displace the genre of the introductory study. It offers paragraph-length statements detailing the thesis of the work, the context of its occurrence, the reasons for its being written, and descriptions of its style. In so doing, these statements parody a certain kind of reading. There can be no further paraphrase, since one is already provided: a summary by the author himself; what could be more faithful to the text? Of course, not only the role of the literary hack is being interrogated here, but also that of the reader. The reader will go on to read the book. And yet he or she will already have 'in their possession' the 'meaning' of the book, so that to read on will only be to waste time, to extract what has already been mined.

But lest we be too hasty, let me examine the last sentence. Two sets of inverted commas, two terms displaced. First, knowledge is marked as the object of possession: it's what readers have 'in their possession'. That is, the meaning of the book is possessed, by analogy with a commodity, insofar as it is made the object of a mental *representation*. We shall have occasion to return to the axis that links representation by concepts to commodification and exchange in our section on the space of political representation. Second, 'meaning' has come to be identified, for our purposes, with the *representable content* of a phrase. This is in contradistinction to the pragmatic instantiation of a phrase, its 'eventhood'. It should be stressed that the particularity of the identification of meaning with representable content exceeds the simple form/content distinction endemic to traditional literary history, in which form is thought as utterly representable, a second-order content, a modifier of meaning. Lyotard's later work is very much concerned with the distinction of the eventhood of the event (the 'it happens', the *quid*) from its meaning or content ('what happens', *quod*).

The nature of this insistence on performativity can be aligned with Derrida's strictures on Austin's distinction of constative from performative content in phrases. The point would be in Lyotard's terms that performativity is not a second order content (the meaning of the 'it happens') but is radically heterogeneous to meaning, cannot be reduced to a content in the same way or at the same time. In 'Signature Event Context' Derrida recognizes Austin's shifting of the issue of meaning from the axis of truth to that of *use* by the introduction of performativity.[2] However, he insists upon the instance of literary activity (which Austin evades in a footnote) to point to the fact that performativity cannot be finally reduced by means of the total determination and description ('saturation') of the context of performance. Performativity cannot be translated into purely constative content ('X said Y in context Z, modifying the meaning of Y as follows...'). Derrida is mainly interested in proving that there is no phrase that can be purely constative, that can be exhaustively identified in terms of its literal meaning.

The excess of the performative over constative meaning, according to Derrida, cannot finally be subsumed under the category of 'intentional meaning' to meaning in general as the determinant nature of the being of all phrases. He insists upon the dramatic to indicate that the performativity of phrases cannot be a matter of conscious, present intention, since 'failure' in these cases is not simply accidental, but a structural necessity of each performance (or actors could not 'marry' on stage). Derrida draws this disruption of oppositions towards a 'graphematics' of the signifier which blurs communication or intention from the beginning, siting resistance in a 'writing' which will not be simply 'the decoding of a meaning or a truth' (Derrida, 1982: 321–30). Lyotard insists that attention to the event should not be thought simply as a fault internal to textual representation (in this sense, he might accuse Derrida of limiting the event to the negative moment of the failure of meaning). For Lyotard, it is not simply the case that there are events that deconstruct the rule of meaning; one has to judge how to judge them, one must do something with events, speak after them by linking phrases to them, despite the fact that events offer no fixed criteria as to what we might do or how we might do it.

Thus, attention to the event resists the reduction of reading to the extraction of meaning content (or its formal modifications). Lyotard insists that the time of reading cannot be understood as the quickest possible extraction of the meaning of a work. The crucial impact of Lyotard's work on literary-critical studies lies precisely in its insistence upon the irreducibility of reading as a practice, an insistence that can give rise to manifestos such as 'we do not interpret, we read' (*EL*: 117). Reading comes to be, for Lyotard, a process of the linking of phrases, and as such instantiates a 'space-time' or a 'universe' alien to that of either interpretation or theory. That is to say, reading is contrasted to theory and to interpretation in that it shares a temporality and a positioning with aesthetic and ethical judgment. Reading is neither on the inside (interpretation) nor the outside (theory) of a text as body: it disrupts the stable boundaries that might establish the text as body. Likewise, Lyotard is explicitly not a historian, as he states in 'A Memorial for Marxism' (*P*), because he doesn't participate in socio-historical assumptions about time. The time of reading as site of resistance is to be opposed to both the timelessness of theory and the accountable, teleologically unified and organized 'time of extraction' that characterizes the process of hermeneutic interpretation.

Thus Lyotard's account of reading, like his accounts of judgment and of phrase-linking, has neither a stable space-time nor a unified subject, but rather is the site of a *resistance to the rule of the concept*. Accordingly, there can be no 'theory' or 'epistemology' of reading that does not deny reading as a material practice. Reading is precisely what theory and interpretation cannot abide, since reading is a process of listening out for events *as events*, refusing to reduce events to their 'meaning', whether that meaning be their content (interpretation) or their conditions of possibility (theory). Here is the difficulty of reading events, as Lyotard describes it in *Peregrinations*:

> To become sensitive to their quality as actual events, to become competent in listening to their sound underneath silence or noise, to become open to the 'It happens that' rather than to the 'What happens', requires at the very least a high degree of refinement in the perception of small differences.
>
> (*P*: 18)

Reading is directed at the event in its singularity, its radical difference from all other events. Reading does not ask what is the case, but what a 'case' is, what it is that an event is before it has been accounted for, before cognition intervenes to determine the meaning of an event by means of a concept, before it is reduced to just 'another case of the French tendency to revolt', for example. Throughout Lyotard's work, reading as event will raise up the figure against discourse, the libidinal skin against the organic body, a narrative pragmatics against the rule of 'meta-' or 'grand narratives', an aesthetics of the sublime against the sociology of art, an ethics against the totalitarianism of the political. All of these terms will have to be explained, and that explanation will be the matter of my subsequent chapters. They can be linked in the first place in the sense that reading as a deconstructive process abides in Lyotard's writings as a resistance to the rule of understanding as conceptual reduction, and in the second place in that there is a consistent political allegory by which that rule by concept is the function of both capitalism and state bureaucratic totalitarianism. I shall delay fuller consideration of the extent of this rephrasing of the temporality of reading, this parodic displacement of the commodification of reading in terms of knowledge gained, until my last chapter.

Let it suffice here to admonish ourselves with Lyotard's description of the reader of *The Differend*, the reader who is in the midst of being provided with a handy paraphrase of the entire text in the shape of a 'Preface Reading Dossier'. Lyotard notes that the reader should be:

> A philosophical one, that is, anybody on the condition that he or she agrees not to be done with 'language' and not to 'gain time'. Nevertheless, the present reading dossier will allow the reader, if the fancy grabs him or her, to 'talk about the book' without having read it.
>
> (*LD*: xiv)

The lesson of this philosophical reading, reading that dwells on the minute but radical differences opened up in language, is what Lyotard has to teach literary critics. It is in his refusal to give up language in the name of 'meaning', that Lyotard's work is most pressingly addressed to literary critics. His ironic assault on the acceleration of paraphrase is not an ivory tower insistence on literary leisure, but is part of a general attack on modernist logics of conceptualization in the name of speedier circulation. Such logics would include both capitalist structures of commodification and exchange and the communicative or hermeneutic rationality common to structural linguistics, semiotics, and political philosophers in the tradition of Jürgen Habermas. Thus we can see that the attack on paraphrase, as a philosophical joke, is part of a general rephrasing of the scene of reading, theory and interpretation, a rephrasing usually named 'deconstruction' which marks the crucial relevance of Lyotard's work to Anglophone literary criticism. In other words, in order to understand why there is a problem with writing a short introduction to Lyotard in the usual periphrastic mode, we need first to consider the impact of deconstruction upon the status of paraphrase.

THE PROBLEM OF PARAPHRASE II: THE EVENT AND THE NECESSITY OF DISTORTION

Geoffrey Bennington's excellent *Lyotard: Writing the Event* expresses just such worries: how to produce a short introduction to the work of someone concerned to resist claims to put an end to language and gain time. Bennington's book adopts the strategy of trying to 'ape its object'.[3] The demand I hear in Lyotard's work is not one of repetition in the English sense, but of performance, as in the French *répétition* – which may refer to each singular rehearsal or staging of a drama. This text performs a more studied drifting away from Lyotard, twists Lyotard's work in order to make it question the *disciplinarity* of English Studies. Yet at the same time, this book aims to be an 'accessible' study of Lyotard in the sense given to accessibility by Lyotard in *Just Gaming*:

> it demands of the writer of books that she get out of the solitude and irresponsibility in which she writes and that she put herself in a position of partnership in which she asks questions and gives replies.
>
> (*JG*: 8)

Such accessibility offers the reader the access of the interlocutor rather than the spectator.[4] Put another way, if Bennington offers an account of Lyotard, I try, at times impatiently, to pose the question 'Why Lyotard?'.

This book, then, is not an introduction to Lyotard, but an introduction of Lyotard. Specifically, it's an introduction of Lyotard to the discourses of Anglo-American cultural criticism.

Here he is

And before looking at what that might mean, let's pay attention to the performativity of an introduction of someone, rather than to an introduction to someone's work. We are dealing here with a presentation rather than a representation of Lyotard, a distinction that will become urgent in our discussion of *The Differend* in Chapter 3.

If we try to think about the performativity of introductions this may become clearer. When one says 'here is Lyotard', one is performing a presentation, not a representation. Additional phrases ('he teaches at U.C. Irvine these days') are not to be judged on the grounds of exhaustive truthfulness, but only in reference to the effects of the performance. Nor is it enough to claim to make a 'representative' selection of descriptive phrases in order to represent a person in introducing them. One might avoid long-windedness, but one would also ignore (at least) the instance of the addressee as a factor determining the nature of the introduction. One is not concerned with accurate description of a *person* but with an act of introduction that may do justice to a *situation*, a 'case' in which speaker, addressee, referent (Lyotard) and meaning (what significance one may attach to the name Lyotard: philosopher; Frenchman; etc.) function variously as pragmatic instances.[5] To confuse the performativity of an introduction with a claim to accurate description is to be socially inept; to confuse the performativity of this introduction with the exhaustive representation of an *œuvre* would be politically inept.

As we shall find, to pay attention to the performativity of a statement or phrase, precisely to the extent to which it problematizes its constative content, will be a peculiarly Lyotardian move. In politics, it will cause him to break with Bolshevism because what the party says (that the workers must be liberated) is radically undermined by the way it says it (from the position of the dominator) (*DPMF*: 153). Or, as Lyotard puts it in *Instructions païennes*, the intellectual Left's critique of power is vitiated by the fact that 'in the pragmatics of their narrations one finds an exemplary machinery of domination in miniature' (*IP*: 16).

As we have seen, an attention to the performativity of an event is not simply a matter of putting a statement of meaning (a signification) 'in context', in order to understand the fuller signification of an enunciation. Lyotard's argument is that the performativity of an enunciation, the eventhood of a statement's taking place, is radically *singular*. To say something once, and then to repeat it, is to make two different statements. The radical insistence of deconstruction is that this difference of context cannot be exhaustively described. This is because any third phrase that sought to describe the difference, to put the phrases 'in context', would in its turn have its own singularity, would be another event. A phrase may seem to be 'about' another phrase, but since the two phrases exist as singular events, we might more properly say that the second phrase comes *after* the first, claiming to link onto the first phrase by virtue of a common referent. In this sense, however, the two phrases can never be identical in the pragmatics of their occurrence.

The observation is commonplace, so stated, but it has major implications for our understanding of what the stakes are in history, politics and criticism. First, the singular eventhood of the phrase stands as a *figure* which disbars the possibility of its ever claiming to be an entirely literal description, displaces the rule of meaning. The discourse of logocentrism since Plato rests upon the identification of meaning with being: to tell the truth is to produce a phrase whose meaning can state the being of a thing or phrase exhaustively. Lyotard's investigation of figurality moves towards a consideration of the temporality of the event as the site of a deconstructive resistance to logocentrism.

Second, the singular eventhood of phrases leads towards a resistance to the condition of metalanguages which claim to provide a history, a theory or a politics of culture, a grand narrative or set of phrases which might transcend the order of phrases that it describes in order to reveal their true meaning. And it is in this sense that Lyotard proposes a rephrasing of culture, as we will see later, in terms of *little narratives*. Thus a respect for the singularity of phrases (or little narratives) evokes a redescription of reading as the site of invention rather than cognition. Instead of considering reading in terms of its descriptive or constative fidelity, reading must be understood primarily as an event or act, a performance which should be judged in ethical terms.

Third, the understanding of aesthetics in terms of singularity evokes an art of *invention* rather than mimesis. Lyotard's writings on aesthetics do not understand art as primarily representative, but as the search for the limits of representation. In this sense, we should understand Lyotard's account of postmodern aesthetic invention as characterized by a transformative *displacement* of the field of representation rather than the innovative *discovery* of new modes of representation characteristic of the modernist avant-garde.

Fourth, the fact that phrases elude the order of literal description makes politics a matter of judgment rather than knowledge, an ethical rather than a social concern. This produces Lyotard's politics of the differend, a politics of rhetorical dispute without finality. Politics is no longer the metalanguage which can authoritatively determine the literal meaning of phrases by calculating their 'political effect', as is claimed by much of the literary-critical 'Left'. The necessary rhetoricity of phrases intervenes as the condition rather than the instrument of politics. To put it another way, the political is no longer the genre that can reveal the final, true, meaning of political rhetorics. If each phrase is radically singular, the nature of the links we may make between phrases is a matter of dispute. Put simply, *The Differend* proposes a *rhetorical politics* rather than a political rhetoric, in that the political is the contest over the way in which to deal with the difference between singular phrases, not the literal instance where the true effectivity of all phrases is revealed.

If the singular eventhood of phrases is always reduced by the discursive claim to exhaustive description, the claim that the essence of phrases is their meaning, then paraphrase is ruled out. How are we to refigure the genre of the introductory study? Here we can turn to an interview in which Lyotard addresses the repeated criticism that he is a faithless and partial reader, an inaccurate paraphraser of the texts he studies:

> I remain continually surprised by the surprise that my readings of works provoke in my readers. I can't seem to make myself feel guilty for any disrespect but I ought to feel that way out of incongruousness. I must be a bad reader, not sufficiently sensitive or 'passive' in the greater sense of the word, too willful, 'aggressive', not sufficiently espousing the supposed organic development of the other (?), in a rush to place it in the light of my own concerns. 'Wild' if you wish (but my concerns are cultivated); 'impious' certainly in the sense whereby Plato judges as impious the belief that the gods (here the works I read) are corruptible by petitions and gifts .... Rather I would say: one writes because one hears a request [*demande*] and in order to answer it; I read Kant or Adorno or Aristotle not in order to detect the request they themselves tried to answer by writing, but in order to hear what they are requesting from me while I write or so that I write.
>
> (*Diacritics*, fall 1984, 18–19)

A reading does not seek to answer a descriptive exigency of faithful paraphrase. Reading is not a matter of mimetic representation or conceptual critique: it is an ethical practice. Lyotard is not here advocating a 'free-for-all' (as the lazy, immobile, reader may have inferred). Reading should do justice to a text. But what is it to do justice to a text? It is not a matter of mimetic fidelity to what the text says, of affirmative or negative description of its discursive content, but of what the text does. It doesn't ask what the text means or signifies but 'What demand does the text make? How am I addressed by it?'. Here we touch upon the problem of justice and the division of prescriptive from descriptive phrases that will be addressed in our discussion of *Just Gaming*.

For the moment, let's focus on the fact that to write about a text is to link another phrase to its phrases. This is demanded by *The Differend*. The question of which phrase to link to a phrase of Marx, of Freud, of Wittgenstein, of Lyotard, is a radically ethical one. The question for this book is not what to say *about* Lyotard, then, but what to say *after* Lyotard. What phrase to link to Lyotard? And the rejection of mimetic fidelity to the content of the set of phrases named 'Lyotard' as a determining criterion has already been evidenced in these pages. Lyotard hardly talks about reading, except in negative terms in *Discours, figure*. It is primarily as a literary critic that I am going to listen to the demand that Lyotard makes on me, so as to twist his writings towards a concern with rhetoricity and with reading. This is not so much a distortion of the content of Lyotard's books as an attempt to do justice to the event of his writing.

This book will link a selective series of phrases onto Lyotard's writings in order to trace the relation of his singular intellectual peregrinations to the problems of literary criticism. To call these linkages 'partial' or 'distorted' would be unjustly to apply criteria belonging to the cognitive language game. It would be to treat an introductory presentation as if it were a summary representation determined by a 'reality' rather than a pragmatic move. Our partiality will not be a problem, since we won't have attempted to provide an accurate summary or a faithful copy.[6] Rather than an account, Lyotard demands from us a *performance*, a *work*. Thus, the periphrastic linkages that this work makes, its explanations, summaries, simplifications, vulgarities, should be judged in terms of their performativity rather than their accuracy. This is not a representation of a person that might be accurate, or even representative. It is an act of introduction which seeks to do justice to its pragmatic situation as an event, involving a speaker (myself), a referent (Lyotard), a meaning (all those descriptive phrases) and an addressee (you). You must judge it in terms of whether it does justice to its situation.

In the present case, this work will consist of three large chapters combined with a divided, mobile, supplement. The supplement should be read to disrupt any tendency of the chapters to form themselves into a dialectical pattern which might allow a determinate result, a revealed meaning. The supplement marks a belatedness which disrupts any claim to extract a methodology of reading from a reading of Lyotard. After Lyotard, it will not be a question of applying Lyotard; this will not have been a preparation for 'Lyotardian readings'. Rather, the mobile supplement will attempt to think what it is to have performed an act of reading belatedly, after Lyotard.

THREE NON-DIALECTICAL SECTIONS

Our first chapter will examine the ways in which Lyotard has sought a term, most often in the realm of the aesthetic, that will allow a sense of the irrepresentable to arise. This chapter will concentrate on Lyotard's first long book, *Discours, figure*, in its analysis of the figural, of rhetoricity, as a deconstructive evocation of incommensurability rather than a second order modification of signification. The aesthetic of incommensurability is the attempt to set to work, within and against the system, an otherness that cannot be exchanged. Obviously, this otherness cannot itself be the object of a representation, lest it become another commodity rather than an other to the rule of the commodity. On this basis, Lyotard provides a powerful deconstructive displacement of the rule of semiotics (inspired by Saussurean linguistics) in contemporary cultural and psychoanalytic criticism. This pre-eminently deconstructive citation of that within representation which cannot be represented, that which disrupts the closure of representation, has proceeded under various names in Lyotard's later writings. If the 'tensor' or maximal intensity of the libidinal band marks the point at which Lyotard succumbs to the temptation of inhabiting a pure space 'beyond' representation, a metaphysics of desire as he himself admits, the readings of Figure, Event and Sublime effect rigorous deconstructions of the conceptual spaces of discourse, identity and experience through which the rule of being as self-representation is established.

The second chapter is devoted to postmodernity as a temporal figure. The pragmatics of narrative form an exemplary trope through which Lyotard has sought to pursue this displacement of the rule of representation, by which the real or true history is the story which narrates itself, which gives itself as always already story, from which representation is (apparently) absent because always already there, in the nature of things before they need to be represented. In Lyotard's continuing investigations of narrative pragmatics, narrative itself becomes a figure that cannot be reduced to logocentric representation, since the figure of narrative cannot be represented without recourse to another narrative. I shall trace Lyotard's postmodern aesthetic of experiment as an analogous attempt to phrase the process of cultural production in terms which do not reduce the artwork to a commodity and knowledge to information. Narrative is thus a further term in the displacement of the rule of representation by concepts, one to which Lyotard has been prepared to lend a particular weight in his analysis of the political.

The third chapter concludes this introduction by examining the sites at which the analysis of incommensurability produces displacements of the political as a representational field. The pressure of the assault on theory and critique proceeds from a worry about the function of the exclusivity of theoretical closure. To call this worry political would be to neglect the pragmatics of political discourse itself: the way in which the theory of political oppression carries with it the oppression of political theory. Thus, this final chapter will examine the way in which Lyotard's work problematizes the political as an order of representation (the function of the political in the West since Plato). Put another way, the political is not the final meaning of representations, but one kind of apparatus, along with others (such as visual perspective, realist narrative, theoretical discourse) for the reduction of heterogeneous singularities to a unifying rule of representability within which all is recognizable. Politics, then, is not simply a question of who is represented, since the exercise of domination is the effect of the representational *apparati* that have governed the understanding of cultural experience. For example, under capitalism the function of commodification is to submit all events to the rule of capital by reducing them to representations of value within a system of exchange. Existence is thus determined as an effect of representation. The politics that seeks to 'represent legitimate aspirations' is itself the subjection of desire to the rule of capitalist commodification and exchange. Theoretical 'critique' is itself merely the nihilistic inversion of this movement, either the simple attempt to make commodities circulate in the opposite direction within a system itself functioning in terms of binary oppositions, or the ultimate capitalization whereby the system may know itself as commodity. According to Lyotard any politics that remains within the realm of representation is necessarily complicit with the exclusionary politics that have oppressed women, workers, ethnic and sexual minorities, and others as yet unrecognizable.

It is important to realize that this is not a position of despair. Rather, this awareness pushes towards a politics of the irrepresentable, a politics which would not be *recognizable* as such within the terms of represented experience. In this 'context', the final chapter will turn to examine the deconstruction of the political in terms of phrase analysis in *Just Gaming* and *The Differend: Phrases in Dispute*, and the move towards an 'ethics of reading' that this enjoins. Appropriately, this section will conclude with a presentation of Lyotard's latest work on the Immemorial (that which is unrepresentable to memory and yet which will not be forgotten) as the sketch of a practice of *reading* that may furnish a site of cultural resistance, the evocation of a radically alternative temporality to that of the working of capital. If the avant-garde intellectual was always the product of a capitalist or totalitarian enlightenment (*Tombeau de l'intellectuel*), Lyotard still has praise for the modernist avant-garde's work of anamnesis, the failure to forget that does not allow itself the solace of representation. The irrepresentable figures sensed by deconstruction impose a work of anamnesis that has characterized, and ought still to characterize, the resistant reading of culture.

AGAINST THEORY

We cannot introduce Lyotard as one more theorist, the latest, most modern, news from France. His interest in the postmodern continues only as long as the postmodern may resist becoming the newest, most sensational, modernity. Nor is Lyotard a 'theorist'; quite the contrary. Just as his postmodernity claims to make no temporal breaks, so his thought ceaselessly denies the pretensions of theoretical distancing, of epistemological breaks. Lyotard's work has been vilified in the Anglophone academy in the name of the political suspicion of theoretical excesses.[7] Terry Eagleton, in a *Times Literary Supplement Review* of 20 February 1987, classes Lyotard's work as at the same time too little theory, in that it refuses the condition of 'total social critique' (ibid.: 194), and too much theory, the product of an ivory tower ignorant of 'present struggles' (ibid.: 194). Eagleton's analysis proceeds less from the position that it claims, the defence of '*political opposition to the system*' against the theoretical disengagement of 'jaded Parisian post-Marxism' (ibid.: 194), than from a defence of theory against any analysis of the politics inherent in theoretical discourse itself.

Lyotard is not a theorist. Lyotard's decisive entry into the French academic scene is an insistence that, after 1968, theory ought to be recognized as part of the problem, not as a potential solution. Theory, that is, is an order of discourse that acts to establish the exclusive rule of a network of oppositions between concepts or signifiers. His abiding interest in Freud places psychoanalysis as the opening of theory to a constitutive uncertainty, a founding hesitation concerning the certainty and closure of hermeneutic models. Lyotard's attacks on the negativity of theory and critique in de Saussure, Marx, Lacan and semiotic analysis do not represent any naïve affirmation of experience (itself a theoretical construct in reference to a subject), but a deconstructive disruption of conceptual reduction.

Glossary

A little more than an index, something less than a master-key, the following gives some indication of how one might begin to think about what is at stake in certain possibly unfamiliar key terms in this book. I am more interested in the potential for directing the reader around the work (so as to link up discussions in possibly unexpected ways) than in providing authoritative paradigmatic definitions of terms. It would be most upsetting were readers to think that learning this glossary by rote might stand in for reading the book.

ANAMNESIS, *see Immemorial.*

BLOCKING TOGETHER. A mode characteristic of the figural, in which two incommensurable elements (such as the visible and the textual) are held together, impossibly, in the 'same' space: a kind of superimposition without privilege. *See* Chapter 1(G).

DIFFEREND. A point of difference where the sides speak radically different or heterogeneous languages, where the dispute cannot be phrased in either language without, by its very phrasing, prejudging the issue for that side, being unjust. Between two language games, two little narratives, two phrases, there is always a differend which must be encountered. As such, the differend marks a point of incommensurability, of dispute or difference where no criteria exist for judgment. The differend marks a point where existing representational frameworks are unable to deal with difference without repressing or reducing it. The task of art and politics is to evoke or testify to differends, to exacerbate them so as to resist the injustice which silences those who cannot speak the language of the master. Justice can only be done if we preserve the differend as to the nature of justice, in politics, aesthetics and philosophy. *See* Chapter 3(C).

DISCOURSE. The condition of representation to consciousness by a rational order or structure of concepts. Concepts or terms function as units oppositionally defined by their position and relation within the virtual space of a system or network, a space that Lyotard calls *textual* or perspectival. The calculation of such relational positions is the work of *ratio*, or reason. The condition of discourse apprehends things solely in terms of the representability by or within its system, as *meanings* or significations that discourse may *speak*. *See* Chapters 1(A), 1(C), 1(G), and 3(A), 3(B).

ETHICS. A mode of *judgment*, drawn from Lyotard's description of Aristotle, that proceeds without criteria (such as moral principles) but only as regards the ethos of the judgment, its status as a judgment that claims to do justice. *See* Chapter 3(C).

EVENT. An event is an occurrence, as such. 'Not a thing, but at least a caesura in space-time' (QP,11). That is to say, the event is the fact or case that something happens, after which nothing will ever be the same again. The event disrupts any pre-existing referential frame within which it might be represented or understood. The eventhood of the event is the radical *singularity* of happening, the 'it happens' as distinct from the sense of 'what is happening'. It leaves us without criteria and requires *indeterminate judgment*. It is impossible to decide whether events happen all the time (without being noticed) or very rarely (and are always noticed). The former seems more likely. *See* Chapter 2(B).

EXPERIMENT or **INVENTION.** As distinct from innovation, experiment does not discover new modes of representation so much as displace the rule of representation in disrupting the field or frame of discursive consciousness. It is a mode of proceeding without criteria in the field of the arts, or in reading, that has much in common with *indeterminate judgment*. *See* Chapters 1(I), 2(G) and 3(D).

FIGURE. The figural is an unspeakable other necessarily *at work* within and against *discourse*, disrupting the rule of representation. It is not opposed to discourse, but is the point at which the oppositions by which discourse works are opened to a radical heterogeneity or *singularity*. As such, the figural is the resistant or irreconcilable trace of a space or time that is radically incommensurable with that of discursive meaning: variously evoked throughout Lyotard's writing as the visible (figure/ground), the rhetorical (figural/literal), work, the Unconscious, the event, postmodern anachronism, the sublime affect or the thing. *See* Chapters 1(D–J), 2(A–C), 3(C) and 3(D).

IMMEMORIAL. That which can neither be remembered (represented to consciousness) nor forgotten (consigned to oblivion). It is that which returns, uncannily. As such, the immemorial acts as a kind of *figure* for consciousness and its attempts at representing itself historically. The prime example is Auschwitz, which obliges us to speak so that this event remains an event, so that its *singularity* is not lost in historical representation, so that it does not become something that happened, among other things. The task of not forgetting, of anamnesis, is the task of the avant-garde, which struggles to keep events from sinking into the oblivion of either representation (voice) or silence. *See* Chapters 2(I), 3(D).

JUDGMENT, INDETERMINATE or REFLECTIVE. Names the kind of judgment characteristic of Lyotard's account of the aesthetic (drawn from Kant), *ethical* (drawn from Aristotle), or political (drawn from Lyotard), a judgment that proceeds on a case-by-case basis without pre-existing principles or criteria, inventing the rule of its judgment as it goes along, by *experimentation*. Nor does the judgment ground a criterion that may subsequently be used as a principle. Rather, each judgment is itself the object of another indeterminate judgment which takes the first as a case. Each judgment necessarily raises the question 'was that a good judgment?', for which no evaluative criteria are given in advance. In this sense, each judgment has the specificity of its own *language game*, which no subsequent language game may exhaustively dominate without injustice. Lyotard characterizes this mode of discourse as 'literary discussion' (*RP*). *See* Chapter 3(C).

LANGUAGE GAME. A term drawn from Wittgenstein which insists upon the pragmatic *singularity* of uses of language. Each language-act carries with it a series of pragmatic instances, along with a set of implied rules. As such, it has a specificity that evokes *indeterminate judgment*. Injustice would be the erection of determinate principles of judgment which claimed to be translatable without loss into other language games. *See* Chapter 3(C).

MODERNISM. The conception of consciousness as primarily a historical project, the discourse of a subject who achieves autonomy by understanding itself as the narrator of history. Modernism is characterized by the *grand narrative* of the progressive emancipation of a universal subject of history, the proleptically autonomous speaker of a *discourse* of knowledge (Enlightenment), humanity (republican democracy), will (romanticism) or history (Hegel, Marx). *See* Chapter 2(C), 2(D).

MODERNITY, predicament of being in. Used in *Just Gaming* to name the figural displacement that precedes and constitutes *modernism*'s claim to impose the discursive order of *grand narratives* of a rational subject (Enlightenment) or a subjective will (romanticism). Lyotard renames this as *postmodern*. *See* Chapter 2(C), 2(D).

NARRATIVE, GRAND. A story that claims the status of universal metanarrative, capable of accounting for all other stories in order to reveal their true meaning. Grand narratives claim to totalize the field of narrative so as to organize the succession of historical moments in terms of the projected revelation of a meaning. They thus offer to suppress all *differends*, to translate all narratives into themselves without loss, to make everything speak their language. Grand narratives link elements in parallel, either in reference to an object (classicism) or their narrator (modernism), so as to unify events into the total history of *x* (nature or the human spirit, for example). *See* Chapter 2(D), 2(E).

NARRATIVES, LITTLE. Narrative understood as a non-finite series of heterogeneous events of narration which resist incorporation into *grand* or meta-*narratives* by virtue of being discontinuous and fragmentary. As such, they are analogous to *language games*. *See* Chapter 2(D).

PAGAN. A mode of action characterized by the impiety of proceeding without criteria, making a series of site-specific *little narratives* that work as ruses rather than the embodiment of overarching rules or strategies of discursive conduct. Paganism implies *indeterminate judgment* in that it shares *postmodernism*'s incredulity towards *grand narratives*, subscribes to no theoretical piety, whether of the political Left or Right. Specifically, Lyotard's use of the term is part of an attempt to rename political struggle once politics is no longer thought of as the neutral space of the clash of *grand narratives* as to the nature of the political. The term is largely dropped by the time of *The Differend*, perhaps because it tends to romanticize the problem of political judgment (it's hard to stop paganism from becoming another religion). *See* Chapters 2(E), 2(H) and 3(B).

POSTMODERNITY. This is not thought by Lyotard in a periodizing sense (what comes after, or breaks with, *modernism*), but as a kind of temporal *figure*. The postmodern is thus an alien temporality that in a sense precedes and constitutes *modernism*, always inscribing the possibility of a radical revision of modernism against itself, specifically in the thinking of the event. *See* Chapter 2(A–C).

SINGULARITY. The radical specificity of *events*, their radical, once and for all 'happening' or eventhood, and hence their heterogeneity or sheer difference from all other events. To put it another way, singularity is what is lost in translation (*figure*, in this sense). *See* Chapters 1(E) and 2(B).

TENSOR. Point of maximal intensity of desire: a name for the *singularity* of the *event* in the erotogenic register of the libidinal band.

TEXT. The discursive reduction of space to a virtual grid of unmotivated oppositions (characteristic of structural linguistics and visual perspectivalism). In textual space, the singular happenings of things are units of value to be recognized and decoded in terms of their meaning within a system rather than seen as events. *See* Chapter 1(B), 1(C) and 1(F).

Mobile supplement I: after the event

> [T]he irreconcilable: [is] what, belatedly [*après coup*], I realize I
> have always tried to keep distinct – under various names – work,
> figurality, heterogeneity, *dissentiment*, event, thing.
>
> (*LI*: 12)

If this book were a machine for accelerated learning, then it would fall
into precisely the trap that the introduction and 'The Time of Politics'
(Chapter 3(D)) outline – it works to prevent reading from becoming
resistant, from partaking of the temporality of the event. What follows
is a supplement, in Derrida's sense – it is both a part of each chapter
and of the book as a whole, and yet apart, a foreign body for each. In
Lyotardian terms, we might say that it works across the regulated
spaces that determine the system of this book, blocking together
what the structure works to keep apart. Thus, this section appears as a
figure for Chapter 1, an *experiment* for Chapter 2, and a *link* waiting
to be made onto Chapter 3. If the book is a machine, then this
section may be plugged in at any point, so as to set the book to
work.

If this mobile supplement is plugged into Chapter 1, it will function
figurally in its direction of the analysis of aesthetic form towards work
as the literary critical supplement for formal readings.[1] If it functions
as a little narrative, serially mounted onto Chapter 2, it will act as the
socio-historical displacement of any grand narratives of cultural
pragmatics – the postmodern at work in this modernist text. If it is
linked onto Chapter 3, then work becomes the locus of a *differend*, the
unspeakable that any socio-political discourse seeks to consign to
oblivion.[2] The problem would then be to find a means of testifying to
the necessity of judging the traces of work, given that any determinant
criterion of judgment must necessarily put a stop to work by virtue of

1

its very instantiation as conceptual criterion. We must stop work, in order to recognize it as 'labour'.

Yet if this section may be plugged in at any point, the plugging in of this extraneous element, even as it sets the machine to *work*, grinds the gears in an identifiable direction, will introduce a certain *play* to the machine, a loosening of its drive belts as they are twisted so as to function in relation to an exteriority, an application. To apply is also to ply, crease or fold, causing friction. This mobile supplement marks one such possible fold.

Strange effect for an introductory survey. The supplement, that which comes before, seems incomprehensible, when it occurs. You will have to read this book in order to return and activate the contingency of these linkings, later on. Those who approach this book with an absolute commitment to linear diachrony in historical narrative had better skip to Chapter 2 right away. Those who approach this book with a stake in the recognizability of forms, the possibility of decidable interpretations, had better pass by the supplement and insert it after Chapter 1. Those who demand that the political should provide them with a ground, a last resort for knowing 'which side we're on' in the face of the kaleidoscope of ideological illusion of late monopoly capitalism, had better turn to the 'last instance', to Chapter 3, before reading this supplement.

Of course, if you have ever been in the grip of an affect, if a certain uncanny belatedness has ever displaced your capacity to refer sense-impressions back to a determining instance called 'human consciousness' or 'the course of history' or 'political strategy', then you might just skip ahead to the end of this book so as to read the second part of this supplement. To fold the book in this way would be to read the supplement before the criteria have been offered to you that will allow you to make a determinant judgment as to its nature, location in time, or political effects. This would be very disruptive, and quite improper for an introductory survey.

2

1

Figure

(A) FIGURE AND DISCOURSE

Discours, figure is a lengthy and frequently difficult book that covers a lot of ground. The history of art, poetics, the philosophy of language, structural linguistics and psychoanalysis are all discussed in terms of a distinction between the discursive and the figural. I have to begin by offering some preliminary sense of what is at stake in the two terms which make up the title of Lyotard's book. This book explores the nature of the distinction between discursive signification (meaning) and rhetoricity (figure). Since the figural is explicitly resistant to the rule of signification, saying what the terms 'mean' is problematic; the differences marked at this point will need to be developed through the rest of this chapter. To begin with, discourse is the name given by Lyotard to the process of *representation by concepts.* Discourse, that is, organizes the objects of knowledge as a system of concepts (units of meaning). Meanings are defined in terms of their position in the discursive network, by virtue of their opposition to all the other concepts or elements in the system. Discourse thus imposes a spatial arrangement upon objects which Lyotard calls 'textual', a virtual grid of oppositions.

For Lyotard, the structural linguistics of Ferdinand de Saussure exemplify this discursivization of textual space, reducing all effects of language to meanings produced by the play between signifiers. Language is understood by Saussure as linguistic representation, in terms of the tabular system of opposed elements which make up language. In the field of figurative space, the order and proportion of Renaissance perspective performs a parallel discursive reduction of the visible to the representable. As in the *costruzione legittima* of Duccio's *Maesta*, the geometrization of perspective determines the visi-

3

bility of objects as their relation to other objects on the spatial grid of the perspectival plane (*DF*: 202–8). The rule of discourse is thus the claim to order being as a structure of meanings, to identify existence with the representable by the establishment of the exclusive rule of a network of oppositions between concepts or signifiers.

Against the rule of discourse in figurative and textual space, Lyotard insists upon the figural. It is crucial to understand that the figural is not simply opposed to the discursive, as another kind of space. Lyotard is not making a romantic claim that irrationality is better than reason, that desire is better than understanding.[1] If the rule of discourse is primarily the rule of representation by conceptual *oppositions*, the figural cannot simply be opposed to the discursive. Rather, the figural opens discourse to a radical heterogeneity, a singularity, a difference which cannot be rationalized or subsumed within the rule of representation. *Discours, figure* evokes a *difference* or singularity of objects (A is not B)[2] which cannot be thought under the logic of identity, as an *opposition* (A is defined by not being the rest of the system). The discursive system cannot deal with this singularity, cannot reduce it to an opposition within the network. The object resists being reduced to the state of mere equivalence to its meaning within a system of signification, and the figural marks this resistance, the sense that we cannot 'say' everything about an object, that an object always in some sense remains 'other' to any discourse we may maintain about it, has a singularity in excess of any meanings we may assign to it.

The figural arises as the co-existence of incommensurable or heterogeneous spaces, of the figurative in the textual or the textual in the figurative, for example. *Discours, figure* itself works to move from a series of oppositions (the figurative line to the textual letter, for example) to find an irreducible difference at work in each opposed identity (the graphic letter has a plastic force, as in mediaeval manuscripts; the plastic line performs an arbitrary conceptual demarcation of space, as in modernist art). In the subsequent parts of this chapter, we will trace the function of figurality in structural linguistics, political space, visual perception and conscious knowledge.

(B) DECONSTRUCTING TEXTUALITY AND VISION

It is this move from opposition to difference in the analysis of representational systems that characterizes Lyotard's account of the work of deconstruction. Lyotard's claim is that the discursive is

4

always necessarily interwoven with the figural and vice versa, despite the fact that the discursive claim to accurate representation or full understanding rests upon the repression of figurality. This displacement of the rule of representation is of major relevance to contemporary debates in the humanities. The sociological move that has grounded the expansion of the field of English studies in the last two decades is based upon an assumption about culture as representation: copulation (a pre-cultural activity) becomes 'sexuality' (an object of study), once you start talking about it. The sides of this debate have tended to be very strictly drawn between traditionalists (who tend to believe that the world and human activity pre-exist attempts to represent them) and advocates of 'cultural studies' (who claim that cultural representations structure human activity and consciousness of the world). The significance of deconstruction, and particularly of Lyotard's account of figurality, is that it provides a way of thinking about cultural representation that rests neither on the naïve realist assumption that representations are purely secondary to the reality of things, nor on the claim that 'everything is culturally constructed'.[3]

In this way, Lyotard offers a deconstructive account of the function of rhetorical figuration, an account which has much to teach by virtue of its implication in the transformation of our understanding of cultural representation. I am calling Lyotard a 'deconstructive' thinker, despite the fact that he has harsh things to say at times about 'deconstruction'. This is primarily an effect of translation. As we shall see, Lyotard's criticism of Derrida for excessive 'textualism' comes, as it were, from the other side of deconstruction; it is an insistence that to claim that everything is in the grip of rhetoricity by virtue of its being a text is to ignore the figural function of the non-textual.

In *Discours, figure* Lyotard is concerned to attack the notion that everything is a text by insisting that the sensible field of vision functions as a figure for 'textual space'. In these terms, it may seem odd to identify Lyotard's work as 'deconstruction', since one of the major slogans by which deconstruction is identified is a mistranslation of Derrida's '*Il n'y a pas d'hors-texte*' as 'there is nothing outside the text'.[4] The point of difference here is an important one with regard to the question of what a text is, though Lyotard's critique of 'textualism' stands more as a corrective to misunderstandings of the impact of deconstruction. Lyotard works with a very restricted account of textuality in order to refute the claim that everything is indifferently a matter of representation, to insist that there is always a figural other to textuality at work within and against the text. On this basis, he

5

criticizes Derrida for containing the deconstructive force of the figural by identifying it wholly with the internal problematic of linguistic signification:

> One does not in the least break with metaphysics in putting language everywhere, on the contrary one fulfils metaphysics; one fulfils the repression of the sensible and of *jouissance*.
>
> (*DF*: 14)

Lyotard's insistence on the opacity of the signifier as the figural condition of its double appeal to the textual and the visible, rather than as merely the loss or failure of meaning, is important here. Derrida and de Man have been read as producing a deconstruction which merely theorizes the impossibility of meaning. Lyotard attacks Derrida for first presuming that there is only language, and then thematizing the visible (perception, reference) as merely an impasse within language, the product of the uncontrollable nature of the oppositional differences by which the signifier functions, the product of the 'play of the signifier':

> It must be seen that the arche-writing invoked [by Derrida in *Writing and Difference*] is not a writing in the strict sense, the inscription of arbitrary signs on a neutral space, but is on the contrary the constitution of a thick space, where the play of hiding/revealing may take place. Difference is not opposition, the former constitutes the opacity which opens the order of reference, the latter supports the system of invariances at the level of the signifier or of the signified.
>
> (*DF*: 75)

The disagreement here is not absolute: Lyotard is arguing that the clash between difference and opposition is not the product of a flaw internal to the structural functioning of language but is the effect of the figural co-presence of the incommensurable orders of the textual and the visible in language. It's not that the opposition between signifiers runs out of control in signification, as Derrida inclines to claim in 'Structure, Sign and Play' (Derrida, 1978). Rather, according to Lyotard, language simultaneously draws on two heterogeneous negations: that of opposition (text) in signification and that of heterogeneous difference (vision) in reference. Lyotard is not an opponent of deconstruction *tout court*, but of a post-structuralism which contents itself with pointing out the epistemic impasse of structuralism.

In the first place, *Discours, figure* seeks to move beyond this impasse by juxtaposing the Saussurean structuralist account of linguistics with the phenomenology of vision elaborated by Merleau-Ponty. Lyotard's book aims to deconstruct the rule of semiology by showing how vision functions as a figure for the structural linguistics on which semiology is based. Vision deconstructs structuralism in that it is both necessary for structuralism and absolutely heterogeneous to it. This should not be misunderstood: Lyotard will go on to deconstruct the phenomenology of vision in its turn, moving from Merleau-Ponty to Freud to evoke the work of unconscious desire as a figure for the phenomenology of conscious perception.

Discours, figure establishes an opposition between textual and figurative representational space, between reading and seeing, and then deconstructs that space to evoke a figurality at work in representation. But not a pure figurality, either. If *Discours, figure* seems to open as a praise of the visible over the readable, of three-dimensional plastic space over the two-dimensional linguistic and conceptual space of the textual grid, the opposition between a good identity and its bad counterpart is turned to reveal a heterogeneous clash of the two spaces. In *Dérive à partir de Marx et Freud*, Lyotard spells out a political analogy: just as we can read the figural displacing the rule of representation, so we can imagine the overthrow of political space. The figural here becomes a quasi-symptom of a 'political unconscious', opening onto a space of social desires and possibilities that are as yet unimaginable within political representation.[5] Figure and discourse are necessarily and impossibly co-present, as constitutive and disruptive of representation.[6] *Discours, figure* opens with the visible as more figural, the textual as more discursive. The titling of a later chapter 'Fiscourse Digure' marks the extent to which the book has worked to deconstruct the opposition on which it is based, to find the discursive in the figural ('Digure') as well as the figural in the discursive ('Fiscourse').

The opposition of the textual to the visible is, covertly, an opposition between structural linguistics and phenomenology. Lyotard counterposes Saussurean linguistics, as the strongest account of the possibility of a purely textual space, to an account of vision which draws strongly on Merleau-Ponty's phenomenology of perception, in the interests of neither. Lyotard displaces Saussure's account of language in terms of signification by insisting upon its inability to deal with vision and with reference, which function figurally at both its limit and its centre. Saussurean linguistics, as the rule of the textual over the visible, effects a suppression of seeing by reading. Lyotard reintroduces the visible to structural linguistics, not as an alternative, but as the necessary yet heterogeneous complement to the textual. The juxtaposition of Merleau-Ponty and Saussure, the tracing of this necessary clash of textual and visible space, amounts to a deconstruction of both structural linguistics and phenomenology, as we shall see.

(C) STRUCTURAL LINGUISTICS AND TEXTUAL SPACE

In order to grasp the force of Lyotard's evocation of the figural, it is first necessary to work through the way in which Saussurean linguistics offers an exemplary determination of textual space. The influence of Ferdinand de Saussure's structural linguistics on contemporary critical theory should not be underestimated. Indeed, the distinction of 'critical theory' courses in universities from traditional histories of literary criticism lies in the taking of Saussure, rather than Plato and Aristotle, as a starting point. The semiotic project of art historical and literary analysis of objects as cultural signs begins with the 'Saussurean revolution'. The three major characteristics of Saussurean linguistics are the rephrasing of language as an object of theoretical rather than historical analysis, his description of the sign, and the unmotivated and differential functioning of signs in the process of signification. First, according to Saussure, although language may have a diachronic history of development, it always functions synchronically, as a *structure* or system extended at a single point in time.

Second, language is a system of signs. Signs are not the names or symbols of things, but are themselves divided between a *signifier* and a *signified*, a sound and a concept. The signifier is primarily the phoneme in speech, more generally the linguistic term. It should not be confused with a word (which may be composed of one or more signifiers) because it is a pure unit of value. The signifier never appears in isolation, for if it were to it wouldn't signify. Signifiers are combined into signs by their being linked to a signified, a meaning. Just as a signifier is not a word, so a signified is not a thing. The signified is a transcendental concept of understanding, a unit of meaning. The sign 'tree' is thus composed of the phonemes or signifiers which make up the word (or their graphic equivalents) and the concept or idea of a tree which is the signified. No actual tree is involved in this process, though an actual tree may be identified by reference to the presentation of the concept 'tree' by linguistic signs.

Third, the functioning of the signifier is *unmotivated* (or arbitrary)

8

and *differential*. The signifier is unmotivated in that there is no continuous or direct relation between signifiers and signified: there is
nothing 'fishy' about the combination of signifiers in the word 'fish'.
This may seem obvious, but the long history of magic, or of biblical
exegesis, or of poetry, all participate in the attempt to find a motivated
relationship between language and meaning. For example, reciting
the Lord's Prayer backwards in the attempt to be evil (rather than
simply adding in a few negatives) rests on the assumption that the
material arrangement of signifiers is directly connected to their meaning. In a less arcane mode, we may be inclined to think of onomato-
poeia as a case of words in a directly motivated relation to their
significations, but as Saussure points out, French dogs tend to wail
'*ouaisouais*' rather than 'woof woof', a fact one is disinclined to set
down to dismay at being born in the wrong place.

A weaker form of the claim for continuity between signifiers and
signified would concern the nature of the signifying function. Whilst
there may be no innate relationship between the signifier and the
signified, associations may nonetheless accrue over time, so that the
word 'fish' directly evokes the concept of a fish. If we no longer want to
claim that Adam chose names for all the animals that corresponded to
their essences, we may yet wish to claim that the process of language-
acquisition is one of learning to name things correctly, to fit the word
to the thing. Against this, Saussure makes the radical claim that the
functioning of language is differential. The collocation of phonic
signifiers 'fish' does not signify the concept fish, but marks the absence of all other signifiers, thus causing the identification of the
concept fish to arise by elimination.[7] The totality of paradigmatic
elements (lexis) and their syntagmatic possible relations (grammar)
makes up the *langue*, the total structure of a language at any given
point. The meaning of a given enunciation (*parole*) is determined by
its differential relation to the *langue* rather than in direct reference.
'Fish' does not evoke fish directly, it evokes the absence of all other
possibilities of the *langue*, leaving only fish as its signification. Meaning arises only indirectly, by differential comparison with the totality
of the *langue*. On the one hand, signifiers are eliminated *syntagmatically*;
for example, a verb might be impossible at a certain point in a
sentence. As the ensemble of grammatical determinations, syntagmatic differentiations establish the kind of linguistic unit that is
required (not a verb, etc.). On the other hand, a *paradigmatic* differential function specifies the signification of the linguistic term by
distinguishing it from all other terms that might occupy the same

9

position within the syntagmatic system of the sentence (not frog, not cat, etc.). As Saussure puts it, 'the most precise characteristic of signs is in being what others are not'. Since Saussure was a resident of Geneva, we shall call this the 'Swiss cheese theory of language', in which a sign appears not as a morsel of cheese, but as a hole.

The implication of this insistence on the unmotivated nature and indirect functioning of the sign is that meaning is a matter of signification rather than reference. Meaning arises as an effect of the internal functioning of the linguistic structure rather than by virtue of language's grip upon the world or the world's entry into language. Reference is not to the world but is an effect of language, so that the world is identified in reference to the structure of the *langue*. Nor is this specific to spoken language; it affects all forms of signification. The massive impact of Saussure on cultural criticism proceeds from the fact that the process of perception itself becomes a function of the *langue*, in that the concepts by which mental representations are ordered are themselves differentially determined in the structure of the *langue*. There is thus no thought before language that is not merely amorphous. Furthermore, since the *langue* is culturally specific, the field of cultural activity becomes entirely self-referential. There are no raw data of perceptions, concepts, or meanings that are not differentially determined within the general structure of the *langue*. There is no meaning that is not culturally constructed. Matters of gender or race, for example, would be significant only insofar as they were inscribed within the system of differences that makes up the *langue* of a culture.[8] The attraction of this understanding of culture is precisely that all elements in culture become transparent to the critic, who merely decodes them by reference to the ensemble of the culture within which they function. The linking of Saussure to Marx in the work of the early Barthes and his *epigones* is so powerful precisely because Marxism supplies a strong description of the total *langue* of Western culture as a capitalist mode of structuring differences.[9]

The importance of *Discours, figure* is that it mounts a critique of Saussure which does not simply counterpose an undifferentiated 'reality' to the account of culture as a system of differences.[10] Lyotard begins by describing Saussure's account of the functioning of language as pre-eminently *textual*. For Saussure, signifiers are purely differential units which have value (signify) insofar as they are recognized as elements in an invariable system. It is the absence of motivation or direct relation between signifying elements and their signification which determines textual space, the space of arbitrary codes. In Lyotard's terms, textual space is space which is pre-eminently flat, two-dimensional.

Saussure's description of linguistic space is flat because the arbitrary and differential functioning of language is discontinuous. The disembodied system of conceptual significations spreads out as a table because the only distinction between concepts is a result of their relative position within the structure elaborated by the *langue*. Thus, the process of reading is merely one of decoding, effected by a switching between the system of oppositions and the linguistic term. Just as the Saussurean understanding of language is as a structure of oppositions, so the act of signification is understood as one of opposition. Textual space is the space of pure *opposition*. In structural linguistics, only two terms are operative at any one time: the element and the totality (the whole cheese and the cheese hole, to return to our example). As Saussure himself points out, there is no stronger connection between 'fish' and 'fishes' than between 'fish' and 'table', since the signification of each is determined solely by its opposition to the totality of all other elements in the *langue*.[11] The referent may be connected, but the *value* of each term depends solely on its relations to other elements.

(D) THE PHENOMENOLOGY OF THE VISIBLE: MERLEAU-PONTY

To this understanding of language as situated in virtual two-dimensional space, as the combination of elements which are nothing in themselves, merely the empty or transparent marks of pure oppositionality, *Discours, figure* opposes an account of the phenomenology of perception which draws heavily on Merleau-Ponty's writings on vision.[12] Merleau-Ponty's account of visual space is opposed to structuralism's account of textual space. The seeing eye participates in the visible world it views: the eye moves in order to see. This corporeal involvement is what Merleau-Ponty refers to as the chiasmatic imbrication of subject and object in perception.[13] Bluntly, where Cartesian optics presume the eye as a virtual point of the reception of light, the exact counterpart of the vanishing point in perspectival construction, phenomenology insists on the corporeality of the eye.[14] This corporeality is not merely mechanical; it is the way the world paints itself on the rods and cones of the retina, the agitation of the two eyeballs in focusing:

My body makes a difference in the visible world, being a part of

it; that is why I can steer it through the visible. Conversely, it is just as true that vision is attached to movement. We see only what we look at. What would vision be without eye movement?
(Merleau-Ponty, *The Primacy of Perception*, 1964: 162)

Visibility is not merely a matter of passive object and distanced subject. Instead, subject and object come together, bruise against each other, in an act of perception. Put another way, the world is not simply extended in flat virtual space, always already given as if it were a perspectival painting.[15]

Lyotard thus analogizes the space of representation determined by perspectival painting with that evoked by Saussurean linguistics. He attacks the twin assumptions of the linguistic term and the visible element as determined simply by their opposition to other terms in the structural totality of the *langue* or their relation to the extended grid of perspective. He insists that neither is simply a transparent unit whose apprehension is a matter of decoding its relation to the whole. For Lyotard, language is as much given to be phenomenologically seen as it is to be read or decoded. The eye moves, it participates in the visible, lending an opacity to the visible as a resistance or friction on the retina. And this friction is a continuous or motivated relation.

In order to begin to understand what it might mean to evoke the figural, we must begin by looking at the ways in which Lyotard finds the visible functioning as figure within structural linguistics. However, and this is perhaps rather difficult to grasp, Lyotard is not simply attacking the textual space of structural linguistics from the ground of the visible space of phenomenology. Rather, he is arguing that vision appears as a figure in the textual conception of space, and that textuality appears as a figure in the phenomenological understanding of perception. The critique of Saussure is thus carried forward on two main counts: (i) the referential distance of the visible at the margin of discourse, and (ii) the opacity or visibility of the signifier at its centre. First, Lyotard evokes referentiality and designation as both necessary for language and yet unable to be contained within it as mere effects of the internal functioning of the system or *langue*. Second, Lyotard insists on the necessary role of the phenomenally visible within the transparent textual space of Saussure's account of linguistic structure, lending an opacity or thickness to the signifier and its functioning. In each case, there is a crucial shift from *opposition* to *heterogeneity* as characteristic of the differential nature of the sign. A heterogeneity, a difference that cannot be reduced to a

12

matter of opposition within a structure or system, is what marks Lyotard's account of figurality as post-structuralist or deconstructive.

(E) OPPOSITION AND DIFFERENCE/ SIGNIFICATION AND REFERENCE

The heterogeneity of the visible consists in its function as a negation of language, an evocation of the non-linguistic, which cannot be contained *within* language, signified by it. Lyotard distinguishes two kinds of negation at work in language: a negation of pure *opposition*, which characterizes the Saussurean description of signification, and a negation of radical *difference*, which characterizes the referential or designatory function of language. The merely oppositional negation of signification founds textual space, whereas the radical difference introduced in reference is characteristic of the visible. Saussure poses language as a closed system of signifiers and signifieds. Lyotard accepts that the linguistic signifier functions differentially, but insists that this is not the whole story: that this ignores the difference of the visible evoked in linguistic reference or in the plasticity of the line in the letter.

Let us begin by looking at the incommensurable presence of visible and textual space in the way reference functions as a figure for structural linguistics. According to Lyotard, reference and designation ground the function of language, but they do so at the cost of introducing the alterity of the visible to the textual space of linguistic signification: 'To speak is always to speak of something, and this dimension of reference, which the structuralist method ignores on principle, is nothing other than the presence of the distantiation of seeing in the experience of discourse' (*DF*: 31). Saussurean linguistics, as we have seen, inscribe the differential functioning of language entirely within the system of signification. The only difference for language is the opposition of one signifier or one concept to all others in the *langue*. Thus a tree can only be apprehended because the system of opposed elements in language posits a concept 'tree', a value internal to the system, with which an actual tree can be identified. The function of reference, by which language points at objects outside itself, is entirely subjugated to signification, by which language assigns meanings to things. A thing can only be pointed at insofar as language can give it a meaning.

Reference is necessary even for Saussurean linguistics because the linguistic unit functions in two ways at once. On the one hand, the signifier establishes a value internal to the system, by opposition to all other signifiers. On the other hand, the signifier indicates or points to the concept or signified. The sign is thus both the counterpart of all other signs *and* the counterpart of the concept (*DF*: 94). The function of the sign is unmotivated or arbitrary in relation to all other signs, but the sign participates in a sensible order: that of reference and designation, of indication.

In insisting that through reference language encounters 'the depth of the visible' (*DF*: 27), Lyotard does not argue against de Saussure that things have a real pre-linguistic meaning.[16] Rather, the capacity of language to point, to refer, to indicate, is not itself a matter of meaning. Pointing, the referential or indicative function, is both necessary to and disruptive of signification. That is to say, it is *figural*. Reference does not introduce language to a reality that cannot be signified; rather reference and deixis as linguistic functions of pointing cannot be reduced to signification because they introduce to the functioning of language a difference which cannot be reduced to oppositionality. To put it crudely, the difference between 'a tree' (a value established within the linguistic system) and 'this tree' (a designated object) is not a difference that can be exhaustively described in terms of a variation in *meaning*.

Why is this the case? Why does pointing function as a figure for signification? In the case of reference, pointing invokes an exteriority to language, a world of things: a relation between language and the non-linguistic. In the case of deixis, pointing invokes a space of designation, a location. The reduction of reference ('this tree') to signification ('a tree located at point X on the map') is the drawing of the object into a conceptual *schema*, the interiorization of the object as a value within a system. Signification is thus the overcoming of the difference of exteriority and its replacement by the opposition between elements in the differential system of the *langue*. Against this, Lyotard argues:

i) that the difference of referential exteriority cannot be reduced to and signified by an opposition;
ii) that this radical heterogeneity is a necessary condition of signification by oppositions. This is because the non-linguistic, the distance of reference, is both the other of discourse and its condition of possibility.

We need at this point to clarify how Lyotard uses the notion of linguistic *negation* in order to distinguish between his account of reference and Saussure's account of signification. The distinction of reference from signification concerns the kind of *negation* of language that each carries with it, the kind of relation each establishes between language and the non-linguistic. On the one hand, in signification, the negation of language is internal to the functioning of the *langue*; negation establishes the gaps between linguistic units, the gaps that distinguish the terms from each other and so permit them to function by opposition. Thus the non-linguistic enters signification solely as the absence of language permitting a separation between terms, the gap that allows us to distinguish 'frog' from 'French'. On the other hand, reference poses the non-linguistic as the silent alterity of objects at the edge of discourse, a distinction between the linguistic phrase 'that tree' and its referent (a non-linguistic object). Reference negates language externally rather than internally; rather than being a gap *within* language, the non-linguistic is the distance of the referent at the outer edge of language.

Lyotard insists that the exteriority of reference is lost in signification. Signification is by definition the interiorization of things within the conceptual structure of discourse as signified values, and yet that exteriority is the price that we must pay in order to make language usable, to let it speak of things (*DF*: 50). Thus, reference functions as a figure in that language encounters its negation, not as the pure absence of language (the opposition of language to its absence that holds elements apart within the system of oppositions) but as another kind of space, that of the visible (a radical heterogeneity which is not in simple opposition to language). Reference evokes a quasi-visual negation of language by the non-linguistic: a negation which is incommensurable with the oppositional negations internal to the tabular textual structuration of language. Reference, language's pointing outside itself, introduces the heterogeneity of the visual as negation of language to the purely oppositional negations intrinsic to the linguistic system of signification, and it introduces this heterogeneity even as it lends discourse the possibility of signifying. As Lyotard puts it, the figure 'is something of another kind that is lodged within discourse and lends it its expressivity' (*DF*: 51).

The strong example of the way in which the pointing of language evokes the visible in its negation of language is the function of designation, as Lyotard describes it in his critique of Hegel's *Phenomenology of Spirit*. Designation is the indication of the 'here and now' by deixis. The signifier of indication, such as 'here', does not function analogously to the arbitrary or differential signifiers of the *parole*. The 'here' does not eliminate the terms from which it differs, it is not posed in simple opposition to all other terms (the 'not-here'). Rather, the designation works by a continuous or motivated differentiation of elements: 'here' may be opposed to 'there', but it is proximate to 'beside', 'below' or 'beyond'. The 'here' is not reducible to the signification or meaning 'point x' on a map, because it is not discontinuously established in opposition to all other points on the map. Instead, it inhabits a kind of curved or continuous space: the phenomenal space of the visible:

> The indicated place, the *here*, is apprehended in a *sensible field*, as its focal point no doubt, but not so that its surroundings are eliminated as is the case in the choices that a speaker makes; they remain, in an uncertain and undeniable presence, curvilinear, the presence of that which lies at the edge of vision, a reference absolutely necessary to the indication of place, as Hegel understands, but whose nature is completely different from that of a linguistic operation: this latter refers back to a discontinuous inventory, vision refers to topological space....
> (*DF*: 38)

Designation is one example of the failure of structural linguistics to account for how the system of language might move outside itself to account for anything other to it. Designation is figural in that it introduces visible to textual space, in that it applies a continuity to a linguistic field which in principle only allows shifts between discrete elements. Place can only be designated in the continuous proximity of before, behind, above and below. The designation of place thus participates in the continuity of what Lyotard calls a 'sensible field'. This is not like linguistic space in that it is not chopped into little bits, and it is not a matter of identifying a discontinuous bit by its opposition to all other discontinuous bits within a system. The continuity that designation introduces to space is thus also the introduction of motivation to the signifier of designation, of a non-arbitrary relation between elements. The quasi-visible space introduced by designation is thus absolutely heterogeneous to the unmotivated function of linguistic space.

Just as structural linguistics cannot account for the referential or designatory function of language, just as reference or designation function figurally for linguistic space, so the fact of speech itself introduces a heterogeneous or radical difference to the system of oppositions in language. Saussure presents us with purely discontinuous units recognizable as elements in an invariable system, functioning by opposition. Significance is the product of a switching or commutation between the signifier (1) and the system (n−1). Lyotard points out that the movement of commutation is at odds with the *disposition* of elements on the horizontal plane of oppositions (*DF*: 101). The opposition of the term to the system establishes its value, or signification, within the horizontal plane. Yet the act of commutation considered as act invokes a space that is alien to that of the structure, a vertical relation as it were, in which one element is picked out from the whole and then folded back in opposition to it. Like the visibility of the letter as a line, the act of commutation lends a sensible opacity to the transparent and arbitrary linguistic elements whose only being ought to be their pure relation to the rest of the system. The possibility of commutation implies a depth which the structural table of invariant distances denies (*DF*: 60). The point is that structural linguistics cannot account for how the horizontal elements of the network organize themselves into the vertical axis of language-use, how the system might give rise to the rhythm of a phrase. Since, for Saussure, the *langue* only speaks to itself (all signification arises internally to the structure), it cannot make any difference whether the *langue* is 'in use' or not. To put it another way, the event of language use is more than simply something which structural linguistics ignores, it functions as a figure, necessary to and disruptive of the horizontal network of oppositions that characterizes the structuralist description of language.

(F) THE FIGURAL OPACITY OF THE SIGNIFIER: PLASTIC LINE AND GRAPHIC LETTER

Let us recapitulate. The last three sections have traced an encounter between textuality and vision at the *edge* of discourse. We have seen how the functioning of language introduces a figure to linguistic space as it seeks to grasp its other: reference, designation and commutation are figures for structural linguistics. In this section, I want to examine the encounter of reading and seeing on the *inside* of discourse, in the signifying unit. If the presupposition of Saussure is that the signifier is the transparent and arbitrary bearer of a concept, Lyotard insists upon the functioning of the visible as a figural 'thickening' of the linguistic signifier itself. Against the claim of structural linguistics that signifiers are nothing in themselves, that they function merely by opposition, Lyotard finds a figural opacity in the signifier which cannot itself be made into a matter of meaning.

Let me sketch the terms in which Lyotard finds the opacity of the signifier as evidence of a figural force at work within the virtual textual space of structural linguistics. If textual space is supposedly immobile, a tabular structure of fixed distinctions between transparent or unmotivated elements, figural space appears inside textuality in two ways: first as motivation and continuity between elements; and second as a depth and opacity for elements themselves. Rather than participating in the abstract space of the table, elements 'stand out', with the depth of figures visible on a ground.

First, Lyotard opposes figural motivation to the arbitrary or unmotivated quality attributed by Saussure to the sign. That arbitrariness does not merely concern the unmotivated relation of the sign to the thing. Saussure's account of signification also establishes an unmotivated relation of textual space to the body of the reader, which Lyotard calls the 'graphic' function of the letter. There is no value to the plastic forms of letters – their capacity to signify depends simply on their oppositional graphic distinction. All that is required of 't' is that it be distinguishable from all other letters. The actual plastic shape of the letter is irrelevant. At the same time, all that is required of the reader is the recognition of this distinction: the different corporeal engagement of the retina in tracing the line of 't' or of 'r' is utterly irrelevant to their function, which in each case is merely to distinguish themselves from 25 other characters, from the absence of character, and from diacritical marks. The letter functions purely in relation to its opposition to the rest of the disembodied system or code to which it belongs (we are back with the discursive model of the Swiss cheese). In itself, the letter is transparently decodable, existing purely in the virtual textual space of the code or system.

Lyotard contrasts this to the plastic function of the line. The line is *seen* rather than read; it functions by an appeal to corporeal resonance rather than to the code; it is a figure on a ground rather than an arbitrary mark. As such it has an opacity, in that it is visible by virtue of a certain 'resistance'. We can think of this resistance in the first place as simply phenomenological, as a friction on the retina constitutive of the act of seeing. In this sense, it is clear that vision as a function of the eye is excluded by Saussure – letters or signifiers are elements to be read with the immobile eye, recognized and decoded rather than viewed (this reading is absolutely equivalent to 'hearing'), not seen with the moving or phenomenal eye.[17] Thus, the various alterations in the plastic form of the letter 't' owing to hand-writing make *absolutely no difference* to its function, unless they alter it so much as to occupy an alternative oppositional relation in the system. All forms of the letter 't' are the same as long as they can be recognized as such, as long as they don't look like an 'r'. And yet of course the letter is made up of a line which must be seen in order to be recognized, whose function as arbitrary and unmotivated unit is dependent on the motivated plastic continuity of the line in order to establish it.

More importantly, for Lyotard the line marks a figural space, it has the quality of a trace of the unrecognizable; it evokes an unreadability that is constitutive of the very possibility of recognition. The line defines objects to which concepts are matched. Yet the line has no concept, is purely plastic. The act of matching the corresponding concept to an object, the act of recognition, of understanding, of mental representation consists precisely in the suppression or forget-ting of the trace or line, and the situation of the concept-thing in the virtual space of its pure opposition to all other concepts in a system of understanding. By analogy, we might consider the status of the line in perspectival construction: the line establishes the distances and con-tours of perspective, but the successful perspectival construction is one in which the plastic force of the line (its vibration – a function analogous to colour) is entirely lost in favour of the pure extension of objects in the three-dimensional space of their interrelation. The construction of virtual or textual space is the forgetting of the line as figure and its replacement by the thought of space as pure neutral support. This move is, according to *Discours, figure*, the definitive feature of logocentrism as the identification of being with meaning. In order to identify being and meaning, all objects must be enclosed within a field of signification: their difference must be reduced to opposition.

In the textual space of signification, the heterogeneity of the figural line is thus reduced to the reversible and oppositional graphic dis-tinction of the letter. The letter signifies by virtue of its opposition to the rest of the system from which it comes. On the other hand, in the plastic space of vision, the line wanders, differently. And the two spaces cannot be finally separated; the plastic function of the line works figurally even in the most prosaic page of text. To read the letter as line, as is always possible, is to render the graphic letter's transpar-ent function as signifier opaque. To put it another way, reading the line in the letter evokes an unrecognizable activity, a seeing devoid of any meaning, underlying the claim to decipher the letter as recognizable meaning. Lyotard points out that the letter cannot be entirely reduced to its literal function within a system of signification. The very literalness of the letter functions as a figural or rhetorical excess over 'literal' meaning, an excess that is, moreover, constitutive of its very inscription.

It must be recognized however that Lyotard is producing more than a phenomenological critique of Saussureanism for having 'forgotten' the corporeal engagement of the body.[18] Thus, for example, Lyotard points to the extent to which the distinction of gesture from language, of movement from speech, in Merleau-Ponty is itself dependent on language: the phenomenology of gesture is not so much an alternative to language as it is one more attempt to think linguistic metaphor, rhetoricity (*DF*: 57). *Discours, figure* argues that the line functions as a figure in the letter: that the transparent recognizability of the alphabet's letters is founded upon an unrecognizable, opaque, plastic function of the line which it attempts to suppress in the interests of its functioning. That is to say, letters function insofar as differences in the inscription of the 'same' letter are repressed, insofar as letters are recognized rather than seen. To see the line in the letter is to shift to a corporeal engagement with plastic value, with a corresponding loss in readability (*DF*: 216). At the same time, however, it is possible to see the letter functioning as a figure in the plastic value of the line: when in medieval illustrations the positions of the body are conventionally coded, when pictures offer themselves as texts for the unlettered.

As a result, in evoking the line in the letter Lyotard is not arguing that the plastic, corporeal or sensible is inherently figural, but that there is always a figural coexistence of the plastic and the textual, of the line and the letter. The figural is not the alternative to the textual: it does not signify in opposition to signification by opposition. Rather, the figural is the blocking together of the incommensurate, the clash of heterogeneous plastic and graphic spaces. To put it another way, the figural is not another kind of representation (corporeal, phenomenological, visible); the figural is other to representation, the entry of the heterogeneous into representation. Furthermore, the figural is not an other to representation that can be represented as 'other', the pure negative of representation, the line as opposed to the letter. If we try to evoke a pure corporeality of the line ('real space'), Lyotard will remind us of the potentially arbitrary signifying function of the line (its work of demarcation).

This figural opacity should not be confused with the 'materiality of the signifier' which some cultural critics have sought to extract as the lesson of deconstruction. The 'materiality of the signifier' has been the banner under which deconstruction has been reinscribed within Marxism's struggle to uphold the material against the ideological. According to cultural critics such as MacCabe, deconstructing Saussure means that the signified is revealed as merely the illusory or ideological effect of the combination of signifiers.[19] To read the materiality of the signifier is to refuse ideological illusion and show the mechanism by which dominant discourses are produced.

The problem with this approach, however much attention it might seem to devote to the formal properties of language, is that it is resolutely concerned with purging language of all figural or rhetorical deformations. The materiality of the signifier is its literal truth, and its literal truth is materiality. To put it another way, the materiality to which cultural critique refers is not that of the signifier; rather, 'materiality' is in this case the *meaning* of the signifier, the grand transcendental signified. All signifiers mean 'materiality', all texts are read to show the signifier saying 'look how material I am'. The material differentiality of the signifier is reduced to pure indifference: all signifiers, without distinction, mean 'materiality'. At which point, since Marxism says that the emergence of materiality incarnate is the historical destiny of the proletariat, the meaning of all texts is literally political.[20]

Lyotard makes the counter-claim that the materiality of the signifier is only resistant if it is figural. For Lyotard 'it is not by virtue of its "materiality" that language participates in the sensible, it is by its figural quality that it may come to the same level' (*DF*: 51). That is to say, only if its materiality may not itself be the object of a signification, a meaning; the materiality of the signifier is its otherness to signification. The redescription of materiality as not a property of objects, but a resistance to conceptual representation is the starting point from which Lyotard elaborates a politics of the figural. As we shall see in our chapter on the politics of representation, the concern for the figural as opposed to the discursive demands that we rethink the material. Rather than taking the material as the literal truth of discourse, as opposed to the ideological abstractions of rhetorical or figural language, Lyotard thinks the materiality of rhetoric to produce a politics which ends up finding materiality to be an effect of the temporality of language. Materiality is not the rough objecthood of things extended in time, it is the temporality of the event which conceptual representation seeks to efface by identifying being with literal description.

The figural, then, is not the alternative to textual representation by signification, not a pure anti-logocentrism (a nonsense); rather, it is the blocking together of heterogeneous spaces (such as the textual and the visible).[21] Lyotard's version of deconstruction is an attempt to make this co-presence of radically different spaces into something more than a contradiction or an impasse. The opacity of the signifier is not a pure objecthood outside language, a simple beyond of representation. Rather, it is the mark that representation only functions by virtue of a necessary and impossible encounter with its other, the encounter that is the condition of the figural. The figural is that which, in representation, makes us aware that there is something which cannot be represented, an other to representation. In this respect it is like the *immemorial*, that which cannot be remembered (made the object of a present representation) but cannot be forgotten either.

For example, Lyotard proposes this figural function as appropriate to the paradox that the Holocaust presents for representation, as Adorno delineates it. In 'After Auschwitz', Adorno says of the application of conceptual cognitive representations to the event of the Holocaust, 'If thought is not measured by the extremity that eludes the concept, it is from the outset in the nature of the musical accompaniment with which the SS liked to drown out the screams of its victims' (Adorno 1973: 365). To make the Holocaust a concept rather than a name, to claim that the death camps could be the object of a cognition, a representation by concepts, is to drown out the screams of its victims. After Auschwitz, history is no longer a rational unfolding. The summit of reason, order, administration, is also the summit of terror. Calculation and accounting encounter the mathematical sublime of railway timetables and of genocide at the same time. If history could remember the Holocaust adequately, we would have forgotten its horror. It is an ethical necessity that the Holocaust haunt us, that it cannot be remembered but cannot be forgotten either. The event must be immemorial. This 'administrative murder of millions' has imposed a debt to the dead that cannot be integrated into a life: no atonement is possible. No atonement, but a postponement into an after-time, the time of Primo Levi as survivor, haunted by the fear that he may awake to find himself once more in Auschwitz, having dreamed survival.

Two implications. As Lyotard remarks in *Heidegger et 'les Juifs'*,

22

Adorno's greatness is to have recognized that, after Auschwitz, art can only be historically responsible as event, rather than representation (*HJ*: 79). Art must not exchange the affect of the Holocaust, the emotion which moves us out of representation, for a representation that claims to give a cognitive signification to the Holocaust. The Holocaust is an opaque sign, one which is not given up to meaning. If this opacity is a 'materiality', then that materiality cannot be a matter of meaning, of understanding. An aesthetics of pathos is required, an aesthetics responsive to the limits of representation, to the sense that something is trying to be said which cannot be said. Thus, in its displacement of representation, deconstruction does not return us to a pure being or truth that might precede representation: deconstruction is the aesthetics, ethics and politics of the incommensurable.

(G) POETRY AND PAINTING: THE AESTHETICS OF THE INCOMMENSURABLE

Having in the preceding sections established the framework within which Lyotard argues for the figural as the other which semiotic or phenomenological theory rejects, I now want to turn to Lyotard's account of the work or labour of art as the practical evocation of figurality. *Discours, figure* thinks the incommensurable in spatial terms: as the co-presence of radically heterogeneous spaces in the formal mode of the artwork's presentation of itself. Thus for example Masaccio's trinity on the walls of Santa Maria Novella in Florence is remarkable for the way in which both medieval and Renaissance pictorial space are *impossibly* co-present, a yoking together of heterogeneous accounts of representation that testifies to the limits of representation, and indicates that art, like desire, is at work here (*DF*: 200–6). Likewise Lyotard echoes Merleau-Ponty in praising Cézanne's deconstruction of vision. According to Lyotard, Cézanne's achievement is the *simultaneous* presentation of both the focal zone and the curved periphery of foveal vision in painting Mont Saint-Victoire, which Lyotard claims amounts to showing the condition of visibility itself. The condition of visibility is the density or thickness of the visible (as in the distance of reference), which is lost once viewing is understood in terms of vision, of the transparency of an object for a subject. For both Cézanne and Masaccio, the image is divided from itself by its simultaneous participation in radically different spaces, and the effect of this is to *testify to something that cannot be represented*. To testify, not to represent. Not to represent the irrepresentable but to make us aware that there is something other than representation.

This description of aesthetic incommensurability may sound familiar to those aware of Lyotard's writings available in translation. Here is Lyotard on the distinction between modernism and postmodernism in aesthetic production:

> Here, then, lies the difference: modern aesthetics is an aesthetic of the sublime, though a nostalgic one. It allows the unpresentable to be put forward only as the missing contents; but the form, because of its recognizable consistency, continues to offer to the reader or viewer matter for solace and pleasure.... The postmodern would be that which, in the modern, puts forward the unpresentable in presentation itself; that which denies itself the solace of good forms, the consensus of taste which would make it possible to share collectively the nostalgia for the unattainable; that which searches for new presentation, not in order to enjoy them but in order to impart a stronger sense of the unpresentable.
>
> ('What is Postmodernism?', *PMC*: 81)

In Lyotard's later writing, he appropriates the term 'postmodernism' as a way of introducing figurality to the thought of history as a mode of representation; postmodernism for Lyotard is primarily an understanding of the historical event as composed of simultaneous and heterogeneous temporalities: a kind of temporal irony.[22] Lyotard's developing switch from politics to ethics, his insistence on the necessary indeterminacy of judgment and his elaboration of the 'differend', is a search for the incommensurable in the socio-political domain, the point at which a radical difference is at stake in political dispute, a difference which any 'settlement' will necessarily suppress.[23]

Before discussing the figural temporality of postmodernism, I want first to trace the deconstructive account of figurality elaborated in *Discours, figure*. In the linguistic field, this amounts to a deconstructive rewriting of rhetoricity in terms of the incommensurable. In the domain of painting, the account of anamorphosis which Lyotard gives may serve as exemplary of the deconstruction of the space of pictorial representation.[24]

Lyotard accords responsibility for evoking the figural to art.[25] As he puts it:

> The position of art is a denial of the position of discourse. The

position of art indicates a function of the figure, which is not signified, and this indicates this function both at the edge of and within discourse. It indicates that the transcendence of the symbol is the figure, that is to say a spatial manifestation which linguistic space cannot incorporate without being overthrown, an exteriority which cannot be interiorized as a *signification*. Art is posed otherwise as plasticity and desire, curved extension, in the face of invariance and reason. . . .

(*DF*: 13)

Poetry is the search for motivation in language not through direct contact with the real but through the twisting or rhetorical torsion of the flat table of linguistic space to the point where it becomes itself continuous, motivated, both in the traffic between words (e.g. in designation) and in the relation of words to (a) the *surface*, and (b) the *event* of their inscription. The figural work of art is to block together the motivated and unmotivated in language. It is important here to dwell on the notion of 'blocking together' as a kind of overprinting, as of two images when we cannot say which is superimposed on the other, when they occupy the 'same' space whilst remaining distinct. Herein lies Lyotard's distance from the New Critical praise of poetry as ironic or 'tensional'.[26] The New Critics demand that poetry *harmonize* incommensurability into a 'verbal icon' or 'well-wrought urn', an autonomous unity. Lyotard insists that heterogeneous spaces be blocked together, incompossible (irreconcilable, unable to be placed or related together) in their difference rather than fused into an identity.

Discours, figure concentrates on the work of art in terms of the formal relation of poetry and painting to the surface of their inscription: this is the basis of the parallel between rhetoricity in language and anamorphosis in painting. More important, and to be developed in Lyotard's subsequent work, is the motivated or figural force of the relation of language to the *event* of its inscription. To put this another way, *Discours, figure* is concerned to elaborate an account of the working of figurality in terms of *spatial form*: as poetry in language, as anamorphosis in painting.[27]

The analogy in painting to the force of poetic rhetoricity as constituent and disruptive figure for language is anamorphosis. Anamorphosis rests upon the figural clash between the quasi-unmotivated geometric perspective and the quasi-motivated force of curvature and diffusion in vision. The 'textualization' of the visual by Renaissance perspective or Cartesian optics is an attempt to understand objects as

25

in principle visible from a singular, immobile, point. The effect of this
is to reduce vision to an affair of geometry, of straight lines, to exclude
curvature and anamorphosis. The immobilization of the eye flattens
the visual field around a focal centre, projecting the visible as a stable
image clearly visible as on a transparent screen (*DF*: 157). Against
this, Lyotard insists upon the presence of the heterogeneity of curved
space in vision: of the foveal periphery alongside the focal centre, of
the evanescent, diffuse and elliptical margin inseparable from distinct
vision. The difference here is not a matter of quantity, of less distinct
vision, but a radical heterogeneity of quality, a different kind of seeing
at the margin of vision, constitutive of the event of perception. Renaissance method erases peripheral vision by understanding it as less
clear, rather than as the other of distinct vision. Lyotard thus juxta-
poses clear and diffuse vision as *heterogeneous* components of the visible. Anamorphosis plays upon the co-presence of curved and
geometric space in the visible:

> The play of two imbricated spaces forms the principle of the
> anamorphic picture: what is recognizable in one space is not
> recognizable in the other. The good form of representation is
> deconstructed by 'bad' forms: the skull in Holbein's picture, in
> the portrait of Charles the First.
>
> (*DF*: 378)

Anamorphosis is the realization in painting of the co-existence of two
radically heterogeneous spaces of representation; as in Holbein's
Ambassadors or the anamorphic portrait of Charles I discussed by
Lyotard, the death's head often forms the mark of the radical difference of the two spaces – the bar of death is the disjunction of the two
spaces in which vision is inscribed.

Lyotard picks on the example of the *veduta*, the 'distorted' projection of a townscape, as an example of the deconstructive force of
anamorphic vision. Viewing such a projection, focusing on any one
spot, displaces all others into curved or diffuse space, produces an
anamorphosis. To apprehend any one of the possible thoroughfares
or ways of constructing the city is to deform all others. This offers us a
useful way of thinking the difference between deconstruction and
pluralism. For pluralism, the city would offer a number of different
focal points amongst which we might choose indifferently, the choice
of one excluding the others. Deconstruction insists that our choice of
focal point makes a *difference*, produces the anamorphosis rather than
the exclusion of other points of view (*DF*: 184). We live *in* the city, not

outside it, any 'perspective' or point of view is implicated, not detached. A perspective is never reducible to the rational distance of a position. Anamorphic painting, that is, insists on the support of painting as material, not as a transparent screen. Points of view are not in indifferent, unmotivated extension in flat rational space, as pluralism insists. Rather, the point of view is always wagered against, and deconstructed by, the continuous or figural distortion in which it is implicated. The implication of opposing the construction of the city from a single point, of taking a unilinear perspective on history, is not that all points are the same, that anything goes. Rather, everything is at stake in the different kinds of continuities, distortions and motivations produced by a point of view. As we shall see, the necessary and disruptive figural anamorphosis of vision is closely paralleled in Lyotard's accounts of the figural necessity of anachronism in the writing of history as definitive of the postmodern condition.

By analogy, poetry is the anamorphic combination of motivated and unmotivated signifiers in the field of language. Mallarmé is Lyotard's example of a poetry that reveals discourse to be haunted by a figural clash between the unmotivated space of linguistic signification and the motivated space of visual figure.[28] Mallarmé's *Un Coup de dés* shows this by means of an attention to such 'formal properties' as typography:

> Mallarmé robs articulated language absolutely of its prosaic function of communication; he reveals in it a power which exceeds communication: the power to be 'seen' and not simply read or heard; the power to figure and not merely to signify.
>
> (*DF*: 62)

It is important to note here that poetry is not being radically abstracted from ordinary language by Lyotard; poetry is for Lyotard the point at which the *inevitable* figurality of discourse, and discursivity of figure, arises; where figure is to be found *at work*:

> This book-object contains two objects: an object of signification (made up of signifieds linked according to the rules of syntax), which says 'there is no notion (signified) abstracted from the sensible'. We *hear* this object. And in addition, there is an object of significance, made of graphic and *plastic* signifiers . . . made, really, of writing disturbed by considerations of sensibility (of 'sensuality'). The first object makes us understand the second, the second object makes us see the first.
>
> (*DF*: 71)

The distinction here between 'signification' and 'significance' is a distinction between *meaning* (as the abstract concept signified by the operation of the *langue*) and *sense* (the fleshly resonance of things, their effectivity in the sensible world). The figurality of poetry is to show the necessary co-existence of these two radically heterogeneous (unmotivated and motivated) modes of being for the sign. Mallarmé's writing in *Un Coup de dés* shows three kinds of figural operation, according to Lyotard. These operate at the level of the space of inscription, of the signifier and of the signified. First there is the figural force of inscription as an event in the field of the sensible, as well as the discursive, a recognition of the letter in the line that distributes signifiers according to a motivated order of plasticity, not simply in arbitrary and differential signifying functions. Examples of this are the spatial rhythms of typography and the temporal rhythms imposed on reading. In Mallarmé's use of the double page, for example, the blanks or gaps between signifiers do not simply have the oppositional function of negation, they do not serve merely to hold linguistic elements separate so as to allow them to function oppositionally in relation to the *langue*. Rather, they create effects by virtue of the motivated rhythms that the spacings establish, and their corporeal resonance with the viewing eye. Second, literary form itself works as figure, something which is not signified in discourse but which works over the linguistic figure. Finally, there is a figurality in the order of language at the level of the signified, the figurality with which classical accounts of rhetoric try to deal. This is the figurality by which a metaphor effects a distortion of meaning that exceeds analogy, that cannot be reduced to a comparison: to say 'rose' for a loved one is in excess of saying 'my love and a rose share the following qualities'. This the figurality of the rhetorical trope. That is to say, the rhetorical swerve of the trope is not merely a matter of the substitution of one sign for another; it is the blocking together of a discursive *comparison* between two discontinuous elements and the suggestion of a motivated continuity between them. The impact of Lyotard's rewriting of rhetoric as a matter of figural incommensurability rather than the discursive modification of meaning requires more detailed consideration.

(H) DECONSTRUCTION AND FIGURAL RHETORIC

Discours, figure upholds the figural against the textual. The implication of Lyotard's critique of Saussure is not so much that Saussure is wrong as that structural linguistics, in imposing the rule of discursive meaning, seeks to reduce the effect of the figural, of rhetoricity, to a mere second-order modification of meaning. We have seen how Lyotard deconstructs Saussure's constant privileging of the textual over the visible to show that the visible functions persist within structural linguistics as at the same time its margin and its centre. It is both absolutely excluded and absolutely necessary. Saussure's strong account of the rule of meaning as signification, a discourse of pure textuality, has also grounded a semiotic account of rhetorical language as simply a second-order modification of signified meaning. The critical significance of deconstruction has been to a great extent its refusal to think the rhetorical as reducible to signified meaning. *Discours, figure* provides an account of the irreducible figurality of rhetoric which is particularly useful in helping us to see how the challenge to the rule of signified meaning does not leave us in the position of saying 'everything is meaningless'.

Current debates in literary theory proceed from a difference over the function of rhetoric. The crucial distinction is between an instrumentalist conception of rhetoric and the deconstructive account of rhetoric as the constitutive displacement of the logocentric possibility of meaning. For traditional literary humanists as well as devotees of 'cultural studies', rhetoric is understood as the instrument by which significations are ordered and disposed. Rhetoric is thus a modification of a signification by means of a second-order signification. The analysis of rhetoric is a matter of setting signs in contexts that will allow us to determine their true signification: working out whether 'chicken' means 'barnyard fowl' or 'coward'. Crucially, however, the meaning that the analysis of rhetoric determines is literal rather than rhetorical, the effect of the combination of a signification with its second-order modification. To put it schematically, *signification A* ('chicken') plus *rhetorical modification B* (metaphorically applied to a human being) gives *signification C* ('coward'). The persistence of this understanding of rhetoric is thus the persistence of the rule of signification in the understanding of cultural objects.

On the other hand, deconstruction thinks rhetoric as *figure* rather than *instrument*.[29] Rather than being a modification of meaning, figurality is necessarily present to signification whilst radically heterogeneous from it. Figure thus evokes a difference which cannot be regulated, cannot be understood as the ratio of alteration between signification A and signification C. To put it another way, the difference that rhetoric makes to signification cannot itself be reduced to another meaning. The metaphorical linking of cowardice to the chicken does not simply render the unfamiliar understandable in terms of the known (define the abstract concept of cowardice in terms of the concrete and domestic chicken) but also makes the known chicken in some sense unfamiliar. This chicken will never be the same again, because we can never be sure whether or not a usage is rhetorical, whether cowardice is a literal or metaphorical attribute of a chicken. The deconstructive analysis of rhetoricity insists that there is no meaning that can be decisively separated from the condition of figural language, that there is no meaning that is literally literal. By a characteristic deconstructive move, rhetoricity, which discursive representation appeared to exclude or banish to the margin, is found to be at the centre, at work constituting and structuring the possibility of that representation. For example, clarity in speech consists in banishing the interference of rhetorical figures which give rise to ambiguities, yet 'clarity' is itself a rhetorical figure, a metaphor for the absence of metaphor. Figure is not a simple exteriority that cannot be interiorized as knowledge, but is the opacity or disturbance that marks the operation of representational interiorization as an operation, a process. This refusal to reduce rhetoricity to a matter of meaning disrupts the theoretical assurances of structural linguistics, stylistics, semiotics and 'cultural studies', the analysis of representations in terms of their political 'meanings'.

Lyotard opposes the deconstructive reading of figure to two major forms of its reduction – semiotics and phenomenology. On the one hand, phenomenology produces a metaphysics of presence by thinking the figural disruption as the pure expressivity of *gesture*, on the other hand semiotics reduces the figure to a swerve or displacement internal to the order of signification, a matter of *stylistics*, as it were.[30] Lyotard steers a course which at times risks falling into the first of these traps; it is hard to see how he is distinguishing himself from a claim that the figural reveals the expressive function of language, language's participation in the sensible world, as a pure alterity to signified meaning. In expression, according to phenomenology, nature enters language (things become words) and language enters nature in discovering its own depth or volume (words become things). But Lyotard importantly refuses this possibility of pure expressivity:

It's clear where this metaphysics of continuity errs: ... the language of nature which it invokes as the basis of the nature of language is not a language .... Language begins with the loss of

30

nature; the links between understanding and sensibility are not direct, unless we reintroduce teleology. Art is doubtless one of them: it gives matter for speech, and supposes for its production someone who speaks; it does not speak itself, *stricto sensu*, but the link that it attempts is always threatened, critical, mediated, constructed. Nothing less natural.

(*DF*: 293)

Language and the world do not share a nature: there is a supplementary violence to the operation that makes words into things, a violence that makes things into words, produces discontinuities, disruptions and immotivations in the world. If expression is a figure for signification, violence is a figure for expression. To put it another way, the figural is not the coming to consciousness of the sensible, but the subterranean distortion and violence of the unconscious. It finds the sensible (motivated) in the abstract (unmotivated) and the abstract in the sensible.

In the case of semiotics, Lyotard's attack on the reduction of rhetoric to stylistics is a refusal to allow any mere formalism to restrain figural distortion at the level of signification, as a second-order modification of meaning, so that in metaphor one would simply pass from a first signified to a second one, assuming a fundamental identity in nature between the two meanings. Lyotard insists, on the contrary, that:

> Metaphor ... is poetic not when it refers back to an already written *langue*, or to any code generally recognized by speakers, but when it *transgresses* it. And the transgression does not consist in passing from an ordinary language (of signified A) to a supposed affective language (of signified B); but in the use of *operations* which do not *take place* in language A.
>
> (*DF*: 318)

Metaphor, that is, is only figural when there can be no retranslation of its excess back into ordinary language, when it is an excess over meaning (signification), rather than just a surplus of meaning. Thus for example, Blake's sick rose is figural insofar as it resists being decoded as merely a multiplicity of significations (lost innocence plus venereal infection plus corrupted church, etc., etc.).[31]

Specifically, semiotics treats the rhetorical trope as a particular kind of *sign*, one which is a homogeneous part of the linguistic code as a whole, though with a certain specificity to its mode of functioning.

31

For example, in Barthes's 'Rhetoric of the Image', the 'rhetoric' of the image consists in the way in which a sign has both denotative and connotative significations.[32] The denotative or literal significance of the sign has an ideological connotation added onto it. The important thing to note here is that the rhetorical connotation of 'Italianicity' in the assemblage of fruits in a pasta advertisement is an additional, secondary, *meaning*.[33] The connotation that rhetoric carries with it has an extra meaning, but it is still another meaning, the co-existence of connotation and denotation is in no sense heterogeneous or incommensurable. The connotation of rhetoric is another communication, not the other to communication that the figural evokes. The theory of connotation reduces the figural to the linguistic order of the code (which Lyotard calls the space of 'writing'). 'Connotation' permits the decoding of rhetoric, 'the reduction of its polysemy, the flattening out of its opacity, the conversion of the object of vision into a readable object' (*DF*: 318). We are here very close to Paul de Man's rejection of the reduction of rhetoric to either grammar or intention. De Man insists, in *Allegories of Reading*, on rhetoric as introducing an incommensurable co-presence of heterogeneity, most notably in the two readings he proposes for the last line of Yeats's 'Among School Children' (de Man 1979: 11–12). The difference is that for de Man these are two heterogeneous *meanings*, rather than meaning and its figural other, as for Lyotard.[34] For Lyotard, semiotic analysis renders the figural recognizable, a mere surplus of literal meaning. In the place of this homogeneous add-on, Lyotard proposes that we understand the excess of rhetoric as figural, evoking the affect or sense that marks the co-presence of the incommensurable in language.[35]

For Lyotard, what makes rhetoric figural is the co-existence of *incommensurable* terms. Rhetoric evokes an incommensurability at three levels:

(1) in the functioning of metaphor;
(2) in the situation of metaphor within the system of tropes that constitutes rhetoric;
(3) in the relation of rhetorical or figural language to the communicative function of literal language.

In each case, this deconstructive account of rhetoric is opposed to the claims of semiotics to provide an account of rhetoric in terms of signification.

There is, first, an incommensurability within metaphor that displaces any attempt to understand metaphor as a vehicle of the communication of concepts, the site of cognitive understanding of signification. Semiotics takes off from Jakobson's understanding of signification in terms of the twin poles of metaphor and metonymy as paradigmatic and syntagmatic substitution. One term comes to *stand for* another. If they are similar but not continuously connected (rose, love) then the substitution is paradigmatic. If they are contiguously connected (horse, cavalry) then the substitution is metonymic. For Saussure, the syntagmatic and paradigmatic functions of the sign are indissociably linked, and function homogeneously in signification. Jakobson's 'Two Types of Aphasia' (in Jakobson 1971) dissociates the two as metonymy and metaphor, under the predominant rule of metaphoric substitution.[36] Lyotard stays with Saussure in finding the metaphor and the metonym to be indissociable; however, unlike Saussure he insists that the twin functions of contiguity and discontinuous similarity are radically *heterogeneous*: that theirs is an incommensurable co-presence.

Lyotard's reading of rhetoric in terms of the incommensurable involves first of all a reading of metonymy as continuous or motivated connection against the predominance of metaphoric or discontinuous substitution that characterizes semiotic accounts of figurative language (even when, as for Lacan, unmotivated substitution is called 'metonymy'). The emphasis on discontinuity, once paradigmatic and syntagmatic axes have been dissociated, is due to the fidelity of semioticians to Saussure. As we have seen, the function of the sign is pre-eminently metaphoric, a matter of unmotivated substitution; the appearance of connection (by which the word fish comes to seem 'fishy') is merely the erroneous effect of historical sedimentation. Semiotic analysis may be thus characterized as the reduction of the metonym to the metaphor in the sense that contiguous connection is understood as the matter of a substitution. And as we have seen, structural linguistics insists that the determination of the value of a signifier rests upon its discontinuity, its opposition to all other terms. The role of linguistics as master-discourse for semiology rests upon the determination of all signs as reversible substitutions. Metaphor, for semiotics, is the application of the characteristic relation of the signifier to the signified to the relations between a signifier and another signifier. 'Rose' stands for 'love' as 'love' stands for the concept of love, by arbitrary and differential substitution. The appearance of a motivated connection that we tend to think of as characteristic of metaphor is in fact itself a signifier positioned in immotivated and differential relation to a further, connotative signified. The apparent continuity of 'rose' and 'love' is merely a signifier functioning by substitution for a supplementary signified such as 'pretty but has thorns'. For semiotics, the distinction of metaphor from metonymy in this analysis is *itself a metaphor*: continuity does not lend a motivated function to the signifier, rather 'continuity' functions as an unmotivated signifier. Thus, rigorously applied, for semiotics 'there is no figure of language, only rules, no figure of speech, only controlled operations, and the figure enters language only at the stylistic level...' (*DF*: 258; 'Dream Work' *OLR* (*Oxford Literary Review*) 6.1: 20).

Lyotard insists that metaphor is never a matter of a substitution that might be reversible, that might be authorized by a code (we all know that 'rose' means 'love'). The figural function of metaphor begins with a substitution that defies the code of communication, that transgresses it: it goes 'too far':

> In the poetic metaphor, substitution is *precisely not authorized by usage*, is *not* inscribed in the paradigmatic network surrounding the supplanted term.... When the substitution is authorized we no longer have anything like metaphor in Lacan's sense of a *figure* of style. We have simply an instance of a choice between terms which stand in a paradigmatic relation to each other, any one of which would serve equally well at that particular point in the chain. Hence the choice of one of them at the expense of the others results in no overloading, no 'over determination' of the statement.... The true metaphor, the trope, begins with the too-wide gap, the transgression of the range of acceptable substitutes sanctioned by usage.
>
> (*DF*: 254–5, 'Dream Work', *OLR* 6.1: 17)

According to Lyotard, rather than a second-order mode of signification introduced so as to apply a concept to the unfamiliar, metaphor is a kind of poetic metamorphosis that cannot be understood in terms of a reversible substitution, where one term would 'stand for' another. The transgression of the code by the too-wide gap means that the functioning of the code is suspended: one term does not *eliminate* the other, substitute for it as an accepted equivalence. Rather, both terms are co-present, in a manner analogous to anamorphic effects in painting that I discussed in the preceding section. There is no single underlying semantic value that would underpin the reversibility of the two terms. The effect of metaphor is not one of comparison around a single signified, rather an incommensurability arises between two terms on the ground of the 'same' meaning.

34

Metaphor is thus a kind of metamorphosis, introducing a radical incommensurability, the co-presence of two heterogeneous meanings in what should be one space that displaces the possibility of purely cognitive comprehension of language as the sign of a concept.

Likewise, the relation of metaphor to other tropes such as metonymy is itself figural rather than discursive. As we have seen, metaphor and metonymy are indissociable yet incommensurable, in Lyotard's account. The figure of language is always both metaphoric and metonymic in its function, both motivated and unmotivated, given both as substitution and as continuation. The 'going too far' of the substitution unauthorized by the code is also a displacement of the axis of paradigmatic discontinuous similarity towards a 'mere juxtaposition' (Breton's surrealist metaphor drawn from Lautréamont: 'as beautiful as the chance encounter on a dissecting table of a sewing machine and an umbrella' is an example) which supposedly belongs to the axis of contiguity, syntagm, metonymy.[37] To put it another way, metaphor and metonymy are always co-present, but there can be no simple translation or equivalence between them; the attempt to reduce the contiguity of a metaphor, to think metaphor as pure similarity, is like the attempt to think the letter devoid of the plasticity of the graphic line.

Motivated and unmotivated are incommensurably co-present, refuse to be controlled, purified, kept apart as the terms of a simple *opposition*, of visible to textual, of metonym to metaphor, even of 'literal' to 'rhetorical' language. Figural language is incommensurable with the pure functioning of the *langue* in signification or communication. The mark of this incommensurability is the sense in which the event of a poem, for example, cannot simply be retranslated into critical discourse. There is a figural singularity to the poem: it doesn't just speak another language (which could be retranslated either into common English or into the descriptive metalanguage of structural linguistic analysis), it introduces the figure as other than language as structure of signification.

In the case of signification the sign is arbitrary, unmotivated: the terms of comparison are reversible. The terms of figurative language are irreversible: to say 'my love is a rose' is *not* the same thing as saying 'a rose is my love'. This irreversibility, or continuity, introduces a motivation to the sign: not a direct relation of words to things, but a motivation, continuity or opacity to the relations *between* the supposedly arbitrary and differential elements of the linguistic system. Words become things in their interrelation: an operation which is *heterogeneous* to the complementary process by which things become words, which is the opening of *immotivations*, discontinuities, in the apparent continuity of the visible. The point is that we are always in the condition of figural language: all language is figural, as we pointed out at the beginning of the chapter, yet the figure is also language. There is no pure figure, no pure motivation: which is what the figure of irony is all about. To take the example of irony at the level of intention, the level at which traditional literary criticism has sought to control it, irony is not 'meaning one thing and saying another', but is 'saying what one means' in a way that disrupts the possibility of literal speech or intention, that reveals the inevitable Carollian non-coincidence of meaning what one says and saying what one means.[38] That is, the ironic effect of a text such as Swift's 'Modest Proposal' does not lie in the fact that he 'doesn't really mean it', but in the radical undecidability that it introduces to the question of intention.

Lyotard's account of the inevitable incompossible blocking together of figural and literal produces a more general account of irony as irreducible to a subjective attitude, as constitutive of the possibility of language. To put it crudely, irony's threat is that it takes the claims of language literally in order to undermine the possibility of literal speech, since to take the claim of the literal literally is to reveal the 'literal' as *itself a figure*. Lyotard gives the example of Freudian analyses, where the figural work of desire is traced precisely by taking words literally, which is the figural blocking together of their designation as if it were a signification and the signification as if it were a designation: 'Figuratively speaking one might say that desire, furthermore, takes words literally [Fr. *au pied de la lettre*: at the foot of the letter]; the [literal] foot of the letter is the figure . . .' (*DF*: 248). Freud borrows Silberer's example: when he thinks of a text to be revised as 'uneven [*raboteux*]' his dream shows him 'planing [*rabotant*]' a piece of wood. The figural thus lies in the inevitable, impossible, undecidable co-existence of the radically heterogeneous orders of the figurative and the literal, of the motivated and unmotivated, the visible and the textually encoded, in all discourse. Therefore, 'it is futile to attempt to bring everything back to articulated language as the model for all semiology, when it is patently clear that language, at least in its poetic usage, is possessed, haunted by the figure' (*DF*: 250; 'Dream Work' *OLR* 6.1: 13). The figural is present in discourse in the relation of the signifier to image, of letter to line; in the relation of signified to form, of meaning to the event of its inscription; in the relation of the designated referent to the matrix in which it is given as lost object, of the

36

thing to the distance and difference in which it is constituted (*DF*: 283). And this relation is a deconstruction of discourse by the figural, not the annihilation of discourse.

(I) ACTING ON THE FIGURAL

I want to try to clarify what the stakes are in this deconstructive critique of semiotics, with its refinement of our sensibility towards the function of rhetoric. It's not simply a matter of reading texts better, more faithfully. Rather, our sense of what reading might be has to change. And along with it, our sense of the politics of reading has to change. Although I want to postpone a developed discussion of what a politics that seeks to deconstruct the rule of representation might look like until Chapter 3, it is important to take account of the extent to which *Discours, figure* raises the question of the politics of the figural. 'Politics' here should be understood as the question of what to do once the work of the figural has displaced the possibility of determinate discursive calculation. In this sense, politics is at odds with the political as a realm of knowledge, of strategy and goals; it may appear more like an ethics. Not an ethics because of a focus on individual conscience; an ethics facing the question of judging how to act once one can no longer *know* in advance how to act.

Discours, figure presents itself as a political book. I'm not so much interested in extracting or deducing that politics, since the project of ideology-critique for which it claims to be a prologemenon is dropped by Lyotard. Instead, I want to sketch the ways in which *Discours, figure*, in some senses despite itself, opens towards the refiguration of the political in Lyotard's later work. Rather than a section on 'politics', what follows should be read as a potential link to Chapter 3 of this book. Adopting language which will be discussed there, one might say that in describing figural language in terms of the co-existence of incommensurable terms Lyotard reads the effect of rhetoric as being the evocation of a 'differend', as the site of an aporetic clash between incommensurable languages, a site that has the performative effect of provoking further discussion. Art, as the setting to work of the figural, does not produce closure and mimetic representation, but more art, more reading. One way of characterizing this would be to say that the effect of figurality is to place the reader in an ethical situation. Thus, Hillis Miller is entirely right to recognize that deconstruction tends to produce an ethics of reading. Deconstruction has at times been betrayed into a *method* for discovering the aporetic impasse of representation, a kind of 'spot the *mise en abîme*'. The importance of Lyotard is to have phrased more clearly than any other writer what the *responsibility*, as well as the freedom, of the deconstructive critic must be. He insists that deconstruction does not produce better readings of art, a more rigorous theory of art. Instead, deconstruction is the refusal to allow claims to know the truth of art to silence the ethical demands that art or politics make on us. For Lyotard, the question of the law is always at stake when an 'event' occurs, when an incommensurability is posed within and against the conditions of representation that appear to determine culture:

> There are many events whose occurrence doesn't offer any matter to be confronted, many happenings inside of which nothingness remains hidden and imperceptible, events without barricades. They come to us concealed under the appearance of everyday occurrences. To become sensitive to their quality as actual events, to become competent in listening to their sound underneath silence or noise, to become open to the 'it happens that' rather than to the 'What happens', requires at the very least a high degree of refinement in the perception of differences . . . the secret of such ascesis lies in the power to be able to endure occurrences as 'directly' as possible without the mediation or protection of a 'pre-text'. . . . I am merely arguing that both art and politics are excepted, though in different ways, from the hegemony of the genre of discourse called cognitive.
>
> (*P*: 18, 21)

The account of rhetoric that deconstruction proposes is precisely a refusal to erase the differences that figurality raises by subjecting them to the rule of determinate meaning. For Lyotard, deconstruction escapes being a method in that it is simply the most intimate attention to the potential of radical difference, of incommensurability, and the awareness of both the impossibility of determinate criteria for judgment and the necessity of judgment. It is this that puts Lyotard in an especially useful position in answering the common charge that deconstruction has 'no politics' or is merely the celebration of meaningless 'freeplay'. Lyotard does not merely celebrate the deconstruction of the entire edifice of Western culture since Plato, he asks what responsibility the figural disruption of the assurance of meaning imposes.

Many critics have sought to argue that deconstruction is politically irresponsible at best, nihilist or Fascistic at worst, because it questions the possibility of political certainty. Lyotard's work allows us to understand the politics that is at stake in this questioning. The figural evokes an incommensurability for cognition. To put it bluntly, it speaks at least two irreconcilable languages at once. The position of the reader is thus one of having to make an *indeterminate* judgment, a judgment without criteria, since any criterion would have to belong to one language to the exclusion of the other. No determinate meaning can be assigned to a figure, since figure is precisely the overturning of the univocal authority of determinate meaning. Lyotard's reading of Kant (discussed in more detail in Chapter 3) insists upon this radical indeterminacy to aesthetic and ethical judgment. Thus, reading becomes an ethical activity rather than a process of cognitive recognition, a politics rather than the extraction or application of political knowledge. Our reading is free, since the figurality of the text resists closure. Yet there is an absolute necessity that we read, since even to remain silent about a text is to make a judgment about the nature of the difference that its figures set to work. The reader is now bound to turn the page, but she or he is free to turn it directly to our chapter on politics and ethics at this point.

One might say that the incommensurable co-existence that marks the figural is a 'differend', but one wouldn't be quite right. In *Discours, figure* the event does not yet have the ethical cast that it has acquired in Lyotard's later writings:

> [T]o respond to a case without criteria, which is reflective judgment, is itself a case in its turn, an event to which an answer, a mode of linking, will eventually have to be found. This condition may be negative, but it is the principle for all probity in politics as it is in art. I am also obliged to say: as it is in thinking.
>
> (*P*: 27)

For the event to be placed as the site of judgment without criteria, Lyotard will have to develop the distinction of reflective or indeterminate judgment from cognition into a politics. This is effected in his successive redescriptions of the social in terms of 'narratives' (*Instructions païennes*), 'language games' (*Just Gaming*) and 'phrases' (*The Differend*), the redescription of the social as a cloud of language particles to be traced in our chapter on narrative. In *Discours, figure* Lyotard is still ready to characterize deconstruction as practical ideology critique, with the reservation that ideology, in the age of telecommunications, can no longer be considered merely 'superstructural' (*DF*: 326). According to *Discours, figure*, deconstruction owes its critical edge to its reading of figure against the seductions of linguistic signification. Ideology is thus characterized as the reduction of the sensible to signification; deconstruction evokes a figural other which overturns that reduction (*DF*: 19). As we shall see in the last section, the subsequent shift away from 'ideology' (which implies criteria of truth and falsity) towards the performativity of 'commodification' as characteristic of the representational mode of capitalism is crucial to Lyotard's deconstruction of the space of the political in order to allow a deconstructive politics.

The distinction of the figural politics of deconstruction from a theoretical Marxist critique of ideology such as Althusser's lies in the *affirmation* that deconstruction makes.[39] If Marxism critically *negates* all hitherto existing history in the face of the eventual realization of the historical destiny of the proletariat, showing the ideological false-hood of all representations not firmly grounded in the historical materiality of class struggle, deconstruction overturns ideology by affirmation. Deconstruction does not simply dismiss the 'real' as illusion, nor does it simply uphold the real. Deconstruction upsets the representational seduction of language in evoking the figural; it does not do this in the service of an affirmation of a pre-linguistic real, but as a kind of secondary re-affirmation of the sensible and the work of the unconscious *after* language's attempt to reduce the sensible to mere signification:

> The deconstruction of the articulations of language, bringing with it the subversion of the most deeply hidden categories, is the work of affirmation (*Bejahung*) if one understands by it not a crude affirmation which would place itself *before* language, but a secondary affirmation, a reaffirmation which comes to cover again what language had placed in the open, to block together what it had separated, to confuse what it had made distinct.
>
> (*DF*: 296)

Ideology is thus counterposed to a *performative* rather than constative truth-value of figural *work*, in the unconscious, in poetic rhetoric, in the anamorphic displacement of vision, in the event's disruption of historical representation. As Lyotard puts it in 'Œdipe Juif' in *Dérive à partir de Marx et Freud*, 'The truth *does not speak, stricto sensu*; it works' (*DPMF*: 167). It does not speak because the truth is not the signification of a state of affairs by means of concepts: the truth is precisely what resists signification, reduction to the concept, articulation within the flat and transparent space of the arbitrary oppositional structure of the *langue*. The relinquishment of ideology as a critical term in the subsequent drift of Lyotard away from Marxism is the development of this sense of deconstruction as a performative work (and *not* merely a 'freeplay'). What we should recognize now is that the term 'ideology' in *Discours, figure* covers the rule of representation by signification, the *reduction of difference to opposition* (*DF*: 165).

It is perhaps more productive to borrow a term which owes its strongest elaboration to Derrida's work, and to speak of deconstruction as opposed to logocentrism rather than to ideology, although it is important to realize that Lyotard's sense of logocentrism is wider than Derrida's, at least in the latter's early work. For Derrida, logocentrism is a problematic properly internal to linguistic representation's attempt to account for itself and the world, a metaphysics of representation which works on other fields by analogy, much as we speak of the 'language of the visible'. For Lyotard, the rule of the linguistic analogy is itself logocentric, participating in Saussure's dream of a 'general semiology'. However, the disagreement between Lyotard and Derrida concerns the common aim of upholding the radical singularity of difference against the metaphysical logic of identity which thinks difference as merely opposition. Thus, there is nothing different to being, merely non-being, nothing different to presence, merely absence, and so on. Derrida's elaboration of *différance* has been a long attempt to uphold the supplementary trace of radical difference which separates the terms of an opposition, and which is foreign to both: the bar that falls between presence and absence, evoking a difference uncontainable within the terms of that binary opposition. Lyotard's disagreement has been to refuse to accept that trace as essentially written or linguistic. For Lyotard, writing is *par excellence* the reduction of difference to opposition, the flattening of space into an abstracted system of recognizable oppositions between units which owe their differential value to opposition rather than motivation (*DF*: 155). Whilst Lyotard's corrective to the rule of the linguistic analogy is useful, his denigration of writing owes more to a definition of it as that which is at odds with the figural than to a detailed tracing of the history of the writing-effect in Western discourse.

Logocentrism as a cultural system for Lyotard would be the function of language, of writing, of textual discourse in replacing the figural by signification so as to render the unknown recognizable, so as to allow difference to be deciphered and assigned a concept within a system of oppositions. The kinds of irreducible singularity that language attempts to render transparent to its system are the incommensurability introduced to vision by the disjunction of curved margin from flat centre; the temporality of the event; the depth of referentiality; the mode of representation of the unconscious; the figural force of poetic rhetoricity. As we have seen, Saussurean linguistics masks differences by turning them into oppositions between terms within a totalizing system of divisions (*DF*:142).[40] Thus, Lyotard opposes Lacan's importation of Saussurean linguistics to the structure and operations of the unconscious. For Lyotard, the Unconscious does not speak, it works; the dreamwork is a matter for rhetorical analysis, not for accounting in terms of structural linguistics (*DF*: 146). Poetic metaphor, as we have seen, evokes a heterogeneous difference, a pure singularity that does not enter the regulated system of linguistic oppositions but departs from it, charging representational values with affects, for example. There is no simple transgression of the system, no pure opposition to the code, but the displacement of the code by figural differences, a displacement which is not the introduction of another kind of code, but which has itself the singular quality of an *event*, a kind of catastrophe, an earthquake as it were.[41]

The seismic event is the effect of the clash of two heterogeneous yet juxtaposed fields – the incommensurable:

> Difference is neither the flat negation that holds the elements of a system apart (linguistics), nor that profound denegation that opens the referential or representative field in the regard of discourse, and if it is the event, the lapsus or the orgasm that come to our pen as examples for beginning to sketch the field of difference, it's not by chance, it is because in these 'cases', unlike in signification or designation, *the division is not that of two terms* placed on the same level, inscribed on the same support, ultimately reversible given certain operative conditions, but on the contrary *the 'relation' of two heterogeneous 'states' at the same time juxtaposed in irreversible anachronism.*
>
> (*DF*: 137)

Discours, figure situates the event as the site at which the earthquake of the figural fractures discourse. Since the 'event' as singular and radical difference to the conceptual temporality of thought recurs throughout Lyotard's work, it is perhaps worth noting the role which the possibility of sheer eventhood plays at this stage. In the space of discourse everything is in place, so that the event can be erased, so that it can seem a simple error, a slip in ordered space rather than the displacement of discourse towards the unrecognizable by the work of truth (*DF*: 135). The event is thus already, in advance of Lyotard's adoption of the postmodern, opposed to the discourse of history. History as a discourse is attacked by Lyotard as the reduction of temporality to language; in historical discourse the event becomes a meaning to be signified, rather than a figural singularity (*DF*: 152–3). The eventhood of the event is the force of sheer happening, which Lyotard later characterizes as the pure 'it happens' which is lost once we try to say 'what happened', to turn the event into a signification by applying a concept to it. The event is thus the quality of temporal difference which cannot be grasped within a conceptual structure of time as past, present and future. Lyotard's turn to the postmodern is precisely an attempt to think the event as figure, to pose the question of how history makes the non-present (past, future) present:

> Difference in the temporal order can be grasped as the non-temporality which that order seeks to reduce.... When we say: what happens *has happened*, the temporal system authorizes us to understand: there is a cause, there is an initial trauma, there's an effect of recurrence of a past event; – and that suffices to repress the event, since a past event is non-event.... But true temporal vertigo is when the event doesn't appear in its proper place where everything is ready to receive it, in the future.
>
> (*DF*: 154–5)

It would perhaps be appropriate at this point to be anachronistic, and to explain the figural force of the event in the light of Lyotard's later appropriation of the language of the postmodern. Therefore, our next chapter will leap from 1971 to the late 1980s to discuss Lyotard's interest in postmodernism as an attempt to seize the term so as to talk about a figural temporality. Our argument has moved from a critique of Saussure to a deconstructive account of the work of rhetoric. One might end the chapter here and move to the issue of the event in postmodernity. However, for the moment, we must talk about psychoanalysis.

(J) PSYCHOANALYSIS: THE CONNIVANCE OF DESIRE WITH THE FIGURAL

Although we have noted the way in which unconscious desire is appealed to as the figure that will deconstruct the phenomenological rule of conscious perception in Merleau-Ponty, up to now in our reading of *Discours, figure* we have almost entirely ignored Lyotard's account of Freudian psychoanalysis, despite the fact that the Freudian account of desire is one of the strong forms of the figural which the book identifies. My reasons for this relative elision are similar to the reservations expressed by Lyotard in his retrospective on *Discours, figure* in the lectures collected as *Peregrinations*:

> Today I wonder if the answers provided by this book [*Discours, figure*] were not themselves too convenient, and that it remains too close to a conception of the unconscious coming directly from Freud.
>
> (*P*: 11)

The title of Lyotard's immediately subsequent book announces a 'Drift away from Marx and Freud'. The reading of Freud in *Discours, figure*, like that of Marx, provokes a 'drift' away from the orthodoxy espoused. Yet it is not simply the prospect of subsequent refinements that have led me to under emphasize the role of Freudian psychoanalysis in the delineation of the figural. To be blunt, fidelity to Freudian orthodoxy is not the argument most likely to influence Anglophone critics to take Lyotard's work seriously. In this chapter, I have preferred to trace the manifesto of the figural in contrast to the Saussurean orthodoxy that dominates contemporary literary theory. However, to make an argument for the figural based on *Discours, figure* without situating it in relation to the unconscious would be to fail to give the reader a sense of the book.

The role of Freud in Lyotard's work is persistent insofar as Lyotard tends always to refuse the limitation of psychic life to a matter of pure consciousness by means of an appeal to primary or unconscious processes. The unconscious is not an alternative reality to which Lyotard appeals so much as a name for an irrepresentable other to representation. Freud thus tends to serve Lyotard as a model for the problematic of an attempt to describe psychic life outside the singular rule of rational consciousness. A strong example of this comes in the essay 'Apathy in Theory' in *Rudiments païens*, where the fecund failure of psychoanalysis to theorize its object fully serves as a model for the limitations of theoretical metalanguages. On the other hand, Lyotard's rewriting of Freud in *Economie libidinale* and *Des Dispositifs pulsionnels* has also produced what seem to me the most unfortunate developments in Lyotard's writing, leading him to describe the former as his 'evil book' (*P*: 13). In a preface to the second edition of

Des Dispositifs pulsionnels Lyotard qualifies the problems common to the attempt of both books to achieve a writing which would be the pure transcription of a pre-conceptual work of desire:

> As for the metaphysics of desire or of the drive which overflows here, may it at least appear as what it was: a blow.

(*DP*: iii)

I shall say more at a later point about the problems of these works: let it suffice for now to note that there is a tendency common to *Discours, figure* and *Economie Libidinale* to use Freud for too easy an affirmation of the unconscious and the primary processes. The unconscious risks always becoming a counter-orthodoxy, the present site of a pure production of energy which can be upheld against system, rationality and economy. The writing of *The Differend* displays a considerable reserve in this respect. Indeed, the later references of Lyotard to the unconscious are hedged about with refusals to let the unconscious serve the modernist function of presenting the unpresentable, the refusal to let the unconscious become the good form of naughtiness, the clear sign of opacity.

Discours, figure moves from the visible to the unconscious in its defence of the figural. It begins by isolating a phenomenological or visual space distinct from language as the site of the figural but moves towards an object constituted by desire; the figural as lost object of desire rather than present object of perception. The designated object is not simply the presence of the visible, with which signification cannot deal, it is 'the visible insofar as it is *lost* ... which places the articulation of the designated or the image with discourse in the field of desire' (*DF*: 284). The importance of Freud is that his writings on desire offer a strong model of the figural: *Discours, figure* turns to the Freudian account of the unconscious workings of desire for the model of the figural *par excellence*. The primary processes of the unconscious function as figures for the rational and conceptual workings of the secondary processes of conscious discourses.

The chapter of *Discours, figure* that deals most directly with the figural work of desire is 'The Dream Work Does Not Think', where Lyotard is concerned to argue that if consciousness is structured by language, the workings of primary, unconscious processes appear as figural disruptions and distortions, disrupting not merely the ordered representations of consciousness, but the space of those representations built in preconscious revision. The four characteristics of Freud's description of unconscious processes upon which Lyotard

45

seizes are the absence of contradiction, intemporality, the free mobility of investments, and indifference to reality (*DF*: 274). All these are violations of the order of discourse. The unconscious is indifferent to contradiction and temporal sequence, it blocks together the heterogeneous in a way characteristic of the figure. The effect of non-contradiction is the anamorphic function of denial in desire. Blank contradiction does not eliminate the element to which it is opposed: the patient's negation of an object is at the same time the presentation of that object:

> 'It's *not* my mother', says the patient. 'We correct: so it is his mother' says Freud.... In negating, for himself, the explicit negation in the phrase, the analyst might seem to do violence to the letter, but only in order to give a dimension of pure literalness, which formalism ignores, that of its detachment from that of which it speaks.
>
> (*DF*: 117)

The literality of the letter functions as a figure here: to deny something is also in a sense to present it. The *difference* between saying nothing and saying 'nothing' is irreducible to the *opposition* between presence and absence upon which the signification 'nothing' rests. The object is incommensurably both present and absent, in a way that parallels Lyotard's description of anamorphosis. The work of desire is to open this incommensurability in our discursive relation to objects, which are constituted (presented) as lost (absent). This 'logical scandal' is the catastrophic event of the figural arising in discourse:

> Truth arises (events itself) as that which is out of place; it is essentially displaced ... no place for it, neither foreseen nor pre-comprehended. On the other hand, everything is in place in the twin spaces of signification and designation, so that the effects of truth may appear simple errors, slips caused by carelessness, poor adjustment of the elements of discourse, poor accommodation of the eye. Everything is ready there for the erasure of the event, for the restoration of good form, of clear and distinct thought. Truth presents itself as a fall, as a slippage and an error: what the Latin *lapsus* means.
>
> (*DF*: 135)

The false and the true appear together, 'not as contraries in a system

... it is necessary to struggle so that the effects of truth appear on the surface, so that its monstrosities of sense appear in discourse, right in the rule of signification' (*DF*: 17).

Second, the temporal condensations that characterize the workings of the unconscious likewise block together heterogeneous temporalities, resist the containment of desire within the logical trajectory of a move from absence to presence, from wanting to having. *Discours, figure* is concerned to insist upon the radically unfulfilled nature of desire, the fact that the work of desire cannot be brought to an end by being fitted into such a diachronic sequence: 'the fulfilment of desire, the major function of the dream, does not consist in the representation of a satisfaction ... but entirely in imaginary activity itself. It is not the content of the dream which may fulfil desire, it is the act of dreaming, of fantasizing, because Fantasy is transgression' (*DF*: 246–7). The work of the dream is thus detached from any logic of wish-fulfilment as the production of meaning and shifted to an insistence on the performativity of dreaming: the truth does not speak, it works; 'Desire does not speak, it disrupts the order of language' (*DF*: 239). In Lyotard's later writings the anachronism characteristic of primary processes is developed in the direction of the event as a temporal figure: our next chapter will discuss the temporality of deferred action (*Nachträglichkeit*) and of the immemorial as crucial to Lyotard's account of the possibilities of the postmodern.

The assertion of a figural force to the free circulation of affects in the unconscious has less positive developments in Lyotard's later writings. The disruption of the restricted or bound energy of logic, system and economy by the work of desire under the principle of pleasure rather than reality is developed in *Economie libidinale* to something perilously close to an affirmation of capitalist socio-economic mobility applied to the discursive order of the organic body. The notion that 'desire constitutes itself as force of pleasure without satisfaction of a need' can be shifted to a defence of the liberating force of surplus value (profit) divorced from the restricted economy of need. This does not seem to be the most helpful argument against the restrictive nature of Marxist reliance on a planned economy. What is important is that Lyotard redraws the Freudian description of desire in terms of the figural co-presence of the incommensurable spaces of the reality principle and the pleasure principle. Thus the simple opposition of reality to fantasy is displaced. The real and the imaginary are co-present heterogeneous spaces: desire borders reality anamorphically in that it is present at the edge of reality as different from it without

being eliminated; desire inhabits reality at its centre as the figural
trace of the struggle to eliminate it:

> Reality is constituted out of the imaginary. What is given first is
> the fantasmatic object. The formation of a 'real' object is a trial
> which corresponds to the constitution of an ego-reality in the
> subject. Reality is only a sector of the imaginary field which we
> have agreed to renounce, from which we have agreed to divest
> our phantasms of desire. This sector is bordered on all sides by
> the imaginary field ... and this emptied sector carries the trace
> of the struggle which opposed the pleasure and the reality
> principles to occupy it: 'reality' is not the fullness of being in the
> face of the emptiness of the imaginary, it carries a lack within it,
> and this lack is of such an importance that in it, in the loss of
> existence which existence bears, that the work of art takes place:
> it is real, it can be the object of identifications and manipu-
> lations before witnesses, assuring them that there is indeed a
> picture or a statue here and now; but it is not real, the *Waterlilies*
> is not extended in the same space as the hall of the Orangery,
> Rodin's *Balzac* is not planted at the crossing point of Raspail
> and Montparnasse in the same soil as the trees of the boulevard.
>
> (*DF*: 284–5)

The artwork is neither purely discursive nor sheer fantasy, it is both
real and unreal, a present object of cognition and a lost object of
desire. This characterization of the artwork in terms of an existence
given up to sheer incommensurability recurs as the postmodern
condition of the aesthetic object, which both is and is not art at the
same time. The significance of this description is less a matter of the
accuracy of a Freudian hypothesis than of the placing of the artwork
as that which deconstructs the opposition of presence to absence,
reality to fantasy, being to non-being, rhetorical to literal language.
The work of desire is thus not a pure alterity to the real, but the clash
of heterogeneous spaces (real and imaginary) that resists the reduction of the artwork to a matter of signification or cognitive understanding. The real and the imaginary are thus analogous to the
rhetorical and the literal in poetic language: attempts to determine
the artwork as a meaning through an opposition of the one to the other
break down in the face of the irreducible difference introduced by
their necessary and incommensurable co-presence.

For example, the dream work is analogous to the function of the
rebus, in which the line and the letter are combined, two hetero-

geneous representational spaces blocked together. In the rebus, which for Freud is characteristic of the dream work, the letter operates in figural as well as textual space. Letters form images, images form letters. The dream therefore gives itself at the same time to two utterly heterogeneous operations: the linguistic, textual act of reading and the visual, phenomenological act of seeing. In the dream work, image relates to text as fantasy to reality:

> The figural is hand in glove with desire on at least two counts. At the margin of discourse it is the density within which what I am talking about retires from view; at the heart of discourse it is its 'form' ... it is a matter of a 'seeing' which has taken refuge among words, cast out on their boundaries, irreducible to 'saying'.
>
> (*DF*: 239, 'Dream Work' *OLR* 6.1: 3)

Lyotard's use of the dream work as an example of a figural force introducing a difference that displaces the ordered network of oppositions characteristic of discourse is important in two ways. On the one hand, if the secondary processes of conscious and pre-conscious are structured like language, as a network of oppositions, the unconscious is not structured like or as a language but is a figural force that displaces the rule of language. This places Lyotard in direct opposition to the Lacanian introduction of Saussurean linguistics to the workings of the unconscious: 'the dream is not a discourse, because the dream work is intrinsically different from the operations of speech' (*DF*: 251; 'Dream Work' *OLR* 6.1: 13–14).[42] Saussurean linguistic science once again provides the strong example of the rule of discourse, of textual space, over the figural force of primary processes. For Lyotard, the unconscious is the space of the figural transgression of the order of discourse, the transgression of the textual by the visible image as object of desire, of visible 'reality' by the de-formations of desire:

> Reverie, dream, fantasy are mixtures to be both read and seen. The dream work is not a language; it is the effect on language of the force that the figural exerts (as image or as form).
>
> (*DF*: 270)

On the other hand, the description of the dream work in terms of the figural is important for the way in which it rephrases the act of *reading*, for the way in which psychoanalysis can be made by Lyotard into a model of an interpretation (if such a term can be used at this point) which does not aim at meaning, an interpretation which does not consist solely in reducing the figural to the discursive. This obviously applies not only to the psychoanalytic analysis of literature but to all reading (as Lyotard's constant analogies between art and the dream work will have suggested), because a long tradition of literary interpretation consists precisely in saying what figurative language really means, of reducing figural distortions to their proper signification.

If the rebus is a figure, a juxtaposition of the heterogeneous fields of articulated language (speech) and the sensible (vision), the question arises of what it might be to pay attention to this composite. The mode of reading which the rebus requires serves as an indication of what it might mean to pay attention to the dream work as activity rather than to seek to put an end to desire, to satisfy desire by revealing a latent content. Lyotard insists that the 'latent content' of the dream is not a meaning to be revealed, that desire does not simply operate as a force that obfuscates a pre-existing discourse:

> Desire does not manipulate an intelligible text in order to disguise it; it does not let the text get in, forestalls it, inhabits it, and we never have anything but a worked over text, a mixture of the readable and the visible, a no man's land in which nature is exhanged for words and culture for things.
>
> (*DF*: 270; 'Dream Work' *OLR* 6.1: 32)

The rebus and the dream work give us an object both to read and see, an object in which sensible forms act as signifiers and signifiers take on sensible forms. On the one hand, the line is read as a letter: the designation of the position of elements is homophonically transposed into a phonemic component. Thus, a picture of someone standing above the word 'time' might be transposed into 'overtime'. The continuous and motivated visible relationship is displaced into functioning as a discontinuous textual signifier. On the other hand, letters appear in continuous and motivated relations, 'inscribed at the same time in graphic and plastic space. The presence of letters or words in the rebus, rather than clarifying it, carries to its greatest height the confusion of the textual and figural. Words, already treated as things by phonetic displacement, can be so treated again in graphic figuration' (*DF*: 303–4).

The point is that this constitutive blocking together of textual and visible cannot be decoded so as to reveal its content in any stable way. The rebus, like the dream, is a figural writing that cannot be interpreted or translated but must be *transposed*, from graphic to plastic, visible to phonetic. There is no stable relation between the two functions, 'there is no rule which controls this displacement' (*DF*: 303). The act of deciphering is thus an elaboration, devoid of 'the constant relation like that which, at least in principle or as an ideal, there is between a text formulated in one language with its translation into another language' (*DF*: 298). To be blunt, having deciphered one rebus cannot help us to decipher another:

> The important thing is that whatever the operations used to construct the rebus, the decipherer doesn't know which he is dealing with: the exact nature of the confusions of place inside linguistic space and the substitutions of a plastic element for a term belonging to language is not indicated in any manner.
>
> (*DF*: 306)

The distinction of the dream from the rebus concerns the fact that the dream work cannot finally be transposed into a linguistic signification. Lyotard's illustration by means of the rebus indicates the demand of *transposition* rather than translation exerted by the figural force of the dream work. The dream work is radically indeterminate by virtue of the absolute heterogeneity of the transformations it performs. Interpretation cannot claim to 'find' the truth, since it must invent the rules by which it works in each case, on a case by case basis. Lyotard's reading of Freud is opening the space of interpretation as indeterminate judgment, which his later concern with ethics will develop. Interpretation thus becomes a work of *elaboration* rather than the decoding of what is already there, as in the analytic rule of 'free-floating attention':

> Thus interpretation is a work in the same way as the dream, it is not a commentary, it is not a metalanguage,it is above all an operative practice which does violence to the manifest organiz-ation of language, to its syntax, to its articulated signification.
>
> (*DF*: 381)

We can't 'just read what's there', we have to *do* something. The co-presence of visible and textual, figural and discursive, the sensible and signification, cannot simply be reduced to a matter of meaning. There can be no determination of the object as its meaning, since that meaning is only given as always already worked over by the alien and disruptive force of the figural. The task of interpretation is to testify to difference, not to reduce it to an opposition: not to make the unconscious speak, or render it conscious; but to manifest it in the work of interpretation. Reading (to depart from Lyotard's restricted sense of the word as the decoding of textual signification) must not claim to reveal hidden meaning, to translate the text into its proper, literal language of meaning; reading must pose itself as an act which sets the text to work, as a work which deconstructs textual oppositions to testify to figural differences.

Discours, figure brings together the workings of the figural and the radical singularity of events, under the signature of the unconscious and the primary processes in a manner that leaves the unconscious in the position of the very meaning it disrupts. The following chapters of this work will trace the development of Lyotard's account of figural work away from a simple opposition of the spaces of primary and secondary processes towards a consideration of the figural in temporal as well as spatial terms, a refusal to characterize the event solely in terms of form. The drift of Lyotard's work away from Freudian orthodoxy comes in a growing reluctance to locate all opposition to the cognitive realm of understanding in the anarchy of the primary processes. Lyotard develops an account of art and politics as sites for an indeterminate or reflective judgment, an account that does not rely upon an energetics of chaos in order to disrupt the hegemony of cognitive rational discourse. *Discours, figure* moves from phenomenology to psychoanalysis in its assault on logocentrism in art, philosophy and politics. That Lyotard should have relied on the chaotic energetics of the unconscious in the wake of 1968 is hardly surprising; that he should relinquish them for an investigation of the figural force of indeterminacy as constitutive of the act and the possibility of judgment is what makes his work of crucial importance to contemporary criticism.

2

Postmodernity and narrative

(A) POSTMODERNISM: FIGURAL TIME

What does it mean to think time figurally rather than as an ordered sequence of moments, to think time otherwise than by means of historical discourse? For Lyotard, the postmodern marks a temporal aporia – a gap in the thinking of time which is constitutive of the modernist concept of time as succession or progress. This temporal aporia is characterized by Lyotard as the time of the 'event' which functions figurally for the modernist discourses of epistemology, historiography, politics and art. *The Postmodern Condition* is most concerned with epistemology, whilst questions concerning the status of a historical discourse on art and politics are raised in *Le Postmoderne expliqué aux enfants*.[1]

The turn towards the postmodern that marks a certain stage of Lyotard's career and by and large his entry into the world of Anglophone 'cultural theory' is thus a transposition of the concern of *Discours, figure* with figures in the *space* of representation into the *temporal* domain. Lyotard's interest in the postmodern, and the interest which it holds for us, seems to me to rest less on his accuracy as a cultural pundit than on his attempt to seize the term 'postmodern' as a site for the rethinking of culture. In Lyotard's words:

> As you know, I made use of the word 'postmodern': it was but a provocative way to put the struggle in the foreground of the field of knowledge. Postmodernity is not a new age, it is the rewriting of some features modernity had tried or pretended to gain, particularly in founding its legitimation upon the purpose of the general emancipation of mankind. But such a rewriting, as has already been said, was for a long time active in modernity itself.
>
> ('Rewriting Modernity', *SubStance* 54: 8–9)

Lyotard is not interested in the postmodern as the description of the contemporary *Zeitgeist*. For him the postmodern comes both before and after modernism, in the sense that it is necessarily present as a figure for modernist discourse:

A work can become modern only if it is first postmodern. Postmodernism thus understood is not modernism at its end but in the nascent state, and this state is constant.

(*PMC*: 79)

In a sense, then, Lyotard's turn to the postmodern is a recognition of the continuing rule of modernism in art and politics, a dominance which may be displaced by the evocation of the postmodern as the figural other that necessarily accompanies modernism. This distinguishes him from a number of other contemporary theorists of the postmodern, who are more concerned either to characterize the flavour of our times or to describe the revolutionary potential of a new way of thinking.[2] As Lyotard puts it in a 1979 note to *Just Gaming*, 'Postmodern is not to be taken in a periodizing sense' (*JG*: 16n). Lyotard refuses to think of the postmodern as a new 'now', a look, the latest fashionable attitude.

This has made Lyotard into a rather uncomfortable bedfellow with other theorists of the postmodern, who tend to be rather more interested in apocalyptic announcements about the end of modernity. To say that the postmodern simply comes after the modern in diachronic succession is to say that it is the most recent modernism. An example of this kind of assault on modernism by the latest modernist avant garde can be found in one of Lyotard's own works, a study of the hyperrealist painter Monory, published in 1984. Lyotard's *L'Assassinat de l'expérience par la peinture: Monory* evokes the challenge of hyperrealism to modernity as the assassination of the model of modernist experience. However powerful the account of modernism which the book supplies, the hyperrealism which the book champions does not so much evoke the figural temporality of the event as transfer the time of the event into a purely spatial arrangement, in which the temporal is frozen or arrested by the snapshot. The gloss of the hyperreal 'reveals' the moment as cliché, as photographic simulation of a moment which is already a simulation, which is photographed precisely because it achieves the order of the pre-packaged, the commodified. And the theorization of this hyperreal moment can only have the same quality, can only be itself a further simulation in the chain of infinite regression. The problem with Lyotard's account of Monory is

54

that it is in this sense closer to Baudrillard's account of postmodernity than to his own other writings. There seems to me to be a stake in distinguishing hyperrealism from the postmodern in that the former doesn't respect singularity but reduces all events to the indifferent order of simulation. The time of the cliché (snapshot) may disrupt progress, yet it still offers a succession of images to a distanced subject that is the site of their synthesis (the epistemological structure implied by modernist accounts of temporality). The only difference is that the succession of images appears as historical impasse because it is modelled spatially rather than temporally, as a matter of levels rather than historical progress.

The understanding of postmodernity in terms of the *event* that Lyotard's other writings propose is radically different from the thought of the postmodern as that of the contemporary historical *moment*.[3] The figural force of the event disrupts the possibility of thinking history as a succession of moments. Lyotard is thus opposed to the majority of writers on the postmodern for whom postmodernity appears as the contemporary critique of modernism; postmodernity as the negative moment of modernist self-consciousness. For example, if modernism is self-conscious artistic practice, postmodernism is usually understood as merely artistic practice conscious of its limitation. Such accounts often point to certain exemplary architectural practices – a distinctly modernist manœuvre, by which process becomes object.

Under these descriptions, postmodernism comes about when modernism loses its confidence in itself, causing art to take on certain formal characteristics: assurance become irony (Hassan), originality become parody (Hutcheon), formal purity become *bricolage* (Jencks), progress become the cynicism of infinite deferral (Baudrillard), authorial voice become dialogue or polyphony ('Bakhtin').[4] For Lyotard, there are two important reservations to such attempts to determine the nature of the postmodern. First, such accounts tie postmodernism to the adoption of an attitude by a subject. That subject is not necessarily an individual, or even bourgeois, but may be authorial (Hassan), cultural (Jencks), historical (Kroker and Cook),[5] or political (Hutcheon). For Lyotard, postmodernism is an event, not a moment in the consciousness of things for the artist, for the people, for the spirit of an age. To understand the event as if it were a state of the soul or spirit is to ignore the eventhood of the event in the interest of taking account of its meaning, to reduce figure to discourse. Second, the identification of postmodernity by means of formal properties will tend to reduce the temporal aporia which the postmodern opens in representation to the status of a problem within representation. To put it another way, once the postmodern is formally recognizable, it is no longer opening up a hole in representation; rather than testifying to the unpresentable, it will have presented it.

Lyotard's account of postmodernism implies that, if resistant to anything, postmodernism resists the assurance of a conscious stance or position of knowledge, critique, or historical survey. This seems to involve a questioning of the political (or the economic) as the 'last instance' in which the truth of all things will be revealed.[6]

For Lyotard, critical negation is not an adequate description of the relation of the postmodern to the modernist idea of history (roughly, the idea of a diachronic succession of moments which is known from a position of transcendent subjectivity abstracted from that sequence). The distinction of Lyotard's writings on postmodernism is that they insist on the appearance of the event as a *figure* for modernist *discourses*, rather than a critique of them. The event appears as figure under the guise of narrativity in culture, anachronism in history, and paralogical experimentation in the arts.

Lyotard adopts the postmodern as an evocation of the figural force of the event in the thought of historical time. The thought of time disrupts historical assurance with regard to the conditions of knowledge, the writing of history, and the status of the aesthetic object. In *The Postmodern Condition* and *Le Postmoderne expliqué aux enfants*, this disruption takes three exemplary forms:

(i)   Narrative introduces a temporality to knowledge in excess of that permitted by the 'history of ideas';
(ii) Deconstruction insists that the possibility of writing history depends upon the effacement of the event of inscription;
(iii) The aesthetic object is detached from the temporality of original creation and repetition so as to no longer be a commodity circulating between artist and critic.

In each case, postmodernism testifies to what Lyotard has called the time of the event. And the time of the event marks a figural incommensurability: that between eventhood and the meaning or signification of an event; that of anachronism in the writing of history, when two incommensurable temporalities are blocked together; that between origin and repetition in the artwork. It is in this sense that the postmodern develops Lyotard's concern with the aesthetics of the incommensurable. For the moment, I want to concentrate on postmodernism as a figure for historical time: the relation of the discourse of history to the anachronism produced by the figural force of the event.

(B) THE EVENT

In order to understand this, it is necessary to be aware of the particular force of the 'event' in reading postmodernity. The event is the occurrence after which nothing will ever be the same again. The event, that is, happens in excess of the referential frame within which it might be understood, disrupting or displacing that frame. History will never be the same, after the French Revolution. That is to say, the Revolution can only be understood elsewhere, in another history, for which it is no longer an event. The event is the radically singular happening which cannot be represented within a general history without the loss of its singularity, its reduction to a moment. The time of the event is postmodern in that the event cannot be understood *at the time*, as it happens, because its singularity is alien to the language or structure of understanding to which it occurs. The pure singularity of its occurrence, the 'it happens' which cannot be reduced to a representation, cannot be identified with 'what happens'. As Lyotard puts it, 'In sum, there are events: something happens which is not tautological with what has happened' (*LD*: 79). To return to our three exemplary instances, the time of the event is that which is unaccountable in representation, appearing as either the difference inscription makes to the temporality of linguistic phrases,[8] or the difference narrative makes to the temporality of knowledge, or the difference unrecognizability makes to the institutional commodification of art.[9]

As the reader will have realized, the figural excess of the eventhood or singularity of the event over any meaning that may be ascribed to the event is very close to the Derridean 'supplement'. The supplement is the 'necessary surplus' that disrupts the propriety and self-presence of logocentric Being in that it is both necessary to Being and yet not part of it. The thought of Being that grounds the distinction of inside from outside, presence from absence, itself relies on an excess that blurs the boundary. The supplement is necessary (inside) and yet excessive (outside), and its work deconstructs the assured self-presence of Being that grounds metaphysics. There can be no plenitude to Being as either origin or finality, since that plenitude is fissured by its reliance on something that is exterior to it, defers onto a difference that flaws its identity.[10]

(C) POSTMODERN FIGURES OF HISTORY:
ANACHRONISM AND THE IMMEMORIAL

In this section I want to look at two of the figures of temporal incommensurability that Lyotard's version of the postmodern evokes. Anachronism is a figure in that its blocking together of incommensurable historical elements shouldn't be understood as a matter of self-contradiction, of conscious negation. Anachronism doesn't just cancel itself out: to disrupt historical succession is not to negate temporality. Postmodernity rewrites history as anachronism: a kind of temporal anamorphosis, in which the present event of writing is not eliminated by the past event that is written about, or vice versa. Rather two heterogeneous temporalities are co-present. Modernist History, as a critical field or science, is founded by and lives from the establishment of a discrete break or cut between a past (the time about which the historian writes) and a present (the time of writing). The modernist historian is not a chronicler, a mere appendix to the story s/he writes, but the absolutely privileged and secure site grounding the possibility of the story. Modernism presents a rigid division, a binary opposition. On the one side the present, modernity, the moment (temporal space) of an overview, of research and writing, secure in its self-presentation precisely because it is modern; on the other side the past, a history that surrenders itself to the gaze of modernity. Postmodernity is not the overcoming of modernity but a disruption of the division that founds and secures it over and against the past.

In postmodern terms, history is not a panoply of past events, written about in an unhistorical present. In Lyotard's postmodern condition, writing and reading cannot be understood as merely contingent or secondary in their effects upon the History to which they happen. On the contrary, they structure History in ways that upset the understanding of it as a procession of moments independent of acts of inscription. Nor is History a purely present act of inscription (nothing other than 'what is said about it now'). On the contrary, the 'it' of historical difference uncannily haunts the 'now' of the historian's discourse. We inhabit neither the distant past nor the distance of the present. Lyotard's confrontation of the modernist conception of historical time with the time of its inscription gives rise to anachronisms which cannot be reduced to the status of historical 'errors'. The time of inscription comes both *after* history and *before* it,

58

since History is in a sense constituted by the possibility of being re-transcribed.

History is always already rewritten because Lyotard thinks the anachronistic temporality of history by analogy with Freud's *Nachträglichkeit*, or deferred action, in which the event occurs both too soon and too late. It occurs too soon to be understood, and is understood too late to be recovered.[11] To follow Freud, the belated quality of the event proceeds from the fact that it only enters consciousness as a re-transcription (Freud 1966: 233). Thus, we might say that although postmodernism is not the age or epoch of psychoanalysis, the postmodern is the working out of a psychoanalytic *temporality*.[12] This displaced temporality characterizes the aesthetic and critical experimentation of the postmodern artist and writer for Lyotard:

> The artist and the writer, then, are working without rules in order to formulate the rules of what *will have been done*. Hence the fact that work and text have the characters of an *event*; hence also, they always come too late for their author, or, what amounts to the same thing, their being put into work, their realization (*mise en œuvre*) always begin too soon. *Post modern* would have to be understood according to the paradox of the future (*post*) anterior (*modo*).
>
> ('What is Postmodernism?' in *PMC*: 81)

Thus, the postmodern is always present to modernist History as anachronism. Anachronisms are not falsehoods; rather, anachronisms are a way of thinking the unaccountable (and yet necessary) phrase-events upon which every act of historical recounting or epistemological accounting is based. This is a denial of a certain kind of history in the interests of a rigorous thinking of temporality, a refusal to think of time as something that *befalls* phrases. History is no longer an envelope or medium within which things happen; our historical awareness is of the conventional modernist account of History as the effect of a certain unacknowledged arrangement of phrases. Modernism bases its claim to legitimacy on the distancing of the knowing subject from the paratactic succession of historical phrases ('and then ... and then ... and then ...'). The event appears for this historicity as a figure marking the time it takes to arrest time and make it an object of knowledge, the noise of the distance that establishes the observer's silent detachment. The event is constitutively invisible to the modernist History that it renders opaque; the event is a figure, not a momentary or incidental lapse on the part of modernism.

The figural force of anachronism means that History with a capital 'H', the modernist critical science, is no longer possible. The end of History opens a demand that we write historically, with an attention to the temporality of our writing. It is in this sense that Lyotard's account of the postmodern is an affirmation of the temporality of the event rather than an account of the simple impossibility of History. As Lyotard has put it, postmodernism is not a break with modernity but a radical rewriting, asking the question of what phrase to link to modernity, to put next.[13] This is the question that historical time poses in the postmodern condition. The absence of determinate criteria by which History may be constructed, once we have become incredulous concerning the discourse of History, means that the adding of our phrase to those preceding (our 'linkage', in Lyotard's term) itself takes on the quality of an event. This amounts to saying that criticism may actually become historically responsible. There is no neutral textual space from which events can be surveyed and given meaning: to give meaning to an event is itself an event.

The event thus marks a gap in historical time in the sense that it seems to inhabit at least two temporalities at once: an unthinkable future history and a past become uncannily present. The reading of that aporia would begin with a recognition of the constitutive impossibility of History, as temporally divided between its status as 'what is written (about events)' and 'what happens (events)'. Postmodernity is the recognition that History as 'giving voice' to the past would be inversely split between the event of writing history, the making present of the voice of the past, and the writing of the historical event, the representation of the past which relegates it to the status of what is to be repeated (*re*-presented). The history of voices forgets the voice of history, and vice versa.

Lyotard's evocation of the historical problematic of postmodernity is significant for the way in which it moves us out of an *impasse* established in the dispute between Foucault and Derrida, a dispute which has continued to characterize relations between critics claiming historical justification for their politics and those concerned to make the category of history a problem – between Marxists or New Historicists and post-structuralists. To remind the reader: Foucault's *Madness and Civilization: a History of Insanity in the Age of Reason* (Foucault 1965) offered to write the forgotten history of the madman, to give a voice to the silent; Derrida's 'Cogito and the History of Madness' remarked that to do so was simply to reinforce the rule of voice over silence, of reason over madness, by giving voice to the silent, by giving madmen their own rationality. Derrida points out that the rule of History as voice that repressed the silent remains intact, with merely a widening of its franchise.

The problems that Derrida indicated in 1964 seem to have been ignored in the Anglophone academy, where 'giving voice to the silent' has been the rallying cry of the attack on traditional literary humanism from critics inclined to display their political credentials. In the United States, the Foucault of *Discipline and Punish* has been adopted within a more flexible historical materialism (a historical materialism which refuses to make up its mind about the relative privilege to be accorded to base and superstructure) to produce the 'New Historicism'. The enormous dominance of the new historicism on the contemporary critical scene proceeds from its status as the keeper of the current claim to relevance. Once, humanists thought that poetry taught us how to live better, or that history was an authentic record of deeds. Thus, its relevance was direct and unmediated. Now, relevance consists in first telling us that culture is indirect and mediated, and then recovering the voices of those silenced by that mediation, giving voice to the oppressed. For those who believe that countering oppression is merely a matter of writing a 'better history', a consideration of the figurality involved in 'giving voice', a deconstruction of the opposition of voice to silence in the constitution of 'history', would be merely an obfuscating or irrelevant theoretical sophistication. Under the guise of history, the past has become the object of study purely insofar as it answers to present concerns: this is the mark of the historian's engagement.

The crucial importance of Lyotard's insistence on the event as a figure for historical representation is not to deny the importance of history as a site of oppression. Rather, it suggests that repression does not simply take place *in* historical representation but that oppression begins in the modernist thought of history *as* representation. Lyotard's account of postmodernity is the evocation of the figural as displacing historical representation, the demand that the writing of History become responsible to the singularity of the event. This pushes us towards a historical writing that seeks to testify to history as a site of dispute, of differends.

The most persuasive argument for this comes in Lyotard's remarks on the condition of historical writing after the Holocaust, which we reviewed in the previous chapter of this book. The task of historical writing is not to give voice to the silence of the oppressed, which would be only to betray that silence. As we saw in Chapter 1, once we claim to represent the Holocaust as part of history, then it becomes just one atrocity among others in the long history of man's inhumanity to man, as West German revisionist historians have argued. In order to respect the impossibility of atonement, of coming to terms with horror by representing it, we have to write a history that will testify to the unrepresentable horror without representing it. We must not give voice to the millions of murdered Jews, gypsies, homosexuals and communists, but find a way of writing history that will testify to the *horror* of their having been silenced. This amounts to the deconstruction of the binary opposition between voice and silence, history and the unhistorical, remembering and forgetting. It's a history directed towards the immemorial, to that which cannot be either remembered (represented) or forgotten (obliterated), a history which evokes the figures that haunt the claims of historical representation, haunt in the sense that they are neither present to them nor absent from them. As Lyotard puts it in *Heidegger et 'les Juifs'*:

> What really preoccupies us, whether historians or non-historians, is this 'past' which is not over, which doesn't haunt the present in the sense that it is lacking, missing. It neither occupies the present as a solid reality nor haunts the present in the sense that it might indicate itself even as an absence, a spectre. This 'past' is not an object of memory in the sense of something which may have been forgotten and must be remembered (in the interest of 'happy endings' and good understanding). This 'past' is therefore not even there as a blank, an absence, *terra incognita*, but it is still there.
>
> (*HJ*: 27)

History, like literature, becomes the site of the recognition that there is something that cannot be said. This is the incommensurability to which the aesthetic may testify, though it has no language in which to speak of it that would not reduce incommensurability to the compatibility of a single voice. In literature the sign of this constitutive impossibility appears as figure (trope) or as affect (sublimity), in history as affect (enthusiasm) or as figure (apostrophe, prosopopoeia).[14] These are all marks of '*differends*', which we shall discuss in Chapter 3. Lyotard's refiguration of the politics of representation under the signature of the postmodern takes place around the name of *narrative*, and it is to this that I shall turn first.

(D) NARRATIVE

Lyotard is perhaps best known for his resistance to the 'grand narratives' of Western politics, aesthetics, and philosophy. The importance of his work is its break with any science of narrative: his insistence that concepts of 'narrative form' should not be allowed to obfuscate the figural force of the pragmatics of performance immanent to narrative. The definitive characteristic of Lyotard's description of the postmodern concern with narrative is an opposition of 'little narratives' to grand or metanarratives. Briefly, a 'grand narrative' claims to be the story that can reveal the meaning of all stories, be it the weakness or the progress of mankind. Its metanarrative status comes from the fact that it talks about the many narratives of culture so as to reveal the singular truth inherent in them. The implicit epistemological claim of a metanarrative is to put an end to narration by revealing the meaning of narratives. This rests upon the assumption that the force of narratives is synonymous with the meaning that may be found in them, that narrative is to be wholly understood in terms of the production and transmission of meaning, that it is a conceptual instrument of representation.

In Lyotard's account, 'little narratives' resist incorporation into such totalizing histories of cultural representation or projects for culture. They do this because of the way in which the *event of performance* (not simply the act of telling but the implicit pragmatics of narrative transmission) functions as a *figure*, so as to displace the scientific claims of narrative theory. For Lyotard, 'narrative' is not a *concept* that allows us to unlock the meaning of culture. Rather it is the rhetorical *figure* that opens culture as a site of transformation and dispute.

Lyotard's consideration of culture in terms of the pragmatics of 'little narratives' is crucial to the postmodern displacement of the assurance of metalanguage in the domains of epistemology, politics and aesthetics. The incidental implication of this for literary theory is that Lyotard's writing signals the breakdown of the possibility of narratology, of a proto-scientific knowledge of narrative and that this breakdown is a marker of our postmodernity with important philosophical, political and aesthetic implications.

(E) POSTMODERNISM AND THE CRISIS OF NARRATIVES [Or: What's Postmodern about Narrative?]

So, we should attempt to sketch the difference that Lyotard's account of narrative as figure rather than as discursive concept, as mark of singularity rather than instrument of signification, makes in the domains of epistemology, politics and aesthetics. First, an account of epistemology in terms of narrative pragmatics attacks both positivism (external description) and efficiency (internal performance) as criteria for the legitimation of discourses. Postmodernity is then an 'incredulity toward metanarratives' (*PMC*: xxiv), whether classical (grounded in appeal to referential truth) or modernist (grounded in appeal to effective communication). Second, postmodernity revalues the aesthetic as a site for the invention of little narratives. Finally, in the political sphere the resistance of political minorities in such 'little narratives' is opposed to the totalizing narratives proposed by capital on the one hand and the 'Revolutionary' Party on the other.

Thus, narrative surfaces as the figural trace of a postmodern condition much after the fashion of epistolarity in Derrida's *The Post Card*. Postmodernity is generally a more or less confused or confusing sense that the stakes have changed once we recognize that politics, art, history and knowledge don't fit together any more within the patterns of temporal succession and rational discourse established by the Enlightenment. And it has something to do with narrative: a rhetoric of narrative that will no longer be confined to instrumentality but that is *both* constitutive and disruptive of the possibility of narration. The rewriting of politics, aesthetics and epistemology in terms of a troubling effect of narrative is a crucial aspect of Lyotard's analysis of the postmodern condition.

Lyotard, after all, has written of postmodernity in terms of a 'crisis of narratives' (*PMC*: xxiii). That crisis means that we can no longer tell a new story (begin another modernity); it means that our understanding of the place of narrative is itself in crisis because we no longer believe in metanarratives.[15] Meta- or grand narratives provide accounts of how the field of narratives might be organized and returned to a centre, origin, or meaning. Grand narratives organize and legitimate the narratives of culture by positing an origin (God) or a telos (universal emancipation) that gives the rule to narratives whilst itself escaping the condition of narration.

The grand or meta- narrative is the organization of the succession

64

of historical moments in terms of the projected revelation of a mean-ing. Modernity's metanarrative is that of a project which works through a rupture with the past that will perform the emancipation of a universal subject of history. This is the story that organizes and legitimates knowledge, reason, and history in modernist accounts. Thus the Encyclopaedia will free humanity from superstition through enlightenment leading to universal knowledge; the dialectic of history will reveal the Hegelian trans-historical Spirit; Marxism will free the proletariat from bondage by means of revolution; democracy will reveal human nature as the people become the subject of a universal history of humanity; or the creation of wealth will free mankind from poverty through the technological breakthroughs of free-market capi-talism. Lyotard points out that these grand narratives have broken down in the face of events.[16]

The breakdown of metanarratives positions culture as a patchwork of little narratives. For Lyotard, a scepticism has led us to understand culture as discontinuous and fragmentary; cultural representations are too disparate to permit a universal point of view. Culture is not one field but a series of local or minoritarian representations organ-ized by narratives. Culture as a site of inquiry is thus dissolved into an expanded field of little narratives. This might seem to be merely a relativizing claim. I don't want to say that everything is narrative, although Lyotard does make this mistake in *Instructions païennes*, where all events, knowledges and practices are understood as narratives, so that consciousness becomes narrative (*IP*: 19). We succumb to the temptation of indifference, once all representation becomes indis-criminately narratological. However, in *Le Postmoderne expliqué aux enfants*, Lyotard distances himself from this 'transcendental appear-ance' (*PMEAE*: 40) by giving up the term narrative and switching to 'phrase' as the elemental term. The difference is that narrative is only one way among others of linking phrases. This doesn't solve the problem, because I still want to be able to talk about narrative, even as one genre among others. It is important to work out how Lyotard is doing more in talking about little narratives than saying that accounts of power, value and knowledge amount to nothing but 'telling stories', producing narratives from a series of indifferently assumed positions.

I think it is possible to have our cake and eat it too if we rephrase the claim that 'everything is narrative' as 'the condition of narrative is unsurpassable'. This shift is what preserves Lyotard's version of the postmodern condition from mere relativist despair. In Lyotard's account of postmodernity, the epistemological condition is marked by a resistance to metalanguages. And it is to this end that he talks about the expanded field of little narratives, about an impious or pagan attitude to knowledge, about minoritarian politics, about language-games or phrases, about experimentation, about judgment without criteria. All of these terms resist becoming metalanguages; so much so that the distinguishing feature of postmodernity, according to Lyotard, is an 'incredulity towards metanarratives'. Before discussing the difference this makes to the claims of theory, politics, and art, I think it might be helpful to work through the displacement of epistemology by the figure of narrative. Lyotard starts off by calling this the predicament of being 'in modernity' (as opposed to modernism, which doesn't recognize its predicament) but in a footnoted postscript to *Just Gaming* he seizes on the term 'postmodernity' to distinguish the displacement of modernism by the condition of its narrativity (*JG*: 16n). 'Postmodernity', then, is the recognition of a narrativity within modernism that disrupts metalinguistic claims.

Lyotard identifies three major epistemic modes of characterizing the relation of narrative to knowledge. For convenience, these may be designated as classicism, modernism and postmodernity, though this should not be taken to imply any simple historical succession, since all three are open at any one time, at least since Augustine.[17]

First, classical positivism legitimates knowledge precisely insofar as it evades the condition of narrative to achieve descriptive anonymity. Truth resides in the objectivity of external description. The narrative pragmatics insisted upon in *Just Gaming* analyse and displace the claim of classicism to objective description.[18] Lyotard's analyses of narrative pragmatics recognize that the conditions of narration are composed of three heterogeneous instances: narrator, narrated and narratee. Classical positivism claims speaker and auditor as mere contingencies upon the truth of the narrated. Knowledge is purely referential, narration a thing that happens to knowledge. Classicism amounts to the privileging of the narrative instance of the referent over those of sender or receiver, a privileging of the referent which is then misrecognized as escape from narration.

Second, modernism is the privileging of the instance of the sender over the referent or the receiver. The legitimation of knowledge is thus in reference to a subjective capacity to know (rationalism) or to will (romanticism). Knowledge is not narrative; narrative is merely the instrument of a subject. Even if modernism acknowledges the narrativity of knowledge that classicism represses, it shares the classical understanding of narrative as concept, which allows a theory of narrative to legitimate knowledge as the effective performance of rational communication (the domination of sender over receiver). Modernist rationalism reduces narration to an effect of consensus between narrator and an anonymous narratee. The horizon of consensus is the production of a total subject who will serve as the end of narrative, whether 'man' (humanism) or 'the proletariat as subject of history' (Marxism). Knowledge may take the form of narrative, but it can only do this as an instrument of a subjective consciousness which is itself abstracted from the narrative, which does not itself require to be narrated.

Crucially, this allows us to distinguish between relativism and postmodernism. Relativism, which classicism dismisses as 'bad faith', appears as modernism's negative moment, a nihilism in the face of the recognition that knowledge is 'only' subjective narration, just 'telling stories'. Relativism says that any claim to classical objectivity is just 'one way of looking at things'. However, relativism must legitimate its own claim to be more than just 'one way of looking at things' by imposing its subjective consciousness as a metanarrative, the way of describing all ways of looking at things. Thus it still answers (poorly) to a non-narrative criterion of efficient communication. Relativism is not so much a break with metalanguage as the preservation of metalanguage even at the price of relinquishing any content to the transcendent subject it installs. *Cogito* becomes *dubito*, but *ergo sum* remains.

The characteristic of both classicism and modernism is thus to erect one instance of narrative to the point where it governs narration from outside, becomes a metanarrative. If classicism privileges the referent, if modernism privileges the sender, then the postmodern condition is one in which no single instance of narrative can exert a claim to dominate narration by standing beyond it.[19] If modernism has suggested against classicism that there is no referent that can be abstracted from the condition of narrative, *Just Gaming* and *The Postmodern Condition* introduce the instances of Judaism and the Cashinahua in order to disrupt modernism by insisting that there is no subject-position that is ultimately outside narration. Briefly to narrate once more the case of the Cashinahua, the narrator is positioned as having already been narrated elsewhere, both by virtue of having previously been an addressee (telling the story as it was told to him) and by having previously been a referent (having been named in accordance with the narrative). Lyotard tells this story of positioning within a chain of already told narratives at least three times in print:

For example, a Cashinahua storyteller always begins his narration with a fixed formula: 'here is the story of ——, as I've always heard it told. I will tell it to you in my turn. Listen.' And he brings it to a close with another, also invariable, formula: 'Here ends the story of ——. The man who has told it to you is —— (Cashinahua name), or to the Whites —— (Spanish or Portuguese name).'

(*PMC*: 20. See also, *JG*: 32–3; *LD*: 152–5)

The pretensions of the modernist subject to be the autonomous origin of narrative are displaced. There is no single and originary speaker: as in Judaism we are addressees of an inaccessible God, so for the Cashinahua we are addressees of immemorial narratives. However, the postmodern condition privileges neither referent, narrating subject, nor addressee. The referent is the object of a narrative; the subject is always already placed within narration. No metanarrative instance makes narrative its object: we are in the expanded field of 'little narratives'. 'Little' because they are short, because they resist being turned into 'grand' or metanarratives. The grounds of this resistance lie not so much in an internal equilibrium between narrative instances as in the way in which language particles are linked together.

Instructions païennes explains this by means of an opposition between parallel and serial disposition. Grand narratives link little narratives in parallel, either around (about) a referent (classicism) or an original sender (modernism). The serial disposition of little narratives (one simply comes after another, and so on in non-finite series) means that no one narrative can become the master narrative organizing the field of language-elements. Narratives clash by virtue of the syntagmatic displacement of preceding narratives by the next, without any narrative claiming paradigmatically to replace all preceding ones by incorporation and negation. That is to say, narratives are to be understood metonymically rather than metaphorically. This underlines the distinction of Lyotard's account of narrative from that of narratology, for which the syntagmatic functioning of narrative is understood precisely insofar as it is transformed into a metaphor for something else (e.g. culture). To put it another way, in the expanded field of little narratives any one language element speaks after preceding ones, not about them. This is what Lyotard refers to in *The Postmodern Condition* as the 'horizon of dissensus', in which consensus is never reached but always displaced by a new paralogical narrative, which does not aim at installing a new consensus but evoking a further paralogical move – its own displacement (*PMC*: 61). This is the pragmatic of *experimentation* characteristic of postmodernity. Crudely, each little narrative does not aim to tell *the* story, to put an end to narrative; rather a little narrative evokes new stories by the manner in which in its turn it has displaced preceding narratives in telling *a* story. Thus, Lyotard's claim is not so much that 'everything is narrative' as that a story is not *the* story, that there can be no narrative to put an end to narratives.

The claim that the condition of narrative is unsurpassable is the recognition of narrativity as a figural condition constitutive of discourse. It means that no metanarrative is possible; there is no criterion for the legitimation of narratives which is not itself marked by the *figure of narrative*, disrupting that criterion's claim to universality. Narrative cannot be conceptualized, made the object of non-narrative, rational discourse. The shift from concept to figure in the understanding of narrative thus marks the specificity of postmodernism. I shall now turn to a consideration of the implications of this for the claims of theoretical, political and aesthetic representations.

(F) NARRATIVE VS. THEORY [Or: Why all this poses a problem for literary theorists]

For Lyotard, incredulity towards metanarratives extends to a pagan impiety towards the claims of theory. Lyotard's refusal of epistemological master-narratives is not specific to his turn to postmodernism: the ground was already prepared by the account of the figural in *Discours, figure* and the accompanying call for 'drift' in *Dérive à partir de Marx et Freud*. *Dérive* takes on the Marxist claim of 'theoretical critique', the Althusserian turn towards a Hegelian Marx, purveyor of the historical science of dialectical materialism. Lyotard is concerned to show the complicity of this analysis with the capitalist social relations whose ideological and dominative nature it claims to reveal. Lyotard evokes the figural in order to attack the claim of theoretical critique to overturn reality and reveal it as merely a symptom of either the economic base (traditional Marxism) or the ideological structure in dominance (Althusserianism). Lyotard is not offering to show the true rationality of communism in place of the illogicality of capitalism: 'We don't want to destroy kapital [sic] because it is not rational, but because it is' (*DPMF*: 12–13). The suspicion of the modernist espousal of rationalism as the ground of social reconstruction that will later emerge in the attack on grand narratives is here understood in terms of the opposition of the figural to the discursive. As we noted at the end of the chapter on Figure, in 1973 the anarchic or deconstructive force is located in the energetics of the unconscious. Lyotard insists upon the lesson of Freud's account of desire for any claim of the avant-garde to incarnate a modernist dream of pure progress:

> It is not true that a political, philosophical, artistic position should be abandoned because it is 'outmoded' ... it is not true that in experience and in discourse the occupation of a position is necessarily accompanied by its critique and leads to a position which would contain the first negatively in overcoming it. This description, which is that of the Hegelian dialectic of the spirit and also that of the enrichment of the capitalist in Adam Smith, is still the thick rope from which the puppets of political life hang their promises of happiness and with which they strangle us. There is a Freud forgotten in such a reading, it is the Freud who dared to write that an investment is never abandoned for a better one, that there is rather at the same time investment in both one region and another of the body (Freud calls it the psychic apparatus) and that the two, unthinkable together, are nonetheless compossible ...
>
> (*DPMF*: 13)

The investments of desire function anamorphically, as it were, the rational linearity of progress is disrupted by the incommensurable co-presence of emotional investments. Historically, this refuses a purely linear narrative of passage from past superstition to present knowledge, the enlightenment narrative of traditional Marxism, even if its critique is dialectical rather than direct. Historical transformations function figurally, disrupting the claim of critique to 'know better': 'the critical relation is still inscribed within the sphere of consciousness, of taking account of, and therefore of taking power' (*DPMF*: 15).

This rejection of theoretical critique does not mean, as it might in terms of the battles of the Anglo-American literary academy, a return to a naïve or assured empiricism. This attack on theory requires nuancing for an Anglophone academy accustomed to thinking of deconstruction as 'literary theory'. The necessity of this nuancing appears when Lyotard counterposes literature to theory in *Instructions païennes* as the road to follow (*IP*: 39). 'Literature' here is to be understood as a series of little narratives which are not accountable to a restricted economy, which are not directed to any single accumulation of intellectual capital. Rather, it is an attempt to upset the assurance with which narratological discourse might claim exhaustively to describe all aspects of narrative's modifications of meaning, to put an end to narration. The metalanguage which speaks of narrative must be reminded that it is itself *a* narrative. The figure of narrative returns to all attempts to speak the literal meaning of narrative. All attempts to reduce narrative's *syntagmata* to a paradigm, to say what narrative is a metaphor *for*, are themselves syntagmatic linkings, narratives. There is no discourse free from figures – the dream of literal discourse, if it were possible, would be the *litotes* of figurality.

This theoretical reduction, the assurance of a metalanguage which does not participate in the set of elements it describes, has been troubled ever since Zeno elaborated the paradox of the Cretan liar.[20] As Lyotard points out, 'theory' is the metanarrative of cognition, of knowledge.[21] A theory is a structure of concepts devoid of any event of narration – governing practice, modified by practice even, but abstracted from the temporal duration of a practice. Theory is, as Lyotard puts it in *Instructions païennes*, a narrative which claims not to be one by virtue of a pretension to omnitemporality (*IP*: 67). The claim to pure metanarrativity is the forgetting by a narrative of its own temporality as act of narration. The radicalism that Lyotard claims for the events of May 1968 in *Dérive à partir de Marx et Freud* is precisely that of having submitted theory to the temporality of events, having made theory into an event, rather than a structure of concepts. This would be paralled by an insistence that we read theory as literature, rather than merely literature as food for theory.

Not surprisingly, *Rudiments païennes* proposes an apathy towards theory, preferring the example of Freud's inability to decide whether he is writing theory or fiction in *Beyond the Pleasure Principle*.[22] At this point in Lyotard's writings, theory is demonized as producing silence, as terroristically claiming the last word (*RP*: 28). However, there is no simple anti-theoretical move, since that would be to accept theory on its own terms, to refuse to recognize that theory's claims to govern reading exhaustively can always themselves be *read* (or narrated, in present terms).

It is not however the case that Lyotard is offering a new *theory* of narrative that will account for our postmodernity. Lyotard's account of narrative as figure disrupts the claims of narratology to offer a positive *critical* knowledge of narrative as a rational concept structuring the organization of signs.[23] Just as he denies that any ultimate meaning can be assigned to narrative as the concept by which a culture speaks itself to itself, so Lyotard's account of narrative as figure denies that narrative analysis reveals the ultimate meaninglessness of culture, the fact that cultural representations are just 'lies'. Lyotard is not claiming that all knowledge is *indifferently* narratological. The figure of narrative is precisely what makes a difference. I want to postpone a full analysis of the difference that a figural consideration of narrative makes until the last part of this chapter.

For the moment, I want to develop the implications of the attack on theory in general in the direction of the aesthetic. Lyotard is thus not suggesting that we give up theory and just talk about things. Rather, he is insisting that the critical function of displacing the assurance of truth and meaning is better understood as the task of practices or performances traditionally considered artistic and literary rather than theoretical.

(G) THE POSTMODERN AESTHETIC: EXPERIMENTATION AND THE SUBLIME

The aesthetic of the sublime and of the experimental that Lyotard sketches in *The Postmodern Condition* and attendant articles is precisely an attempt to situate art as the field of a resistance to metalanguages. As early as *Dérive à partir de Marx et Freud*, Lyotard appeals to the aesthetic in order to rethink our understanding of what cultural transformation might be. Here the aesthetic is the site of invention, where desire works free of the rule of truth. What is important here is the kind of invention of which art is capable. This is not the invention of new, truer, truths (Lyotard dissents from Adorno's claim that art is the workshop of more discriminating critical concepts) but rather an invention that will *displace the rule of truth* (*DPMF*: 20). At this point, he calls art a 'drift', as opposed to the mechanism of conceptual knowledge. This simple opposition of the free to the restricted risks being read as a defence of spontaneism or expressionism, within the contours of a Romantic modernist subjectivity. To avoid the trap of 'free expression', Lyotard refines the notion of art as drift in his subsequent account of art as either 'pagan' or as postmodern paralogical experimentation. Lyotard defines the artwork as that which *displaces* either the author or the audience, or both (*RP*: 237). The 'paganism' espoused in *Instructions païens*, *Rudiments païens* and *Just Gaming* is precisely an insistence on art against knowledge, of art as a matter of invention rather than truth.

If the problem of cultural transformation is that of how the weak can be made strong, the piety that paganism resists consists in claiming that the weak are really, truly, strong, and it is just a matter of stripping away the veils of illusion (whether sinful or ideological) in order to reveal the truth. Piety tells us that the truth shall make you free, that the weak shall be strong. Paganism consists in giving up the opposition of truth to illusion, no longer trying to seize the high ground, to wield power in the name of destroying it, as Soviet and Chinese Communist Parties have done (*IP*: 16). Whereas the pious philosopher aims to speak the truth, the pagan uses ruses and trickery in order not to redefine the truth but to displace the rule of truth. The weak do not become strong, but use ruses so that weakness may overcome strength, as mortals may trick the gods. The function of art is pre-eminently pagan, if art does not aim at mimetic fidelity either to a world (telling the truth), or to a subjective will (creating a new truth of the imagination, a Utopia) but at producing effects, at provoking more art, more invention. Art is no longer in the service of cultural transformation; it *is* cultural transformation, an expanded field of little narratives.

The effects art produces do not add up to new truth, the little narratives do not form a metanarrative of cultural transformation, because they are *aneconomic*. There is no bottom line. Artistic invention does not produce anything that would not itself be subject to further displacement by aesthetic innovation. To put it another way, art is a *series* of little narratives: these narratives are not aiming at the condition of metalanguage, nor do they promise to reveal a new truth.[24]

Perhaps the clearest formulation of the difference of postmodern invention from modernist innovation comes in *The Postmodern Condition*, where Lyotard distinguishes the *paralogism* that characterizes pagan or postmodern aesthetic invention from the merely *innovative* function of art that is characteristic of the modernist understanding of the avant-garde.[25] Innovation seeks to make a new move within the rules of the language game 'art', so as to revivify the truth of art. Paralogism seeks the move that will displace the rules of the game, the 'impossible' or unforeseeable move. Innovation refines the efficiency of the system, whereas the paralogical move changes the rules in the pragmatics of knowledge. It may well be the fate of a paralogical move to be reduced to innovation as the system adapts itself (one can read Picasso this way), but this is not the necessary outcome. The invention may produce more inventions. Roughly speaking, the condition of art is postmodern or paralogical when it both is and is not art at the same time (e.g Sherrie Levine's appropriative rephotographings of 'art photography'). If early modern aesthetic innovation sought a new truth or a new way of telling the truth, if late modernist innovation sought a new truth to the experience of telling, postmodern art does not seek a truth at all but seeks to testify to an event to which no truth can be assigned, that cannot be made the object of a conceptual representation.

In the language of the postmodern, art is no longer a matter of metanarratives; instead it is the site of resistance to metalanguages. Just as the art object no longer forms part of a grand historical narrative of progress, be it technical (Vasari) or spiritual (Hegel), so its claims to mimetic representation are disrupted by temporality. If the early modern or classical artwork sought to represent History or the world as a fixed meaning, a tableau (dismissing the event as a contingency), the historical adventure of avant-garde modernism was the claim to represent or narrate the event itself (from a position nonetheless exterior to it).[26] The art object can no longer narrate either objective reality (History) or its own subjectivity (its 'eventhood'). Art cannot aspire to the metanarrativity that would ground a truth claim. The giving up of claims to either objective (classical or early modern) or subjective (modernist or avant-garde) representation is the displacement of the art object from a position in which it may offer to narrate either the world or itself from a position of exteriority, from a position of metanarrative.

The aesthetics of postmodernity draw attention to the status of the artwork as the displacement of both the historical assurance of classicism (the dismissal of the event as contingency) and the historical adventure of modernism (the claim to represent, or narrate, the event itself from a position nonetheless exterior to it). If classicism offers a description of the concept that would not itself be an event, whereas modernism offers to represent the concept of the event, postmodernism seeks to testify to the event without recourse to the concept that would reduce its eventhood to unity and fixity.

(H) NARRATIVE AND POLITICS

This resistance to metalanguages moves Lyotard to attempt to sketch a politics of the minoritarian in *Instructions païennes* and *Just Gaming*, a rethinking of the field of the political in terms of little narratives. Lyotard demands that we develop the utmost attention to the difference between narratives, more precisely to the radical heterogeneity suppressed when we adopt any one genre to govern the linking together of phrases. The recognition that knowledge-claims are grounded by narratives about what knowledge is and how to get it, does not produce a sophistic relativism. Rather, Lyotard insists that the political is not a decidable state of affairs, since a politics underlies what is named 'political'. The 'politics of narrative' depends upon a certain 'narrative of the political'. There is a politics inherent in the decision to consider certain things, or ways of saying things, 'political'. As Lyotard puts it:

> Everything is political if politics is the possibility of the differend on the occasion of the slightest linkage. Politics is not everything, though, if by that one believes it to be the genre that contains all the genres. It is not *one* genre.[27]
>
> (*LD*: 139)

Politics is not so much a genre as the struggle between genres. Thus, accounts of 'the politics of representation' must extend their analysis to the politics at stake in the grouping of certain representations under the generic name 'politics'. This is not so much a retreat from the political into relativist indifference as the extension of the political into the condition of narrative itself. Narrative is not a purely descriptive concept, but a figure, the mark of a difference; it evokes a politics that remains political (a matter for dispute and difference). Politics remains. It remains in Lyotard's refusal to put an end to difference in the revelation of the true meaning (positivism), or ultimate true meaninglessness (relativism), of history.

Whether libertarian or repressive, the claim to legitimate a prescriptive politics by appeal to a literally describable state of things (actual, theoretical, or Utopian) necessarily totalizes one narrative of the state of things as literal and victimizes those excluded from political performativity. A postmodern politics demands a recognition of the figural displacement of all claims to literal description, of the constitutively figural quality of political narratives, a recognition that entails a judicious respect for the difference of minorities.

All of this suggests that incredulity towards metanarratives is not a position of critique but a recognition of political narratives as constituted by a rhetorical figure (of narrative) for which they are unable to account. Politicians cannot account for the figural quality of their discourse because it claims to be organized by universal rational concepts, not by the figurations of specific acts of narration. Politics claims that either its ideals or its pragmatic compromises belong to the realm of reality, not 'mere rhetoric'. An understanding of narrative as figure insists that the necessarily narrated quality of events marks them as radically singular happenings. No metanarrative is possible because there is no criterion for the legitimation of narratives which is not itself marked by the figure of narrative, disrupting that criterion's claim to universality.

At this point, we might worry that the multiplication of little narratives, Lyotard's account of cultural fragmentation, amounts to a welcoming of the effects of capitalism. And indeed, Lyotard is prepared to ground the breakdown of metanarratives in an empirical narrative about the contemporary condition. This lapse into sociological punditry makes me very nervous. As the diffidence of the prologue to *The Postmodern Condition* makes clear, to claim postmodernity as simply a socio-political *fact* risks leaving us as celebrants of the destabilizing effects of capitalism in its latest 'late' phase.[28] If capitalism develops by indifferent expansion of the rule of commodification and exchange, then the legitimating grounds of the rule of the market will necessarily tend to become themselves occasions for profit, so that they lose their legitimating exteriority. To put it crudely, once we begin to market God, He is no longer so authoritative a ground for capitalist relations.

The effect of dissolution that drives capitalism has indeed been celebrated by Lyotard, in his scandalous book, *Economie libidinale*. There, Lyotard attacks accounts of alienation and emiseration as failing to affirm the liberation of libidinal intensities that accompanies capital's indifference to sites of investment in its pursuit of profit. *Economie libidinale* thus proposes a startling description of industrial 'injuries' such as deafness as in fact sites of *jouissance* for workers, the liberation of sensual potentialities from the rule of the integration of experience into the economy of the organic body (*EL*: 136–8).

Leaving aside the shock value of this reading, the effect of *Economie libidinale* is to force us to run up against the problem of *indifference* that accompanies the dissolution of organizing economies. How are we to discriminate between narratives or libidinal intensities, once we are incredulous towards metanarratives or suspicious of the rule of the organic body, once we have entered the expanded field of little narratives, or been situated on the libidinal band as pure locus for the inscription of intensities?[29] In either case, there is a problem with the temptation of indifference, of the celebration of transgression *tout court* (as Lyotard notes in *Peregrinations*). Just because the present form of capitalism is prepared to abolish itself in search of profit does not mean that capitalism is indifferent to profit. Once, following Deleuze and Guattari, we recognize that capitalism profits from an indifferent transgression of boundaries by the rule of commodification and exchange, there is a problem in distinguishing our own transgression of capitalism's boundaries. After all, making intellectual capital out of the critique of capitalism is precisely the flaw of classical Marxist analysis, proceeding from its naïve faith that capitalism can be brought to heel by the very laws of contradiction that drive it.

If postmodernity is a disaffection from metanarratives, this is importantly something more than the empirical effect of capitalist development in that analysis of the immanent pragmatics of metanarratives allows the identification of injustices. Narrative pragmatics, refined in *The Differend* as 'phrase analysis', do not simply act as conceptual tools for the description of narratives: we're not in the realm of a grand narrative about little narratives. Attention to narrative pragmatics enforces, if it does not ground, discrimination and differentiation among the expanded field of narratives.

In order to understand this, we have to pay very careful attention to Lyotard's insistence throughout *Just Gaming* that justice be separated from truth, that judgment should proceed without criteria. Narrative pragmatics differentiate narratives without grounds because they do not refer narratives to either referential truth or the truth of a just model of narrative. The analysis of narrative is a matter of *performance*, not of truth. Nor is this a criterion of performance in the sense of 'maximum efficiency' (the returning of performance to its 'truth'). Performativity here is the production of effects in and by narratives.

The shift from truth to performance is a characteristic Lyotardian move – as early as *Dérive à partir de Marx et Freud* he insists that we pay attention to the discursive posture of the French Communist Party (PCF), not merely to the signification of its statements (*DPMF*: 153). This is also explicit in *Instructions païennes*, where he discusses the gagging of the proletariat as mute referent of the discourse of a Party alone authorized to speak of and for it (*IP*: 23). As Lyotard puts it in *Just Gaming*, analysis is a question of coming to grips with effects, not discussing truth-content (*JG*: 6). This turn is crucial. Rather than reducing discursive pragmatics to the rhetorical instruments for the presentation of a truth, we are placed in a rhetoric without instrumentality, where reference is merely one instance of a general discursive pragmatic. Reference is not erased; it is simply one aspect of the performance of a narrative. We go from questions of truth to those of performance, from talking about ideology to discussing narrative pragmatics.

At this point is is necessary to distinguish the 'little narrative' from the 'little ideology'. To think of narrative by analogy with ideology would be to remain utterly within the paradigm of sceptical modernism. Lyotard takes his distance from ideology and the representational framework of illusion that it implies. Once rhetorical positioning in a discursive pragmatic is not reducible to a *modification* of content then the field of narratives can't simply be divided into positions which constitute or affect referential claims to truth. Bluntly, the analysis of narrative pragmatics moves us away from the reading of ideology, whether vulgarly positivist or scientifically critical.

For a traditional Marxism, the ideological veil of false consciousness would produce narratives as lies about the true nature of capitalist expropriation. The critique of ideology simply consists of returning narratives to the one true narrative of the economic base. Since Althusser, and sometimes even after Foucault, ideology comes to be considered *constitutive* of social experience, a process without end. The term ideology comes to cover the clash of truth claims (ways of making sense) that are not ontologically but teleologically grounded, in reference to their political effects. We don't discriminate among ideologies in terms of their simple conformity to an ontological truth but in terms of the kind of political organization to which they lead. However anti-foundationalist this move to a strategy of political effects might seem, a referential criterion of *truth* is still operative: accounts of the separation of ideology from falsification are greatly exaggerated. Each ideological narrative can be referred to the metalanguage of political effectivity, which is not in itself simply a question of effect but of mimetic adequacy to a telos. This is still referential, since political effect lends *meaning* to discourse: critique will restore the lost or hidden meaning to humanity.[30]

In these terms, we can see the relation between ideology-critique and narratology as not just a matter of coincidence. Narratology is not just the tool of ever more sophisticated ideology critique; both preserve an instrumental rhetoric under the rule of meaning. Both are concerned to reduce rhetorical aspects of performance to second order modifications of signification.

The question of what kind of judgments we can make without the metanarrative organization of final political goals is perhaps the most difficult one. We are too wedded to politics as the sphere of progress to entertain very much suspicion of the modernist notion of 'progress', despite the evidence of centuries. The move from meaning to performance is a move from ideology to narrative pragmatics in discriminating between phrases. As *Just Gaming* insists, justice is no longer a matter of truth (of mimetic correspondence to an origin or telos) but is pre-eminently something to be *done*. Chapter 3 will develop this implication of a redescription of agency in terms of ethics rather than politics. Lyotard's interest in Kant is precisely for the way in which the Third Critique sketches the terms of indeterminate or reflective judgment in ethics or in terms of the aesthetics of the sublime. This is neither a moralization of the political (here I'm drawing something like a common usage distinction between moral law and ethical judgment without criteria) nor an aestheticization of politics. We aren't talking about Khomeini or Hitler, who claim to determine the political by means of criteria drawn from aesthetic or moral domains. Rather, Lyotard is concerned to insist that the indeterminacy of ethical or aesthetic judgment *forbids* such a transfer of criteria into the cognitive realm of determinate judgment.

To which one might remark that it's all very well to say that justice must be done, but what are we to do? And Lyotard will reply, 'Be just'. Which isn't an answer, because an attention to immanent performativity resists monolithic calculation in two ways. First, we are not claiming to repeat faithfully what is 'in' a preceding act of narration but to attach another narrative to the preceding one that may do justice to it, a justice that is no longer a matter of truth or mimetic fidelity. Second, our analysis does not constitute a theoretical description of narrative, but another narrative, a further performance, one aspect of which is its referential relation to the narrative it analyses and transforms. Other aspects would be our position as senders, and the narratees of our narration. We are not so much judging politics as *doing* them in judging. There isn't a universal model of a just narrative, but an indeterminate idea of justice to which another narrative is responding. It's in this sense that attention to narrative pragmatics enforces but does not ground differentiation among narratives. Once again, the political and aesthetic are being rewritten as fields of indeterminate judgment. This might once more prompt the reader to turn to our final chapter. However, before shifting towards a more explicit consideration of the political in Lyotard's writings I want to turn the issue of narrative back towards our opening, by thinking the implications for literary criticism of the understanding of narrative as a figure.

(I) NARRATIVE AND FIGURE: FROM NARRATIVE FORM TO PERFORMANCE AS EVENT

The distinction between a figural or deconstructive analysis of narrative and narratological theory replays the attack on semiotics in general of our first chapter. On the one hand, for Lyotard narrative is not the object of a discourse, there is no metalanguage of narratology which would not itself be subject to analysis in terms of its narrative pragmatics, analysis as *a* narrative rather than as *the* narrative of narratives.[31] No 'narratology', no return of narrative to the Logos. On the other hand, narrative is not a second order discourse, analogous to the classical conception of the persuasive or decorative functions of rhetoric.[32] Narration is not the tool that enforces a subjective perspective, since the subject that narrates is itself constituted by *being narrated*.[33] Narrativity is thus both constitutive and disruptive of representational discourse (the representation of an object to a subject by means of a concept). A deconstructive figure rather than a concept, narrative necessarily intervenes to disfigure the legitimation of representation. Nor can that intervention itself be exhaustively represented, since no account can be given that would not itself be a narration. That is to say, Lyotard's account of narrative as figure rather than concept amounts to a deconstructive resistance to narratology that is characteristic of postmodernity.

Narratology takes its object, narrative, and shows it not to be natural or real but rather artificial. It shows that narrative is not simply the vehicle of meaning, but constructs the meaning it carries. It thus supplies the true meaning (often socio-political) of narrative to the illusory world of narrations. However, theory's claims to displace the assurance of the real are vitiated by the fact that, finding the real to be an illusion, theory offers to supply the meaning that the world has lost. For Lyotard, this move retains its piety, though at the second order of metastatements about narratives rather than at the first order of narratives about things.

Let us examine in detail how a reading of the figural force of little narratives might upset the claims of narratology. At first sight, the assertion of conflict might seem odd, since narratology can very easily propose itself as a 'rhetoric of narrative'. The distinction to be drawn here is between the rationalist and instrumentalist conception of rhetoric on which narratology reposes, and the deconstructive account of rhetoric as the constitutive displacement of the logocentric possibility of meaning to which Lyotard attaches the figure of narrative.

Narratology is an attempt to conceptualize the function of narrative in the organization of both representations and the knowledge we have of them. It is thus the basis of accounts of cultural programming (as in film analysis). Although it may appeal to a 'rhetoric of narrative' in order to displace claims to referential truth, this is an instrumental account of rhetoric. Narrative is *used* by an individual or a subject of history (the dominant class, the spirit of an age, etc.) in order to advance certain theses or to make knowledge claims which are not *in themselves* matters of narrative but are meanings. A story is told, and the process of analysis is one of stripping away the narrative technology in order to expose either the referential content or the philosophical position that narrative has sought to hide. Although they look very different, both narratology and neo-pragmatism tend to think of narrative as the concept by which cultural representation is organized. For narratology, unacknowledged narrative structures place signs in meaningful patterns; for neo-pragmatism, unacknowledged narrative structures legitimate cognition.

Specifically, narratology reveals the second-order modifications (such as Mieke Bal's 'focalizers') by which the syntagmatic ordering of signs gives rise to meanings.[34] In this sense it is a branch of semiotics, concentrating upon the syntagmatic patterns in which signs are arranged, rather than on the paradigmatic function by which signs become bearers of meaning. Crucially, however, the meaning that narratology reveals is not itself a narrative, but is simply the cumulative signification of all those second-order modifications. If we want to remain Jakobsonian, we might say that narratology is the process by which syntagm is reduced to paradigm, metonymy to metaphor.[35]

Using the techniques of structural linguistics, semiotic narratology reveals narratives as synchronic organizations of elements in patterns of opposition which produce cultural meaning. The appearance of narrative diachrony is stripped away to reveal a synchronic structure of oppositions. Thus, the opening of Genesis tells a diachronic story which merely covers up the coding of male as primary substance and female as defective copy. What appears as narrative sequence (man then woman) bears the cultural meaning of priority as value (man over woman). The process of semiotic analysis has been to reduce the temporality of the narration to a structure of oppositions: the synchronic meaning of the narrative.

As early as *Discours, figure* (1971), Lyotard takes his distance from the semiotic analysis of narratives. Lyotard is concerned to insist that an analysis that seeks to find meaning by erasing the diachrony of performance (the time of narration) in this way is complicit with the very mythologizing function of narrative that narratology claims to unveil. The demystification of narrative by narratology is in fact merely a remythologization at another level. This is because structural analysis merely accentuates the mythic function in narration, which takes a difference (that between beginning and end) and seeks to reduce it to a meaning.

According to Lyotard, the discursive function of myth is precisely to 'tame the difference that it recounts, to place it in a system, that is to transform it into an opposition' (*DF*: 166). Myth takes a difference and seeks to place it within a narrative construct that will lend it meaning. It explains the difference between men and women as a matter of sequence of origin. Narratology takes the temporal difference in a narrative (A then B . . .) and seeks to place it within an atemporal theoretical construction that will reveal its meaning.

The complicity of narratology with the mythic function that it claims to demystify is an effect of their common concern with the revelation of *meaning*. Myth tells how meaning was revealed to the people; narratology reveals how meaning was told to the people. The mark of discursive or textual space, for which Lyotard adduces scientific discourse as the strongest example, is that there is no difference, there are only oppositions. In terms of the Genesis example, sexuality is not a radical difference (A is not B) but a meaning produced by the opposition between terms (A/not-A). Everything is a matter of signification. It is this assumption that Lyotard is concerned to disrupt by considering the *figural* function of narrative.

Lyotard insists on the figural as the mark of a difference that cannot be reduced to oppositionality. The figure always appears in discourse as radically other to discourse, as the trace of a force that necessarily works over meaning (just as the narrative must be told) and yet cannot itself be assigned a meaning. This figural force appears as a 'remainder' (*reste*) that constitutes the possibility of meaning and yet cannot be explained in terms of meaning – it is left over, left out. The figure is the eventhood of an event (its radical singularity) that is excessive to the calculations of the meaning of that event.

That is to say, narrative is a figure insofar as it does not merely produce meanings but marks an *event*. The force of Lyotard's account of narrative pragmatics is its insistence on the figural event of narration immanent to narratives. Lyotard treats epistemology, politics and aesthetics in terms of narrative in order to testify to the force of the event, the event that meaning seeks to reduce to merely the contingency of its manifestation. Postmodernism is not merely the scepticism that says 'everything is just a story', but the attempt rigorously to think the eventhood of the narratives of culture.[36]

The insistence on the event of performance that will later appear in Lyotard's analysis of narratives as pragmatic situations is described in *Discours, figure* in terms of an ultimately unsatisfactory opposition between meaning as the discursive signification (*signification*) of a text and meaning as the expressive significance (*sens*) of an act. There is a problem with the rather too neat *opposition* between the radical difference evoked by expression and the structure of oppositions mobilized in signification: in this respect, Lyotard's analysis doesn't quite mark a radical heterogeneity to signification. Furthermore, Lyotard at this point in his writing on narrative rather too straightforwardly identifies the event of narration with the act of performance, in his use of the term 'expression'. This does not necessarily break with an instrumentalist account of narrative. 'Expression' implies the possibility of a subjective will which would use the performance of narrative in order to express itself, even if it didn't employ the content of narrative in order to signify. However, I want to focus on Lyotard's insistence on the irreducible heterogeneity of the event of telling to what is told. In these terms, the account of narrative as figure provides the basis for an understanding of what the stakes are in his account of narrative.

The event of narration appears as a necessary figure disrupting narratology's claims to describe narrative exhaustively by revealing its cognitive meaning. This holds even for a narratology that offers to describe the event of narration in terms of performance as a modification of meaning. The performance of the act of telling takes time, a time that marks the difference between the beginning and the end of the tale. That difference cannot be signified as the meaning of the story (the synchronic statement of the trajectory traversed as an opposition between two states) without leaving out the time of its happening. The event of telling is both necessary *and* contingent, both primary and secondary. It is figural in that it cannot be contained as merely a second-order modification of meaning.

In *Discours, figure* Lyotard calls the figure of narrative a 'matrix-form' (*DF*: 167). This is a complicated term, with a good deal of local significance in that book that I don't have space to discuss, but it is an attempt to describe narrative form in terms of the pragmatics of performance of narration. 'Matrix-form' is distinguished from 'narrative form' in order to insist that the immanent pragmatics of narrative cannot be reduced to formal considerations secondary to narrative signification (this is not formalism). 'Matrix-form' is an attempt to account for narrative form as irreducible to a matter of structure. However, I think it's more useful to detach oneself more fully from the language of form, and to think narrative as a trope that necessarily accompanies meaning whilst itself resisting meaning. The figure of narrative disrupts the rule of meaning, of the Logos, in that it is an element both inside and outside meaning. The figure remains as the work of signification for which a meaning (signification) cannot be *substituted*, a metonymy that cannot be reduced to a metaphor.[37] The impossibility of signification by substitution proceeds from the radical singularity or particularity of the event of telling.

It is this account of narrative as *figure* rather than *concept* that preserves Lyotard's analysis of the narrativity of political, aesthetic and philosophical discourse from mere relativism. Narratology reposes upon an understanding of narrative as concept, as the object of a representation or a rational discourse which can render an account of an economy of narrative effects in a single language, devoid of the radical difference introduced by the heterogeneity of narrative instances and narrative temporality. The determination of narrative in terms of diegetic reference or communicative performance is the reduction and suppression of the heterogeneity of one of the instances of narration in the name of unity. The claim of narrative as concept is thus that narrative itself may be the object of a description, a communication or a theory (a static network of oppositions) that would themselves be in no sense acts of narration. An understanding of narrative as figure insists that the necessarily narrated quality of acts of language marks them as radically singular. The figure of narrative introduces to discourse the opacity of the specific pragmatics of communication and description, such as the incommensurability of the narrating subject and the subject of narration, the turbulence which the time or rhythm of narration introduces to unity of the narrated. The scene of narration insistently returns to, and disrupts, any attempt to reduce the act of narration to a described content or effected communication. Postmodernism insists that any single metanarrative, whether it claims to speak the 'real world' or the 'theory of narrative', will reduce justice to an effect of power, art to a commodity, and thought to conceptual knowledge (reason).

To sum up, Lyotard's account of the postmodern narrative consideration of theory is thus asymmetrical with the modernist theoretical consideration of narrative, as well as the classical realist dismissal of narrative. The particularity of multiple narratives replaces the unified narrative of multiplicity. The figure of narrative displaces the politics of victimization, the aesthetics of representation and the philosophy of the known. An attention to figure preserves the understanding of the constitutive force of narrative from either theoretical or relativist reduction. Yet one set of problems remains. What is the status of this narrative of classical, modernist and postmodernist art; positivist, verificationist and postmodern epistemology; capitalist, communist and minoritarian politics? Is there a grand narrative of the failure of metanarratives? Yes, insofar as the rigour demanded by Lyotard's *The Differend* falls back into the conceptualization of the postmodern as the avant-gardism of a moment or a movement, of the minority as oppositional rather than heterogeneous. No, insofar as narrative is traced as a figure both constitutive and disruptive of discourse, rather than in simple opposition to representation. No, insofar as it is possible to bear witness to the different in a language that does not seek to exchange its figural narrativity for the consolations of the order, rationality or efficiency of discourse. Lest this be thought too theoretical, let me remind you that you have heard a story, one that was told to me by Jean-François Lyotard.

3

Politics and ethics

(A) THE POLITICS OF REPRESENTATION

This work has avowedly twisted its reading of Lyotard towards the problematics of the literary critical academy. It has sought to emphasize the *rhetoricity* of Lyotard's concern with the figural and to understand his interest in the postmodern as an issue of cultural criticism. It may seem ironic that a third chapter on 'politics and ethics' appears to demand no such distortion on my part. In order to understand the apparently immediate (unmediated) significance of the political for literary theory, we should remember the rule of the political as metalanguage in the realm of literary theory that we discussed in Chapter 2. To be blunt, 'theory' in the literary academy has become a cloak for the political policing of literary texts, in that the ultimate meaning of all theoretical insights is held to be political. This is hardly surprising, since it shares absolute continuity with the long tradition of literary humanism – except that now the 'ultimate significance' of a text is named as a 'political' rather than 'transcendental' or 'essentially human' truth. It is in this light that the justification and relevance of literary theory has been as an interpretative tool to allow us to decode accurately the literal political meaning of texts. Thus, deconstruction has been welcomed insofar as it offers a sophisticated analytical mode that awakens us to the 'hidden' political meanings of binary oppositions in cultural texts, dismissed if it tends to undermine our assurance of the decidable reality, the non-rhetorical nature, of political meaning.

The importance of Lyotard's work is not that it gives post-structuralism a decidable political dimension that it had otherwise lacked. Rather, Lyotard's refusal to think the political as a determining or determinate metalanguage, as the sphere in which the true meaning of false metalanguages (such as 'aesthetic value') is revealed as 'political effects', pushes him towards a deconstruction of the representational space of the political. As we shall see, this induces a shift from the political to the ethical, in the sense that the instances of dispute conventionally determined as political are seen to be more justly considered as sites for indeterminate judgment. Let it be clear that this is not an 'aestheticization of the political' in the sense of the Fascist project. In Fascism, as Benjamin has demonstrated, the political remains as site of determinate judgment, by analogy with the determinant judgments of the beautiful which may be made about art.[1] The political is conceived in terms of criteria which are claimed to be drawn from art (the ugly should be eliminated). For Lyotard, the aesthetic and the political are both sites for *indeterminate* (ethical) judgment *without criteria*. To find the grounds of the political in the aesthetic is simply to replay moments such as the Futurist praise of Fascism and war as more beautiful than democracy and peace. That is to say, the aesthetic is not simply the determining ground of the political.

Just as the aesthetic cannot provide the legitimating grounds of the political, so the political cannot legitimate the aesthetic. Rather, the analogy between the aesthetic and the political is that their grounds of legitimacy always *remain to be decided*. They have always yet to be decided: as we saw in our consideration of the postmodern, art and politics thus become sites for experimentation and struggle. In this chapter I want to begin by tracing Lyotard's deconstruction of the political as a representational order. In this respect, his work can be seen to shift. Lyotard begins in *Dérive à partir de Marx et Freud* by proposing a politics of struggle between the established ratios of the space of political reason and a figural and disruptive force of work. If Barthes announced semiotics as a move 'From Work to Text', Lyotard's rephrasing of the political is an anti-semiotic move from (political) 'text' to (figural) 'work'.

Specifically, according to Lyotard the theatrical-representational apparatus of capitalism enforces the law of absolute exchangeability by way of commodification. Lyotard's insistence on the primacy of commodification in capitalism owes much to Adorno, though he will accuse Adorno of still thinking commodification as a process of falsification. Lyotard does not propose to resist commodification by returning things to a materiality that would be their true nature. Rather, he insists upon a necessary incommensurability that accompanies the reduction to commensurability in commodification, in the same way that the postmodern comes both before and after modernism.

Thus, the figure is the clash of incommensurable spaces of representation; the postmodern is the clash of incommensurable temporalities; the differend is the clash of heterogeneous language games. This specificity is what gives Lyotard's version of deconstruction as the thought of difference (whether formal, historical or ethical) its political resonance. Thus, Lyotard's deconstruction of the political as a determinant instance, his refusal to privilege the political as the metalinguistic realm into which all other discourses can be translated, is nevertheless a constant engagement with the question of what the limits of the political might be.

In his later writings Lyotard moves to a displacement of the political in terms of *time* rather than work. The political is no longer a text, a product-space, to be disrupted by work as process. Rather, the process of capitalist and rationalist commodification or economization is a regime of accountable time which works to reduce the figural force of the event, to commodify it as an exchange-value (for example, by reducing the event to its signification-content, its meaning). Resistance is thus not simply the pure transgression of forms by performance but the attempt to derive temporalities respectful of the event as event.[2]

In order precisely to dislodge the metalinguistic status of the political in literary theory, I shall perform just the kind of twisting of Lyotard's work that initially seemed unnecessary in this chapter, introducing the term 'reading', by way of an analogy with Paul de Man's work, as exemplary of the kind of attention to difference that Lyotard demands in indeterminate judgment. I want to propose 'reading' as a strong term for the attention to the disturbing and aporetic temporality of the event, the way the event opens a gap in the temporality of representation, that has already characterized our description of the postmodern rewriting of modernity. In light of this, in the last parts of this chapter I will turn to an elaboration of a Lyotardian description of judgment in the face of the 'differend', the rephrasing of cultural and political analysis as an ethics of reading.

(B) POLITICAL SPACE

Drift

In *Dérive à partir de Marx et Freud* Lyotard draws the figural into the representational space of the political. This move is perhaps most explicit in his essay on political posters, but it is also generally evident in his concern to think the political alongside the aesthetic in the wake of the repositioning of avant-gardeism after the events in Paris in 1968. As I mentioned in my remarks on 'narrative against theory', the figural drift begun in *Dérive* is not only away from discursive knowledge but also away from the claims of critique to treat discourse as a symptom, to find the errors in capitalism. Lyotard states the problem bluntly: 'All critique of capitalism, far from surpassing capitalism, consolidates it' (*DPMF*: 16) because it negates capitalism by merely inverting it, standing it on its head. That is to say, the problem with dialectical or Marxist critique is that it functions as a kind of photographic negative of capitalism, preserving itself within the same representational framework. In *Dérive*, Lyotard starts to develop a resistance to the representational space of capitalism that does not work by opposition but by *difference*; to deconstruct that space by revealing a figural work, 'another libidinal apparatus, still unclear, difficult to identify ... in a non-dialectical, non-critical relation, incommensurable with that of kapital' (*DPMF*: 17).[3] Lyotard must find a way of unleashing the deconstructive force of figurality against the representational space of capitalism; in 1972, belatedly writing an introduction to *Dérive*, Lyotard turns to the aesthetic. The introduction criticizes the essays for sticking too closely to a Marxist politics.

In the introduction, refusing to share traditional Marxist contempt for the aesthetic as 'superstructural unreality' (*DPMF*: 19), Lyotard gives up trying simply to aestheticize politics: he rejects Adorno's evocation of the aesthetic as the 'workshop of more discriminating critical concepts' (*DPMF*: 20), though he does not exempt the essays in the collection from being seduced by this position. It is a fairly typical move of Lyotard's to publish a collection with an introduction which explains why the essays are wrong, suggesting nevertheless that there might be something worthwhile in the essays, that the political is not inherently the sphere of theoretical rectitude, but of struggle. He will name this struggle 'work' in the early part of his career, and ultimately elaborate it as 'the differend'. In the 1972 introduction to *Dérive* the aesthetic is not appealed to as the ground of determinant judgment (in which, as Lyotard paraphrases Kant in 1988, 'a concept being defined, one must find the available cases to be subsumed under it and so doing begin to validate the concept' (*P*: 21)).

The essays in *Dérive*, however, drift from a position fairly close to the heart of Marxism; rather than claiming that the 'political' must be rephrased, it wants to believe that economistic Marxism has simply failed to take the political into account. In short, Lyotard is trying to be a better Marxist:

> The *theory* of the State has not been written definitively, and it is up to Marxists to do it. . . . It is not Marxist today to relegate the space of the political to the superstructure.
>
> (*DPMF*: 120–1)

Lyotard turns to the state as the site of the political in order to issue a corrective to economistic Marxism. The understanding that the state as the representational space of the political is not merely an ideological apparatus determined by underlying economic factors (capitalist relations of production) is significant. The state places capitalism as not merely a matter of relations of production but of the *re-production* of those relations, as a representational apparatus. Nor is that apparatus secondary or ideological; the state is not so much the instrument or expression of the ruling class as the extension of capitalism. For example, Lyotard claims, taxes are not secondary to market relations, they are the extension of those relations to the salaried classes (some twenty heartwarming pages of *Dérive* are dedicated to proving that teachers are exploited by the state that employs them). Thus there is a revision of Marxism to be performed in the light of the development of the state in capitalism:

> Marx spoke of what he saw, liberal capitalism. We must speak of what we see, capitalism in its imperialist and bureaucratic form (or as completed state monopoly).
>
> (*DPMF*: 149)

However, the overtly Marxist language in which this revision is performed, in which the teacher is proved to be host to exploitation as well as parasite, is important: a major shift is taking place within Lyotard's Marxism. There is a drift away from an understanding of the political as ideological reflection of capitalist relations, to an account of capitalism as *primarily* a space of representation. In Marxist terms, we might say that this is a description of capitalism as political rather than economic:

> [The socio-political is] the empirical space of intuitions and representation. It is not the space of the system which supports it and hides itself there, it's the space where social relations are lived, where the class struggle takes place.
>
> (*DPMF*: 278)

In these terms, it is the 'political' which means that we have to judge 'case by case' (*DPMF*: 151). Lyotard has left this Marxist language behind even by the time he writes the general introduction, but the drift begins here, from inside Marxism.

Even within Marxism, *Dérive* picks up the figural as the site of a resistance to political representation: the way to carry forward the class struggle is not the counter-exploitation of political space for socialist ends but its disruption. An analysis of political posters in 'Plastic Space and Political Space' insists upon the revolutionary potential of the figural as the transgression of textual space so as to reveal a 'political unconscious' (*DPMF*: 276). The work of the avant-garde is thus not to produce left-wing art but to produce an 'anti-art' (*DPMF*: 304) that will deconstruct representational space. This amounts to the political application of the model of the figural elaborated in *Discours, figure*, to the declared end of 'elaborating a model of ideology-critique' (*DPMF*: 277). The further development of Lyotard's analysis consists in extending to ideology-critique the deconstruction of the socio-political sphere of representation that he identifies as the critical legacy of the movement of May 1968:

> If the May 1968 movement can continue to mean anything, it is because it extended criticism to a number of forms of representation, to the union, the party, the institution of culture in general, which 'big politics', including Trotskyism and Maoism, either ignored or considered merely secondary. On the contrary, the movement of May 1968 found these forms of representation to be immediate and persistent obstacles to the liberation of potential critical energy.
>
> (*DPMF*: 307)

Economie libidinale and *Des Dispositifs pulsionnels* elaborate the account of capitalism as a representational space to be deconstructed rather than occupied by socialism. Their analyses are highly problematic, as asides throughout this book have noted. The turn towards a metaphysics of desire, an absolutely an-economic energetics of the unconscious in opposition to capitalism as 'a regulated system for the regulation of growth which permits in principle the introduction, circulation and elimination of ever greater quantities of energy' (*DPMF*: 311), is an unfortunate one, even if it performs for Lyotard a necessary opening up of Marxism to deconstruction. First, and most obviously, desire and anarchy produce a transgression for its own sake which is entirely *indifferent* to the structure it opposes. The pure alterity to conceptual representation which these books demand thus ends up leaving the representational structure untouched, unworked on. The figural comes to be a pure alterity, wholly 'outside' rather than in a relation which deconstructs the opposition of inside to outside. Second, this fall into the 'temptation of indifference' as Lyotard calls it (*P*: 15) thus functions as a simple *application* of a deconstructive method to the political. To put it in Lyotard's terms, 'drift' has become pure departure; a confirmation of the modernist model of the absolute 'epistemological break' with past superstition, even if the break is with the possibility of epistemology itself. In this sense, the intellectual contours of 'ideology critique' perhaps persist longer than might be immediately apparent. The first chapter of Lyotard's *Peregrinations* offers perhaps the strongest defence of *Economie libidinale* that it is possible to maintain in the light of the later work:

> [M]y prose tried to destroy or deconstruct the presentation of any theatrical representation whatsoever, with the goal of inscribing the passage of intensities directly in the prose itself without any mediation at all.... The readers of this book – thank God there were very few – generally accepted the product as a rhetorical exercise and gave no consideration to the upheaval it required of my soul. They were certainly correct to do this, but I could still pretend to myself that I had achieved my goal to the extent that the dominant position given to the forms of writing or style could indicate nothing other than how impossible any argumentation, any debate over the so-called content was, and how all that was possible was the opportunity to like or dislike the signifiers of the text. Thus the book did perform the ruin of the hegemony of conceptual reception.
>
> (*P*: 13)

It may be gathered from this that the writings of the period are not particularly comfortable reading.[4] However, it is important to focus on the displacement of representation that they seek to effect, even if only as a way of clearing the ground for the later reading of art and politics as indeterminate in the aesthetics of postmodernism and the ethics of the differend. *Economie libidinale* and *Des Dispositifs pulsionnels* identify the space of political representation in three ways, and offer three modes of resistance that can serve to deconstruct that space. First, in general, the conceptual order of representation is *theatrical*. Within that space capitalism is, second, the rule of *exchange*, of the commensurability of commodities (the importance lent to commodification in contemporary capitalism gels with the analysis proposed by Adorno and Horkheimer in *Dialectic of Enlightenment*, 1979). Third, the exchange of those commodities is regulated through the economic metaphor of the *organic body*.

Lyotard identifies a node of resistance to each of these instances. To the closed economy of the organic body Lyotard opposes the '*libidinal band*' or 'great ephemeral skin'. To the rule of exchangeability that founds capitalism Lyotard opposes the incommensurability that was characteristic of the figure. Furthermore, his insistence on the effect of *work* disrupts the fixed or textual framework of the theatre of representation. In all these cases, Lyotard is pointing towards a materialism of libidinal or figural energy that refuses to see materiality as a property of bodies, and that insists that materiality shares the radical singularity of the event.[5] According to this logic, the error of Marx was to think the material as a property of things, and thus to conform to the rule of capitalism's systematic regulation of energy through circulation within an organic body. Lyotard proposes to redescribe space, objects and labour in terms that will resist the restricted economy characteristic of the rule of 'kapital'. Let us begin by working through Lyotard's account of how thought is restricted to the concept by being enclosed within the theatre of representation.

The theatre of representation

Lyotard elaborates the 'theatrical-representational apparatus' (*DP*: 255) by analogy with perspectival painting, with the *costruzione legittima* of the Italian Renaissance. The theatre consists of three closed spaces articulated together: the support, the image or stage, and the viewer. In painting, these would correspond to the surface and technology of painting (the medium), the image, and the position prescribed for the viewer by the vanishing point of perspectival construction. In the theatre itself, the three spaces are respectively the backstage apparatus (wings, machinery, star system, etc.), the stage, and the auditorium. These three closed spaces locate themselves in opposition to a fourth, open, one – the space of the real, of the world outside the theatre. There are thus three limits or divisions: of stage from backstage (3), of stage from auditorium (2), of theatre from world (1). Lyotard gives a diagram of this representational apparatus or 'set-up' ('*dispositif*') in *Des Dispositifs pulsionnels* (see below).

Two immediate observations have to be made. First, that the

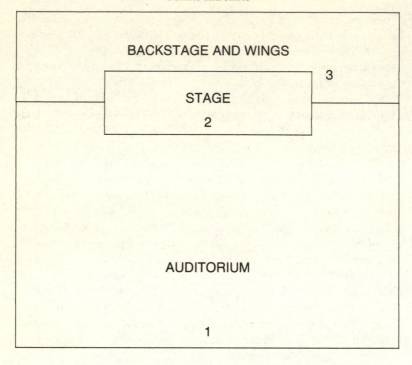

representational system positions its viewing subject *inside* the system; second, that the effect is not one of illusion, but of seduction:

> I should say seduction rather than illusion because the subject who looks into [Brunelleschi's] box, if he is not mad, knows very well that he is not looking at the Baptistry itself. For those who sit in the theatre it is the same.... This representation is not *trompe l'œil* and it is not even illusion, it is seduction in the proper sense of the term: one is divided from oneself [Lat. *seducere*], there is a scission.
>
> (*DP*: 256)

This is significant in that Lyotard's analysis of representation does not consist in decrying its (ideological) falsity, but in considering its *performance* as an apparatus. Much of the difficulty in understanding Lyotard's work comes from the fact that we tend so easily to slip back into the language of illusion in thinking about representation, the language that Lyotard is precisely trying to elude. This characteristic turn away from issues of falsity to questions of performance distinguishes Lyotard's analysis from that of a certain radical dramatics, drama as ideology critique, in which the limit between stage and auditorium (2) is breached (to ask 'who speaks?') or where the limit between stage and backstage (3) is breached to show the apparatus by which the image is constructed. These cases correspond to the classical moves of cultural ideology critique by which the spectator and the image are referred back to the mechanism by which they are constructed and positioned. In each case, however, the limit that separates the 'de-realized' space of the theatrical apparatus from the outside (1) is preserved. Lyotard claims that contemporary capitalism has developed to the point where it can itself make profit from breaching the limits interior to the theatrical apparatus:

> We have the advantage over Adorno that we live in a capitalism
> that is more cynical, more energetic, less tragic. It places every-
> thing (including the backstage apparatus of 'exploitation') in
> representation, representation is self-reflexive (as in Brecht)
> and presents itself. . . . The walls, the entry, the exit, remain.
>
> (*DP*: 111)

Capitalism has caught up with Brecht, as it were.

Lyotard describes the space of the political as a theatre of representation by means of an extended analogy with the disposition of the Greek *polis*. A first limit circumscribes the city from the outside (1). In this spatial model of democracy, the stage is determined as a circle with an empty centre. The limit between stage and auditorium (2) is this circle, which one enters in order to speak. A third limit (3), marking off a backstage apparatus, determines who has the power to enter and speak and how they may do this:

> [W]omen . . . never speak in the centre and therefore they never
> say anything. Not everyone gets on stage. And then you have
> also *processes of effacement*: wealth, friendship, pressure groups,
> rhetoric, which are ways of getting to speak in the centre,
> backstage elements, which have to be effaced so that the politi-
> cal stage can be constituted.
>
> (*DP*: 257)

This analysis reveals that democratic 'freedom of speech' (in the middle) is hedged about by a series of limits and constraints; it also points out that ideology critique, which consists in making visible the backstage apparatus, in breaching limit (3), does not displace the rule of the theatre of representation which is guaranteed by limit (1).

This limit (1), the outer limit of political space, has an effect parallel to that of the walls of the museum on art: 'the putting aside of affects and the privileging of concepts as extraterritorial; the setting aside of intensities and their weakening by means of their staging' (*DP*: 291). Staging within the scene of representation involves two moves. First, it sets up a representation within limits: an 'inside' of representation's theatre as opposed to the reality 'outside' that it is the business of the theatre to represent. 'To stage is to institute this limit, this frame, to circumscribe a region' (*DP*: 59). Thus, culture is inside 'nature' representing it, politics inside 'society', for example. At the same time, however, this representation that copies reality imposes its rule on 'reality', *reduces the real to 'that which can be represented'*. What is explicitly 'off-stage', outside, is staged in that it can only be thought in terms of its potential representation on stage, as the referent of a discourse. The real is the representable. The real is reduced to the absent object of a representation. This is what Lyotard means by calling representation a 'placing outside [that takes place] on the inside' (*DP*: 291). The theatre of representation produces this effect of 'derealization' (the reduction of the real to a representation for a subject) by making everything within it a matter of conceptual representation, a move which Lyotard characterizes as 'theological' in that the outside, the 'reality' which the theatre proposes to represent is kept outside, excluded, and appears in the inside of the theatre only as the absent meaning of the representation, the dead God, the 'Great Zero' as Lyotard calls it. Thus, the move which appears to denigrate representation as secondary to the real is in fact the establishment of the rule of representation, by which the real is merely the absent original of a representation. Being is merely the absence upon which meaning is constructed. This is, for Lyotard, the theology of representation (which we in America are more familiar with under the perhaps excessively linguistic title of logocentrism) that begins with Plato.

For example, 'History' is produced by narrative representation as the external origin ('Great Zero') of that narrative. As the 'Little Libidinal Economy of a Narrative Apparatus: the Renault Company Recounts the Murder of Pierre Overney'[6] suggests, 'History' is the exteriority claimed by the theatrical apparatus of narrative representation (*DP*: 172). Narrative isn't something that happens to history, it produces historical diachrony as its origin:

> The history with which we are familiar, the diachrony of a
> supposed social subject, is certainly not something that narra-

tion comes to transform: either to falsify or betray it, or on the contrary to establish it as authentic; narration ceaselessly produces history.

(*DP*: 174–5)

Thus, temporality is reduced to History, to the diachronic sequence which narrative poses as its origin. In this way, narrative opens up the space of a theatre, with narrative technique inside and the raw fact of history to which narrative refers left outside. Affective intensities, the singularity of events, are thus reduced to merely the neutral fact that is the 'origin' of historical representation. Eventhood is merely the 'Great Zero' of diachronic sequence.

This allows us to understand more fully the grounds of the opposition to narratology that we traced in Chapter 2. A narratological analysis that merely shows that 'history' is constructed by narratives (e.g. Hayden White) remains within this theatre, because it contents itself with pointing to the apparatus by which 'history' is constructed within the theatre, making 'history' into an absolutely inaccessible origin, an even grander Great Zero. In refusing the illusion on stage, narratological critique simply despairs of leaving the theatre. Against this critical negation of history, the claim that there is no such thing as an event, only subjective representations, Lyotard demands a figural affirmation of the event as a singularity irreducible to the theatre of representation. That is to say, the narrative apparatus is never perfectly in place: there is a figural potentiality whereby narrative may be directed to the displacement of origins rather than their installation, where intensities appear 'in their singularity as non-unifiable events, as fragments incommensurable with the supposed unity of the reading body' (*DP*: 175).

The libidinal band and the organic body

At which point, it might be helpful to say something about this affective singularity of the event, this pure intensity, that is being counterposed to the theatre of representation. Briefly, at this stage of his work Lyotard is trying to think the singularity of the event (which I have already discussed in relation to postmodernity). The difference is that here the event is described in terms of energetics: as pure bursts of affective intensity, libidinal investments. It is basically a development of the revision of psychoanalytic desire as figural begun in *Discours, figure*. The 'discontinuous events' produced in a 'theatre of energy' resist the condition of discourse, of signification, of speech, 'they are potencies [*puissances*], intensities, present affects' (*DP*: 96). The libidinal theatre of desire would be devoid of limits distinguishing the exterior from the interior, pure production would replace any representative claim. Desire would have no *meaning*, it would simply aim to produce 'the highest intensity' (*DP*: 98).

I share Lyotard's later repudiation of the 'metaphysics of desire' implicit here, because it heads in the direction of an indifference in which there can be no discrimination between the intensities inscribed on the 'libidinal band', merely the anarchic, arhythmic pulsation of unconscious energy. However, one should not therefore dismiss what is going on in *Economie libidinale* and *Des Dispositifs pulsionnels* as merely wrong or silly (though some of the erotic writing in defence of adultery in the former is rather hard to take, even as strategy). The problem lies not so much in the evocation of the event as resistant to the theatricality of conceptual representation (which is a constant theme in Lyotard's work) as in the way in which the resistance of the event is articulated and characterized.

What it might mean to breach the outer limit that installs the theatre of representation is clearly not the revelation of the constructed or ideological nature of the representations on stage or of the viewer, the kind of critique exemplified in Stephen Heath's writings on cinema.[7] Rather, 'to doubt representation is to show that the theatrical relationship (in music, painting, theatre, literature, cinema) is ruled by a libidinal apparatus that is arbitrary' (*DP*: 110). This does not mean a critique of capitalism so much as a recognition that capitalism is supported by precisely the libidinal irrational intensities that it exists to regulate and exclude. It is this that produces in *Economie libidinale* the kind of praise and revaluation of capitalism that we have mentioned, the evocation of the '*jouissance*' of the industrial worker able to sustain enormous decibel intensities. As Lyotard puts it in *Les Transformateurs Duchamp*:

> [T]here is, in the worst conditions of the worker, a startling contribution, a contribution which can easily be paralleled to the adventure of poets, painters, musicians, mathematicians, explorers, physicists and the most hot-headed *bricoleurs*.... [A contribution] to disrupting the measure of the human condition, to a putting up with situations which one might have considered unbearable. It demands another body, in another space.... In particular an experience of quantity [intensity] without precedent in the rural tradition.
>
> (*TD*: 22)

The disruption of the theatre of representation is to be carried out, not by criticizing it as repressive or false but by showing how its repression and seduction repose upon the irrational libidinal energetics that it is supposed to repress:

> Theatricality and representation, far from being necessarily taken as a libidinal (*a fortiori* metaphysical) given, result from a certain work on the labyrinthine moebian band, a work which stamps these special folds and foldings back whose effect is a box closed on itself filtering impulses and only permitting to appear on the scene those which, coming from what one will thenceforth call the exterior, satisfy the conditions of interiority. The representational chamber is an energetic apparatus.
>
> (*EL*: 11)

Capitalism, itself an energetic or libidinal set-up of a particular kind, is thus to be redescribed and affirmed as the liberation of new libidinal intensities (the capacity to put up with 20 KHz of noise frequency) rather than simply critiqued as 'the growth in the forces of production at any price, even the death of many workers' (*TD*: 23). This seems useful insofar as it does not deafen us to the fact that history has a stutter, that we should be aware of the possibility of differences arising, that dehumanization may not be entirely a bad thing insofar as it displaces the discourse of humanism. However, Lyotard's libidinal energetics seem very problematic in that they fall back into a kind of indifferent celebration of singularity, an affirmation of the event that does not distinguish between the 'it happens' and the 'what happens', because there is only the 'it happens'. That is to say, the analysis of capitalism put forward in Lyotard's writing of this period has a certain shock value as an event, but that shock is too obviously a *value*, too simply a meaning within a system. The irrational and libidinal are being *staged*, as the 'libidinal band', even if Lyotard installs his description of the libidinal band only to say it is indescribable ('One cannot say where one is from any point, any region, because that point or region has not only already disappeared when one claims to speak of it, but, in the singular and non-temporal instant of intense passage, it has been invaded and invested [*investi*] from both sides at once') (*EL*: 25).

Let me take the example of Lyotard's analysis of film, in the essay 'Acinéma' in *Des Dispositifs pulsionnels*: the traditional cinema orders time through narrative sequence and space through perspective, so as to bind the singularity of movements on film into the unity of an organic body, a totality (*DP*: 60). Lyotard describes the functioning of the 'organic body' in the essay on Overney. The discourse of the human body is only one form of the organic body, which is simply any totalizing mechanism working to homogenize and regulate the elements within it; it's a 'body, of which the elements isolated by their respective functions coordinate themselves for the greatest good of the whole following the rule of the *Gestalt*' (*DP*: 178).[8] In general, 'organic body' is Lyotard's way of apprehending the totalizing function of an economy in *spatial* terms. Here, the organic body functions analogously to a 'grand narrative', taking disparate elements and reducing them to a homogeneous unity, by excluding aberrant impulses and channelling those that are recognized into a singular meaning, the constitution of image and the articulation of images into a narrative progression. Against this, Lyotard evokes an 'anti-cinematics' in which either immobility (too little movement) or extreme agitation (too much movement) give rise to intense affects or emotions, impulses which resist libidinal normalization within the totality of the organic body (*DP*: 61).

The account of affect here moves in two directions. On the one hand it leads towards the Nietzschean vitalism of the explicitly senseless 'eternal recurrence of sterile explosions of libidinal expenditure' (*DP*: 56).[9] Each singular movement (e-motion) would bear an 'intensity of extreme *jouissance*' that could not be connected to preceding or succeeding ones in temporal sequence. Time would be merely the succession of present intensities, flaring up and disappearing. The recurrence of intensities would not be the repetition of the same because all time is in the present; there is simply no possibility of memory, since consciousness is not preserved from one event to the next. The problems with this first direction are two-fold: first, all movements that are not recuperable by the organic body are *indifferently* orgasmic; the difference that displaces temporal diachrony or subjective consciousness is a pure unthinkable intensity, so all differences end up being *opposed* to the organic body in the same way. Accordingly, the figurality of the event would be a pure alterity, a Utopia of the absolutely inconceivable. For those of us who have read the opening to *Economie libidinale*, it makes no difference whether we are smoking pot or sunbathing as long as we are assaulting the organic body. Second, the absolute refusal of memory proceeds from a simple identification of memory with the persistence of rational consciousness, as opposed to a purely present moment. Lyotard's later work will refuse the implicit metaphysic of presence here by elaborating the 'immemorial' that I discussed at the end of the first chapter. The *Nachträglichkeit* characteristic of the postmodern parallels the attempt to present the work of the artistic avant-garde as not the instantiation of new 'nows' but as work of 'anamnesis', a refusal to forget the unsayable or unpresentable. This avant-garde of the immemorial attempts to testify to that which cannot be said by the elaboration of a sense of memory as the persistence of affects which will not be forgotten and yet cannot be remembered either, in which affect undermines the possibility of purely present intensity. On the other hand we can trace at the same time an opening towards just such an anamnesic aesthetics of pathos, of sublime incommensurability, in the suggestion that the affect is figural, that it resists being reduced to an exchangeable unit, a value defined relationally in a system. The affect is that of which we cannot speak, in the terms of structural linguistics. The affect, like materiality, is annihilated by being made a message, a matter for semioticians (see *EL*: 58). The importance and the difficulty of this thought should not be underestimated. To return to an earlier formulation, the affect and materiality are not properties of things but are figures, traces of an incommensurability between an event and any representation that might be given of it. Emotion and materiality are rhetorical, in the deconstructive sense, radically irreducible to matters of meaning that might be exchanged in communication or signified in discourse. And this resistance to being turned into exchangeable units within an economy, examples for a metalanguage, moments within a grand narrative, is what marks a displacement of the representational space of the political. In order better to understand this, we need to look at the way in which *Des Dispositifs pulsionnels* and *Economie libidinale* open up an analysis of capitalism as the rule of the commensurable. This will conclude my consideration of the representational *space* of the political, for it is the consideration of the resistance of the incommensurable in terms of the *temporality* of the event that marks Lyotard's turn to a postmodern politics of indeterminacy.

Capitalism: exchange and the incommensurable

Des Dispositifs pulsionnels states the failure of Marxism bluntly in historico-political terms. Capitalism has refused, practically and politically, to come to the terminal crisis that Marx predicted, and the Soviet experiment has produced an oppressive state bureaucracy and a technocracy. This failure, however, is not simply the result of historical accident. The negativity of Marxist critique has sought to find the weak link in the chain of capital, implicitly waiting for capitalism to come up against the limits of its own development, believing that:

> Even as [capital] extends the law of value to new objects ... to make of them 'modern' objects devoid of any other constraint than exchangeability, it approaches a limit which it cannot overcome.
>
> (*DP*: 13–14)

Lyotard insists, on the contrary, that there is no pure 'other' to capitalism's law of exchange, that what is required is to find regions of disruption within capitalism itself. There are two important points at stake here. First, capitalism is characterized in terms of the law of exchangeability; the primary operation of capitalism is one of *commodification*, of the reduction of materiality to exchangeable objects:

> Any object can enter into Kapital, if it can be exchanged. If it can exchange itself, can change itself from money into a machine, from one commodity into another, from labour power into labour, from labour into wages, from wages into labour power, everything, from the moment it is exchangeable (according to the law of value), is an *object* for Kapital.
>
> (*DP*: 17)

Thus, the only law in capitalism is the universal law of the exchangeability of all values: every value is a commodity.[10] The development of capitalism is the growth of *indifference*, in that all commodities may be exchanged indifferently. It makes no difference whether you hold cabbages or linen, as long as their value is the same. Capitalism is indifferent to the object, seeing it as money; indifferent to the worker, seeing him or her as labour; indifferent to the product, seeing it as object of exchange. The only limit to capital is the law of exchange: exchangeability determines value, not vice versa, 'Presumed commensurability ... is the rule or the regime of the capitalist system' (*DP*: 43).

Second, the imposition of the law of indifferent exchange, of commensurability, cannot be thought in traditional Marxist terms, as an alienation of objects from their true nature. Such an analysis, that of

Adorno at his most orthodox, thinks of the true nature of objects as 'that which is *lacking* in capitalism' (*DP*: 116). In this reading, the materiality of objects that is lost in commodification functions entirely *within* the theatre of representation as a 'great zero', as it were, the absent truth of representation. Insofar as it is a pure exteriority, it paradoxically remains within the theatrical model. If there is no grand absence outside, no dead God with which to berate capitalism, then resistance will have to be located inside, in the evocation of the figural necessity and impossibility of *incommensurability*, of the hetero-geneous, the singular, the inexchangeable, for the law of ex-change.

This incommensurability is, of course, that of the 'acinematic' movement that I have already discussed: the singular event that is 'sterile' in the narrative, that refuses to be reduced into a commensu-rable order of communicability, to become a value (meaning) to be exchanged between film-maker and viewer. At this point in Lyotard's writing, the Freudian 'drives' (Eros and Thanatos) are the privileged instances of incommensurability. Lyotard says that they are not two drives (*pace* Freud) so much as two regimes which are not *opposed* but always co-present in their heterogeneity (*DP*: 181–2). The incom-mensurability of the drives is constitutive of desire, in Lyotard's reading of Freud. And, since capitalist commodification is a 'fet-ishism', desire in its figural disruptiveness is always at work within capitalism, displacing the rule of the organic totality of the system of exchange. This is rather a shocking positive revaluation of fetishism.[11] The point here is an important one, however. As Lyotard points out, the assumption that commodity fetishism is bad rests not simply on the 'great zero' of the true nature of the commodity but also upon a suppression of the figural work of desire. The problem, once more, is that the celebration of polymorphous perversity as such leads to an indifferent valuation of transgression for its own sake. The evocation of the incommensurable that will be developed in Lyotard's later writings concerns the temporality of the event. In the essay on Over-ney, the analysis of the narrative apparatus leads in this direction, beginning with the observation that 'the *time in which* the narrator narrates is not and cannot be the time of the history which he recounts' (*DP*: 176). This incommensurability at the root of narrative is of course precisely that which, as we have seen, will be developed in Lyotard's account of the postmodern as figure for modernist histori-cal narration. Narrative thus necessarily fails in its attempt to impose a temporal order on events. The event is not the absent 'real' that the theatre of representation first proposes as its origin, and then reduces to the temporal envelope of diachrony in which bodies move.

The event is described as a 'tensor', an intense singularity, which Lyotard calls 'amnesiac' by analogy with the 'sterile' movements of '*Acinéma*'. History simply cannot remember it, cannot fit it into its narrative sequence of past and present. The event resists becoming a commensurable value in narration (one 'moment' in a historical sequence of other 'moments' [*DP*: 180]), by virtue of its 'inanity' (*DP*: 177). The death of Overney is 'vain' (*DP*: 177), meaningless, it cannot be accounted for in a diachronic history, given a meaning. In its singular intensity it simply doesn't fit into any historical narration of which it might be posed as origin. Lyotard is beginning to elaborate the distinction between the 'it happens' (event) and the 'what happens' (the moment – the event that can be assigned a meaning). However, the event is at this point a pure resistance, absolutely empty, *inénarrable*. The problem with this is that we have fallen back into an *opposition* between the absolute meaninglessness of the event and the discourse of meaning. Paradoxically, all events would then be indifferently, interchangeably, *commensurably* meaningless and incommensurable resistances to the organic totality of history.

This kind of attention to the event as displacing historical time is not specifically temporal; Lyotard is interested in the disruption of time insofar as it opens the time and space of the organic body to the spacelessness and atemporality of the libidinal band. His later writings move from a celebration of amnesia to an insistence on the immemorial, a shift which is effected through a thinking of time as self-divided rather than as opposed to the atemporal, of thought as split between conceptual and reflective judgment rather than as opposed to acephalic intensity.[12] Thus, his location of the postmodern as a figure both within and different from the modern is a rewriting of the event as an *im*pure otherness to historical discourse. We are seized by the event as a figural blocking together of eventhood ('it happens') and meaning ('what happens'), of two temporalities, the immediacy of happening and the mediation of conceptual understanding. Thus, the event is not anti-temporal so much as constitutively belated, *nachträglich*. The political is to be disrupted, not by desire as an other to the space-time of representation inhabiting space and time but by an account of space-time as always split between the singular time of happening and the spatialization of the event as a moment within a discourse of meaning, or a diachronic network of history. And this will not be a simple demonstration of impossibility, a little deconstructive technique: it will point to the necessity and impossibility of justice. We cannot simply transgress the outer limit of the theatre of representation: we have to represent, yet must not represent; that is to say we have to present in a way that at the same time testifies to the eventhood that representation suppresses. We are committed to a justice without criteria, to inventing ways of doing justice, experimenting in search of a justice that cannot be justified in advance.

(C) JUDGING THE DIFFEREND

Kant and Wittgenstein

And it is no transition to say that politics is implicated in this problem of judgment. Bennington is correct in saying that 'Lyotard is fundamentally a political thinker', with the proviso that we place as much emphasis on the word 'thinker' as on 'political'.[13] Lyotard demands that we think about politics, which is not simply a question (as it so often is, alas) of remembering to be aware of what we already 'know' about politics. To think about politics with Lyotard is to place our understanding of the term at risk.

This risking of the political proceeds from Lyotard's challenge to the legitimation of knowledge in general, the concern of *The Postmodern Condition*, which feeds into an account of political action in his later work. *Just Gaming* is concerned to deny the legitimation of political action either in terms of the desirability of a describable state of affairs corresponding to the true nature of things (whether Plato's *Republic* or Marx's primitive Communism) or the achieved autonomy of political entities (whether the self-knowledge of 'we the people' or the self-determination of the Soviet State). This produces a shift to what has been more conventionally understood as the ethical. That there are no grounds for a politics any longer means for Lyotard that the political only begins at the point where determinant grounds for judgment are withdrawn. This is very disturbing to those who wish to believe that their political actions are motivated by a consistent and coherent programme of objectives and strategies. As I have remarked, the current authority-claim of literary theory in the United States is to determine the political significance of cultural texts. Because of this focus within literary theory, the question of a politics without grounds is crucial, since the political, by Lyotard's account, can no longer be assumed to provide the grounds for the study of literature. More nearly, literature, or 'literary discussion', provides the mode of a politics.

In order to work out what such a 'literary politics' might involve, I want to conclude this book by trying to trace what is at stake in the turn towards a politics of indeterminate judgment, an ethics of reading, by looking mainly at two of Lyotard's works available in translation, *Just Gaming* and *The Differend*. First of all, this means a study of Lyotard's appropriation of Kant and Wittgenstein, the former for the question of indeterminate or reflective judgment, the latter for the understanding of language as the locus of events that necessitate such judgments. In each case Lyotard's is an avowedly partial and singular reading, as when Lyotard describes himself in *Instructions païennes* as a Kantian 'if you wish, but [a Kantian] of the Third Critique' (*IP*: 36). Lyotard opposes the Kant of the First Critique to the Kant of reflective judgment and imagination characteristic of the Third Critique, the difference being that in the Third Critique Kant 'cures himself of the disease of knowledge and rules in passing to the paganism of art and nature' (*IP*: 36). *Just Gaming* refines this difference by distinguishing between the rule-bound nature of the First Critique and the capacity of the imagination in the Third Critique as the power of *experimental* judgment without pre-existing criteria which parallels the experimental paralogism of the postmodern aesthetic (*JG*: 17).[14] In cognition, or determinate judgment, we 'know' by applying a pre-existing concept to an object in order to determine its nature: 'this thing is a "tree"'. Indeterminate judgment is judgment to which we cannot apply a pre-existing concept. Its relation to the event is thus clear. When an 'event' occurs, in Lyotard's sense, something happens which disrupts the pre-existent frame of reference, so that we don't know how to understand it, at the time (see Chapter 2(B), 'The Event'). Indeterminate or reflective judgment is required, in which the imagination experiments, inventing ways of understanding the event. It is thus judgment which takes place in the explicit absence of criteria. Indeterminate judgment deals with the 'it is happening', not with the '*what* is happening', with the event rather than with its constative content.

In the case of Wittgenstein, Lyotard, as we saw in Chapter 2, adopts the notion of 'language games' to develop the importance of pragmatic analysis of phrases raised by his concern for 'little narratives'. To summarize brutally the analysis put forward in *Just Gaming* (51–4), culture is an expanded field of language games, which are multiple and heterogeneous. That is to say, 'language games' function here in a manner analogous to the 'little narratives' that I discussed in Chapter 2. Lyotard's use of Wittgenstein's 'language games' insists upon the pragmatic specificity or singularity of phrasings, their resistance to being incorporated into 'grand narratives' or metalanguages. The use of 'language game' evokes the implicit discursive pragmatics of any phrase. The language game is not a subjective strategy, rather a subject is an effect of the language game: games play individuals, rather than vice versa:

> [T]hese are games that we can enter into but not to play them; they are games that make us into their players, and we know therefore that we are ourselves several beings (by 'beings' is meant here proper names that are positioned on the slots of the pragmatics of each of these games).
>
> *(JG*: 51)

Nor are language games situated 'in the world'; reality or the world is a pragmatic position constructed by each language game. A phrase belongs to a language game in that it is a move in the pragmatic universe implied by the language game: each move implies a sender, an addressee and a referent. Thus, to take the analogy of chess, each move carries with it a set of rules governing what moves may be made at any point. These rules situate both the players and dictate the significance of the move. To think about phrases in terms of language games is to insist that 'meaning' or signification is only one element among others in distinguishing the pragmatic effects of language: for Lyotard it is a way of focusing upon the performativity of language.

However, in *The Differend* Lyotard relinquishes the term 'language game' as implying too strongly the notion of a player behind it, and turns to an account of the cloud of language particles in terms of 'phrases'. What is important is the way in which *Just Gaming* links Kant to Wittgenstein so as to insist that doing justice in a field of language games consists of resisting the pretensions of certain language games to provide the rules for other games, to become metalanguages. Thus, in each language game we must try to judge without importing criteria from other games, such as that of theory (which claims to give criteria to all games). The language game, in Lyotard's reading, thus demands an indeterminate judgment, without criteria, on a case-by-case basis. This is a political matter for Lyotard in that the political is inherently the search for social justice, a search that must proceed without pre-existing criteria. Politics, that is, is a matter of indeterminate judgment for Lyotard.

Injustice

Politics is a matter of judgment in that Lyotard identifies politics as a demand for change, an attempt to induce a transformation of reality, inherently prescriptive:

> There is no politics if there is not ... a questioning of existing institutions, a project to improve them, to make them more just. This means that all politics implies the prescription of doing something else than what is. But the prescription of doing something else than what is, is prescription itself: it is the essence of a prescription to be a statement such that it induces in its recipient an activity that will transform reality, that is, the situational context, the context of the speech act.
>
> (*JG*: 23)[15]

The performativity of prescription is directed towards the just action, whereas descriptive statements are formulated in reference to the true. Lyotard's concern in *Just Gaming* is to insist that there is no bridge possible between the just and the true, and that injustice and political terror (totalitarianism) proceed directly from the assumption that the true and the just may be united. Lyotard insists that prescriptives are formulated in reference to an Idea, an *irrepresentable* law (such as 'Justice', in the case of the political) rather than to an object of cognition (such as a description of what society should be).

Political prescriptions as to the 'just' are incommensurable with descriptions of the 'true' because the former refer to an *indeterminate* idea, the latter to a determinate object of cognition. In the case of a prescriptive:

> This phrase presents what ought to be done, and simultaneously it presents the addressee who ought to do it. It does not arise from the true/false criterion since it is not descriptive, but from the just/unjust criterion because it is prescriptive. One may wonder whether it is just or not. But even if it were unjust, it is endowed with sense, just as a phrase is endowed with sense even if it is false. ... However, the sense pertinent for the criterion of justice and the sense pertinent for the criterion of truth are heterogeneous.
>
> (*LD*: 48)

In the prescriptive case judgment is indeterminate or reflective, in the descriptive it is determinate or cognitive.[16] As I pointed out in my remarks on 'narrative and politics' in Chapter 2(H), the moralization

108

or aestheticization of politics is the application of indeterminate judgments to the political as if they were determinate (we know what is beautiful/good, and so we will make society that way). This may not seem to be saying very much if we think that it is clear that the strategies of Khomeini and Hitler are unjust; however, the argument of *Just Gaming* and *The Differend* is more wide ranging. It consists not merely in resisting the transfer of indeterminate judgments to the political *as if* they were determinate but also of resisting *any* determinate judgments in the political sphere. That is to say, the political as a realm of prescriptives, of performance, is not a site for determinate judgment into which aesthetic and ethical judgments must not sneak; the political itself is a realm of indeterminate judgment into which determinate judgments of any kind must not be transferred. Thus the ethical, political and aesthetic are three realms of indeterminate judgment and none must claim to function as a metalanguage, as a ground of determinate knowledge regulating the others.

The representational apparatus is no longer counterposed to a libidinal band, rather we are in a cloud of language particles (little narratives, language games, phrase-universes), and politics is one way of judging how to move among them. In these terms, Lyotard is rephrasing politics as *the art of formulating prescriptions about the social without recourse to metalanguage.* In order to do justice to the multiplicity and heterogeneity of language particles, to avoid reducing their singularity as events to the status of signified units within a metalinguistic discourse, we have to apply indeterminate judgment on a case by case basis. *Just Gaming* and *The Differend* are attempts to work out a mode of attention to linguistic events sufficiently rigorous in its awareness of difference to permit this.

The 'theatre of representation' is rephrased as the rule of one order of phrases (the descriptive) over another (the prescriptive). Where oppression was the capturing of desire in the apparatus of representation, or the reduction of work to text, we are now talking about injustice as the subjugation of political prescriptives to descriptives (cognitive representations). The effect of this domination is to make politics entirely a matter of knowledge, of cognition, a domination which is essentially totalitarian. Totalitarianism proceeds from the claim that an idea can be an object of cognition, that a law can be adequately represented. If the law is thus within the theatre of representation, then determinate judgments can be made in reference to it. The effect of this is to preclude the possibility of dispute, which is the essence of totalitarianism; the terror of totalitarianism consists in saying, for example, that 'we are just because we *know* what justice is'. As Lyotard puts it, in *The Differend*:

> As a general rule, an object which is thought under the category of the whole (or of the absolute) is not an object of cognition (whose reality could be subjected to a protocol, etc.). The principle affirming the contrary could be called totalitarianism. If the requirement of establishing the reality of a phrase's referent according to the protocol of cognition is extended to any given phrase, especially to those phrases that refer to a whole, then this requirement is totalitarian in its principle. That's why it is important to distinguish between phrase regimes . . .
>
> (*LD*: 5)

If I may untangle this rather gnomic formulation, Lyotard is arguing that there is a distinction between the object of an idea and the object of knowledge. The idea transcends representation in terms of concepts. Justice is such an idea, in that the law is irrepresentable, for Lyotard as for the Kant of the Third Critique, the law always remains to be determined, by experimental, paralogical judgments. Lyotard is not being 'idealist', since idealism would consist precisely in believing that the idea of the law can be represented as an object of cognition: we can know what ideals are and try to live up to them. To return to the language of *Just Gaming*, idealism is totalitarian in that it claims to formulate prescriptive statements ('be good') in reference to a determinate idea of the 'good', a knowable good. For historical materialism that knowable good is real but masked by ideology; for idealism that knowable good is opposed to the degradation of the real, the failure of the actual to live up to it. In contradiction to such totalitarian derivations of the just from the true, the argument of *Just Gaming* is that a just politics can only consist in responding to the imperative 'be just' without claiming to know in advance what it is to be just. Politics is thus not a matter of devising strategies for arriving at goals so much as experimenting in search of an indeterminate law, the idea of justice.

What this might mean will perhaps be easiest to grasp by working through Lyotard's argument concerning the nature of injustice. According to Lyotard, political injustice consists in seeking to establish the justice of a prescriptive phrase by reference to a representable order of things (a descriptive statement). Lyotard stresses the impossibility of passage from the true to the just, the incommensurability of descriptive and prescriptive language games (*JG*: 22). Any politics which claims to unite the two seeks to establish a representable law, a determinant use of the idea of justice, and thus leads to totalitarianism, the conception of society as totality which annihilates resistance as, by nature, asocial or anti-social. This conception is founded on the conflation of description and prescription, 'the deep conviction that there is a true being of society and that society will be just if it is brought into conformity with this true being . . .' (*JG*: 23).

This claim to know what justice is produces terror, since on that basis all opposition is silenced as inherently unjust. Lyotard analyses two ways in which attempts to make politics a matter of knowledge in this way produce terror. The first form of terror occurs when political theory, whether 'idealist' or 'materialist', attempts to produce an account of justice as mimetic correspondence to a model of society. The true description of society will legitimate the just formulation of prescriptions as to social practice. The task of politics is to return society to its true nature, whether that nature is believed to be egalitarian (Marx) or hierarchical (Plato). Political theory is the derivation of prescriptives as to how to do this ('arm the workers') on the basis of the model. Practice is merely the instrumentation of the described ideal by means of those prescriptives.

The second form of terror does not focus on the referent of political descriptions (the model of the just society) but on the sender. Justice is made the object of a representation by embodiment rather than by being modelled. 'We the people' is the strong form of this, where the self-determination of a social consensus allows the determination of the law. The law is what the people want, and what the people want is the law. This may seem strange: democracy is being identified as totalitarian, when the terms are usually opposed. However, Lyotard insists that the notion of self-determination is nothing less than the claim to determine the just as a society's knowledge of itself. The law is thus describable as the knowledge or the will of a universal subject, and prescriptives about just action are derived from that description. To provide a quick example, totalitarianism is evident when a society claims to have embodied justice, to represent the law, so that it is able to dismiss any criticism of itself as simply 'un-American' or 'anti-Soviet' or 'counter-revolutionary'. When Lyotard says that there is 'no just society' (*JG*: 25), what he means is that any society which claims to represent the law is immediately unjust, silences any possibility of opposition.

In the first case, political prescriptions are grounded as just insofar as they correspond mimetically to the essence of the social. In this case, politics is a matter of making actual society correspond to a true

111

description of the social, of achieving an accurate political representation. In the second case, political prescriptions are grounded as just insofar as they correspond to the describable will of a subject 'authorized to say "we"' (*JG*: 81). Here, Lyotard is arguing that any attempt to ground justice, to make it the object of a description, a representation, a cognition, is inherently unjust. There can be no just theory of justice, nor any just embodiment of justice in a society. Any such attempts to justify justice install totalitarian terror in making the law a determinate representation, an object of cognition. In each case, one language game comes to function as a *metalanguage* into which all others are in principle translatable.[17] To put this another way, the language game of prescription is being translated into that of description. For example, prescriptive phrases ('respect those in authority') are legitmated by being translated into descriptive statements ('it is natural to respect those in authority'). In this case, an ontological discourse is presumed to be capable of regulating all other kinds of language games. The effect of this presumption of translatability is that anyone who fails to respect authority is condemned as 'unnatural', without origin, and thus annihilated.

Thus, injustice or terror lie in the erection of the notion of a justice which might be justified, the confusion of prescriptive justice with descriptive *justification*. That is, we must perform the difficult feat of thinking about justice without recourse to notions of mimetic adequation. To believe that there might be a representable reality of justice is to light the way to terror. The voice that might speak the law as such always performs the operation of terror, in that to assert the law as literally representable is to silence its victims by relegating the operation of resistance to the condition of transgression. The binary functioning of the law through obedience and transgression has a double terror: it both silences resistance (turns the injured party into a victim) and confines resistance within itself.

The representable law, the prescriptive which claims to be grounded in either a description of the true nature of society, or the will of the universal subject of humanity, or the grand narrative of historical destiny, institutes terror in that it silences resistance by victimization: those who lie outside the law (since the law is the justice of non-metaphorical reality) are unreal, and cannot speak. If description is conflated with prescription, if justice can be justified, then those upon whom the law operates are not oppressed, they simply do not exist for the law. There can be no discussion as to justice, since what justice is has been determined. For example, if one is accused of 'anti-Soviet activities' in a Soviet court, one cannot defend oneself by disputing the law that identifies 'anti-Soviet' with 'unjust'. This is what Lyotard calls 'absolute injustice' or 'Terror':

> Absolute injustice would occur if the pragmatics of obligation, that is, the possibility of continuing to play the game of the just, were excluded. That is what is unjust. Not the opposite of the just, but that which prohibits that the question of the just and the unjust be, and remain, raised. Thus, obviously, all terror, annihilation, massacre, etc., or their threat, are, by definition, unjust.
>
> (*JG*: 66–7)

As you will realize, terror is not incidental in Lyotard's account of politics: our entire understanding of politics as a matter of representation, whether democratic or totalitarian, is terroristic insofar as the political theorist, the state, or society claims to determine what justice is, to derive political prescriptions in reference to a describable state of affairs. If *Just Gaming* refuses the representable law as unjust and demands a practice of reflective judgment, without criteria, a judgment which respects only the irrepresentable law of the idea of justice (see below, 'The Idea of Justice'), it has a problem as to *why* this should be so. What is so important about respecting the heterogeneity of the prescriptive language game, directed as it is to an idea rather than an object of cognition? *Just Gaming* in this sense seems to privilege the prescriptive game exorbitantly. In *The Differend*, however, it is the account of politics as the art of differends, of clashes between incommensurable language-games, that explains what makes judgment without criteria necessary, lest some criterion privilege one language game at the inevitable expense of the other.

The Differend

The Differend is a long book, one that works over the issues central to Lyotard's career in terms of language.[18] Not a *theory* of language, but a persistent attention to the pragmatics of language as crucial to reading, judging, thinking. This is not a claim of a semiotic order – that everything is just a linguistic sign, that all significance is *internal* to a linguistic system or to the language of nature. In this sense, the insistence on the 'phrase' as elementary particle is a resistance to grand narratives or metalanguages.

The Differend works on a case-by-case basis, and its attempts to

testify to differends at every turn are not a method ('spot the differend') but a kind of manual of *asceticism* in the sense Lyotard gives it in
Peregrinations, an emptying of analysis of all cognitive assumptions
that might lead it to pre-judge the nature of the event. *The Differend*
does not propose answers so much as perform a work of reading
philosophy, politics and history (the aesthetic is rather less in evidence) in search of the indeterminate law. It attempts to perform the
kind of reading that might do justice to events in these domains
without criteria. As such, it demands of the reader that she or he set to
work in turn. *The Differend* doesn't so much tell the reader how to
judge as transpose arguments into the language of 'phrase analysis' in
such a way that the necessity of judgment without criteria that the
differend poses appears as fully as possible, in a presentation which
does not prejudge by its reliance on the logocentric criteria of cognitive representation.

You have read more of *The Differend* than you might think, perhaps
most notably in the introduction to this book, but generally in the
consistent evocation of the incommensurable or irrepresentable as the
figural or postmodern quality of the singular event, the 'it is happening' as distinct from the 'what happens'. The work of *The Differend* is
to provide a mechanism of description that will allow the event to be
presented in its singularity, rather than suppressed in re-presentation. The nature of this presentation, and how one might testify to
the event without representing it, have to be worked out in the book.
In order to establish the terms of Lyotard's transcription into the
language of phrase analysis, it is necessary that I presume that you
have not read the book, weaving a certain amount of the paraphrase
already provided by Lyotard in his 'Reading Dossier' into my account
of it.

Phrases

The Differend proposes the '*phrase*' or sentence as the elemental unit of
analysis: 'What escapes doubt is that there is at least one phrase, no
matter what it is' (*LD*: 65). Any attempt to deny this statement simply
proves it, since '*There is no phrase* is a phrase' (*LD*: 65). This does not
mean that the phrase is real or meaningful, since reality and meaning
are themselves effects of certain kinds of phrases or groupings of
phrases. A phrase, then, is simply the empty singularity of an event,
the fact of an 'it happens'. The phrase is thus the unit of the 'cloud of
language particles' and we are faced by a succession of radically

singular events. In Lyotard's terms, there is a phrase; it happens. As to what it will be that has happened, that's a matter to be discussed, a matter for more phrases. The fact of a phrase-event is indubitable solely in respect of its happening:

> For a phrase to survive the test of universal doubt stems neither from its being real nor from its being true (No. 101) but from its being merely what happens, *what is occurring, ce qui arrive, das Fallende*. You cannot doubt that something happens when you doubt: it happens that you doubt.
>
> (*LD*: 66–7)

The 'phrase' is thus Lyotard's most fully developed account of the 'event' as pure happening. It is a way of dislocating the rule of the various discourses which attempt to give meaning to the event. These discourses consist of ways of making links between phrases so as to fit them into patterns. These patterns allow the event to be represented (as historical narrative, for example) by suppressing the singularity of the happening of each phrase.

Each phrase presents a 'phrase universe', it carries with it not merely a meaning but an entire pragmatics (in this sense, it is like a 'language game'). Phrases do not take place 'in context', rather the context is within the phrase, as its implication of the universe of its production, reception, meaning and referent. Lyotard takes the example of the deictic indication of '*here, now* and *I*' as all depending on the universe presented by a phrase. Although they seem to indicate a reality external to the phrase in which they occur, the capacity for that indication depends upon the phrase that presents it (*LD*: 33–4). There is thus no 'space or time independent of a phrase' (*LD*: 76). The taking place of the phrase does not determine the nature of this 'phrase universe', it merely presents it. The four instances that Lyotard identifies as composing this universe are *the referent, the meaning* or *sense, the addressee*, and *the addressor* (*LD*: 14). Each phrase occurs, and implies each of these four instances or poles, but it does not determine their nature: they appear like empty slots.[19] The next phrase will determine the nature of each by the way it is linked onto the slots, so that the instances function as 'valences of linkage' (*LD*: 76).

Lyotard gives the example of a cat raising its tail (*LD*: 77). A linkage onto the addressor would be 'What do you want?'. The nature of the addressor is determined ('you', the cat). A linkage onto the addressee would be 'You're bothering me'. The subsequent phrase situates 'me' as the addressee of the phrase (rather than God, or another cat). A linkage onto the sense or meaning of the phrase would be 'Hungry again?'. The subsequent phrase determines the meaning of the raised tail as a description of the state of the cat's digestion. A linkage onto the referent would be 'They have very expressive tails'. The subsequent phrase determines the raised tail as merely its referent. Note that this last example presumes a different addressee than in the preceding linkage; this is indicative of the extent to which the instance is presented but not determined by the first phrase.

The example of the cat shows that phrases are not confined to language in the conventional sense (one may phrase by gesture [*LD*: 70]), not least because 'silence makes a phrase' (*LD*: xi). Silence is a phrase in that the refusal to phrase 'happens' in the same way as doubting that there is a phrase 'happens'. Once we have realized that silence is a phrase, then we must recognize that there is not simply one phrase but always at least more than one. There are always phrases, one phrase happens, then another: phrases are 'moving objects which form an infinite series' (*LD*: 7). Similarly, there is no last phrase, no end to phrasing, since any identification of the 'last word' on a subject is itself a phrase (*LD*: 85), as is the silence following it.

Linkages, genres

Since phrases are extended in series, each phrase is *linked* to the next one. This linkage is absolutely necessary (since silence is another phrase), yet the nature of the linkage is not pre-determined. One of any number of phrases can be appended, even those seeming irrelevant or inconsistent. Thus, 'to link is necessary; how to link is not' (*LD*: 29).[20] Linkage is necessary but contingent (like reading, as we shall see). There exist a number of ways of attempting to determine the linking of phrases, modes of organization: Lyotard calls these *genres*. A genre supplies a rule for linking phrases, for selecting one phrase to link rather than all the other possibilities. The genres thus function across heterogeneous regimes of phrases, effecting linkings with particular aims in mind. The heterogeneity of phrase universes (their difference) is thus subordinated to a defined goal.

Lyotard gives the example of the phrase 'Charge!' uttered by an officer leaping from the trench. If the soldiers link onto this phrase by charging likewise, they understand it as an exclamation in the genre of persuasive rhetoric, directed at persuading them to perform an action. If they respond by standing around and saying 'Well done', they make a link which understands the first phrase as in the nature of

116

a theatrical gesture, a link which diverts the series towards a comic effect. The genre of the linkage directs the two phrases towards an end (persuasion, laughter). And everything about the nature of the phrase is at stake in the linkage. That is to say, the phrase occurs, and its meaning, its referent, its speaker and its addressee are all determined by the nature of the phrase that is linked onto it. The singular event of the phrase (the 'it happens') is distinct from the determination of the instances of the phrase ('what happens', to whom, through whom, its significance) which is regulated by the link that is made next, belatedly. Whether 'Charge!' is a heroic persuasion or a theatrical performance is determined by the contingency of the next phrase linked onto it. The apparently 'non-serious' linking of applause is not a mistake but a mutiny by metalepsis. This causes us to rethink the hierarchy of 'serious' and 'non-serious', of literature and 'real politics'. A play may give rise to a revolution, a war may be undone by reducing it to farce.[21] And since the multiplicity of available genres are each heterogeneous, they make a difference to each of the instances of the phrase-universe. Genre is a literary term, a term which marks the fact that the choice of a next phrase, the effectuation of a kind of linkage, is a matter of what *Rudiments païens* called 'literary discussion'. There is no universal genre that will determine the one, right, authoritative linkage. It is in this sense that the contingency of linking always introduces a *differend*, a radical point of dispute as to the genre of linkage.

Several linkages are possible, but only one can happen at a time (*LD*: 29). A multiplicity of genres offer a multiplicity of linkages, and to choose one is to suppress all others.[22] Without a grand narrative to tell us which one linking will be the right one, we are committed to understanding our linkings as necessarily involving a question of justice divorced from the question of truth. 'What to say next?' cannot be legitimated as right or true; it can only be considered in terms of how it does justice to the phrase event. Many genres of linkage are called forth by the phrase but only one is chosen. And the importance of this necessity of suppressing other linkages is that the dispute involved is a *differend* rather than a *litigation*.

The differend

The difference between a differend and a litigation is crucial to Lyotard's argument. A litigation is a dispute that takes place according to a single and determinant rule of judgment. A differend, on the other hand, is a dispute between at least two radically heterogeneous or incommensurable language games, where no one rule can be invoked in terms of which to pass judgment, since that rule necessarily belongs to one language or the other. In a litigation, the accuser and the accused speak the 'same language' as it were, recognize the same law. In a differend, they speak two radically different idiolects.

Perhaps the most obvious example of this comes in the clashes concerning aboriginal land rights in the wake of the breakdown of the grand narrative of imperialist expansion. For example, Werner Herzog's film *Where Green Ants Dream* stages the conflict between Australian aborigines and a mining company. The mining company has one kind of claim ('legal title', deeds, etc.). The aborigines have another kind of claim (sacred buried objects). There is not simply a dispute as to who owns the land; the notion of 'property' as such is the locus of a differend. The film stages this in two exemplary double-binds. The aborigines are asked to substantiate their claim by producing the sacred buried objects as if they were 'evidence' for the court. They reply that they cannot do this, because to look at the sacred objects would be a sin, resulting in the death of the viewer. Second, an aborigine hitherto known as 'The Mute' stands up in the court and suddenly begins speaking. The judge asks why he is called 'Mute' if he can speak, and demands a translation. The other aborigines reply that he is called 'Mute' because the rest of his tribe are dead; no one else speaks his language, and he speaks no other. The judge expresses sympathy for the aborigines but concludes that they have presented nothing to the court which is admissible as legal evidence. In each case, the aborigines are not litigants but victims: they have suffered a wrong, and the nature of that wrong removes the capacity to prove it before the law. No tribunal can resolve the case, either way, without victimizing one side or the other, rendering them 'Mute'. Any judgment that claims to have the last word on this case will necessarily victimize one side or the other, since 'the rules by which one judges are not those of the judged genre or genres of discourse' (*LD*: xi).

Nor is this a limit-case, an extreme example, taking place at the outer limits of our 'civilization'; rather the differend is at stake in every linking of phrases. In this way, *The Differend* refines the argument of *Just Gaming* by insisting upon the incommensurability of all regimes of phrases, all genres of linking, not merely the prescriptive and the descriptive:

Incommensurability, in the sense of the heterogeneity of phrase regimens and of the impossibility of subjecting them to a single law (except by neutralizing them), also marks the relation between either cognitives and prescriptives and interrogatives, performatives, exclamatives.... For each of these regimens, there corresponds a mode of presenting a universe, and one mode is not translatable into another.

(*LD*: 128)

Thus, when any linking is made, all other genres of linking 'remain neglected, forgotten, or repressed possibilities' (*LD*: 136). Every phrase is the locus of a differend, in that the nature of every phrase is to be determined by the next phrase linked to it, so that 'every phrase is in principle what is at stake in a differend between genres of discourse. This differend proceeds from the question, which accompanies any phrase, of how to link onto it' (*LD*: 137–8).

The problem raised by the differend is neatly summarized in Lyotard's 'Reading Dossier':

Given (1) the impossibility of avoiding conflicts (the impossibility of indifference) and (2) the absence of a universal genre of discourse to regulate them (or, if you prefer, the inevitable partiality of the judge): to find, if not what can legitimate judgment (the 'good' linkage), then at least how to save the honour of thinking.

(*LD*: xii)

To 'save the honour of thinking' is to 'bear witness to the differend', the prescriptive issued at the end of 'What is Postmodernism?' (*PMC*) as well as in this preface to *The Differend*. In order to understand what this might mean, we first need to look at how the differend is suppressed in the 'theatre of representation' that governs conventional understandings of the political, in the notion of the 'real'.

A world of names

'The Real' is not the rule by which all phrases can be judged, and the appropriateness of a linkage be determined. Rather, the 'real' is the effect of a certain genre of linkage, the cognitive genre, analysed in *Just Gaming* as the hegemony of descriptive phrases. 'Reality', that is, is an effect of consensus about the state of the referent as an object of cognition (*LD*: 4). To which one might reply, with Habermas, that as long as consensus were reached, there's nothing wrong with that; the problem is merely one of achieving a universal consensus by means of more effective communication. Lyotard, however, insists upon the fact that communicative consensus is impossible; that consensus as to the real is always wagered against the differend. This is because a world is made up of a network of names. Names are 'rigid designators' which mark an absolute singularity. What a name means (the sense or meaning attached to a referent) is debatable, but the name is situated rigidly as a mark of singularity: the proper name functions by virtue of its distinctness and locatedness among other names. Even if we give 'Kant' two different meanings (bourgeois lackey, great philosopher), the name seems to mark a single and particular referent. Phrases cluster around names, and dispute over the ways in which they can be used. This might seem to imply that names mark a continuity between phrases, a permanence independent of the 'phrase universe' in which they are presented (*LD*: 40). Indeed, the rule of cognition would claim that the state of the referent could in principle be fixed, either by universal consensus or in reference to an infallible third party such as the eye of God or Nature.

On the contrary, says Lyotard, the single particular referent of the name cannot in principle be exhaustively identified or described, because the name is not 'by itself a designator of reality' (*LD*: 47). It is rigid but empty, as it were. And an infinite inflation takes place if we attempt to list all the meanings that may be attached to a name, which do not so much establish the reality of the referent as defer it indefinitely. As a result, 'the referent of the name *Caesar* is not a completely describable essence, even with Caesar dead' (*LD*: 53). Nor is it merely the case that the meaning of a name can never be finally determined, that consensus is impossible. The name is also the locus of the clash of different genres of linking: descriptive, prescriptive ('Be like Washington') and so on. The name is thus both singular and multiple, identical and different: 'strongly determined in terms of its location among the networks of names and of relations between names (worlds) and feebly determined in terms of its sense by dint of the large number and of the heterogeneity of phrase universes in which it can take place as an instance' (*LD*: 50).

As a result, the name does not designate 'reality' so much as mark reality as the locus of differends. To put it another way, the name rigidly marks the locus of an indeterminacy; a determinate hole in determinacy, as it were. Names do not merely provoke litigations as to what they really mean (who was 'Richard Nixon?'), rather they evoke differends in that they attract heterogeneous genres of phrases. Some-

120

one greets 'Richard Nixon' with the phrase 'You can't be Richard Nixon'. This phrase does not make sense in one genre of linking since according to the cognitive genre the name 'Richard Nixon' can only be the object of phrases describing a currently living human. However, in another genre, the prescription may be made that it is imperative not to be Richard Nixon (the meaning of 'Nixon' is 'political has-been'). A litigation would be an argument as to whether or not an individual is Richard Nixon, a differend arises when the name is put to heterogeneous uses, when there is a metalepsis, 'a change in the level of one's take on the referent' (*LD*: 25). To dismiss this metalepsis as 'nonsense' would merely be to privilege the cognitive genre of linking, to claim that the meaning of the name can only be identical with an ostensible referent. In the rule of the cognitive genre, Nixon is either alive or dead, and all phrases must be formulated in respect of this exigency. By such a rule, we could not speak of Auschwitz, since it is the name of extermination itself, of the removal of ostensible referents. Lyotard invokes the function of the name in order to make the point that names are not determined by reality but are the locus of a struggle as to what the world can be. The name is rigid, but it is empty, indeterminate in its sense or pragmatic situation:

> Reality entails the differend. *That's Stalin, here he is.* We acknowledge it. But as for what *Stalin* means? Phrases come to be attached to this name, which not only describe different senses for it (this can still be debated in dialogue), and not only place the name on different instances, but which also obey heterogeneous regimens and/or genres. This heterogeneity, for lack of a common idiom, makes consensus impossible. The assignment of a definition to Stalin necessarily does wrong to the nondefinitional phrases relating to Stalin, which this definition, for a while at least, disregards or betrays.
>
> (*LD*: 55–6)

Perhaps the most prevalent name in *The Differend* is Auschwitz, which is the model of a name which functions, as we might say, figurally, which cannot be made into a concept.[23] Auschwitz, that is, is a name which cannot be an object of cognition, which disrupts the rule of the real: 'it is not a concept that results from "Auschwitz", but a feeling, an impossible phrase, one that would link the SS phrase onto the deportee's phrase, or vice versa' (*LD*: 104). Auschwitz produces the feeling that something is trying to be said that cannot be said: it witnesses to a differend. This feeling, this pathos evokes the awareness of a phrase absolutely incommensurable with any phrase that offers a knowledge of Auschwitz.

Auschwitz is a name to which no concept should be applied, which can only be betrayed by becoming the object of a representation, a matter for cognition. This is the weight of Lyotard's analysis of Faurisson's critique of the historical reality of the sufferings of victims of Nazi gas chambers. The sufferers in the gas chambers are victims of the double bind imposed by a representable law: to have seen a gas chamber work is to be dead, unable to speak of the wrong one has suffered. The victim is one who has suffered a 'damage accompanied by the loss of the means to prove the damage' (*LD*: 5). In this case we can see that there is a differend between the phrase regime of cognition (for which the Holocaust is indescribable) and the suffering of the victims of the Holocaust. This is a strong example of the injustice of reality, of the hegemony accorded to the cognitive genre by the demand for a representable law, the insistence that justice can be justified, that law can become the referent of description, an object of cognition. Resistance becomes transgression of the real; the victim is silenced.

A simple example of what is at stake in a normative law which links a prescription and description would be the phrase 'Nobody would do x'.[24] To oppose the injustice of that statement by a quibble over terms in the presumption that a consensus might be reached about a literal sense of what it is to be 'somebody' would be to miss the point: any description of what it is to be 'somebody' which could be the basis of prescriptions about the real, the ground of a representable law, would always exclude somebody, though of course it would claim only to exclude nobody, to exclude only nobodies, only women, only blacks, only madmen, etc., etc. These 'nobodies' are victims, those deprived of the ability to phrase their wrongs because their idiolect is not representable before the law. If the law is representable, if justice has a real referent, is an object of cognition, then the terror or victimization is inevitable. Anyone who argues with the representable law is simply to be dismissed as 'mad' (*LD*: 8).

Yet on the other hand, if we cannot make everybody into 'somebody', if the claim to universal subjectivity necessarily involves the suppression of differends, how are we to deal with differends? What might it mean to testify to them without representing them, to do justice to a dispute between radically incommensurable idiolects without resolving it, while still respecting the heterogeneity of

122

phrases? This, for Lyotard, is the task of 'philosophy', as he defines it, to testify to the differend:

> By showing that the linkage of one phrase to another is problematic and that this problem is the problem of politics, to set up a philosophical politics apart from the politics of 'intellectuals' and 'politicians'.
>
> (*LD*: xiii)

'Philosophy' is opposed to the discourse of intellectuals and politicians in that it does not seek to find a determinant criterion by which to resolve differends. This is a very particular understanding of the philosophical genre. The 'intellectual' seeks to make philosophy 'queen of the sciences', the metalanguage which grounds the epistemological or historical rigour of all other language games. In this sense, by understanding any language-game as in principle translatable into the philosophical 'belief-system' that produces it, the 'philosophical' would turn all differends into litigations between opposing philosophies, resolvable before the tribunal of 'philosophy'. On the contrary, Lyotard defines philosophy as a resistance to this metalinguistic pretension to the domination of other language games:

> There is no genre whose hegemony over the others would be just. The philosophical genre, which looks like a metalanguage, is not itself (a genre in quest of its rules) unless it knows that there is no metalanguage.
>
> (*LD*: 158)

The philosophical genre resists metalanguage in that it is a 'genre in quest of its rules', not a universal point of view. It's an experimental genre, the genre of judgment without criteria, which searches for the rule appropriate to an event. Because it has no rules, it does not prejudge the event. Philosophy seizes a differend and testifies to it in the search for a phrase by which it may come to be understood:

> One's responsibility before thought consists ... in detecting differends and in finding the (impossible) idiom for phrasing them. This is what a philosopher does. An intellectual is someone who helps forget differends, by advocating a given genre, whichever one it may be ... for the sake of political hegemony.
>
> (*LD*: 142)

Philosophy is thus a practice of paralogical experimentation, the attempt to do justice to a differend which assumes nothing in advance

123

as to what the nature of that justice might be. 'In order for the wrong
to find expression and for the plaintiff to cease being a victim',
philosophical experimentation seeks out 'new rules for the formation
and linking of phrases ... a new competence (or "prudence")' (*LD*:
13). History will not end, we will never be done with doing justice.
The differend cannot be set aside or fossilized in order to preserve it,
respect for the differend means keeping it open, at work. The parallel
with the postmodern reformulation of the task of the avant-garde is
obvious. What is at stake is not the resolution of a differend, but its
phrasing. Its phrasing because the differend is, by definition, a clash
of heterogeneous language games, so that if it is mistaken for a
litigation the victims are deprived of the means to speak of their
suffering and do not appear:

> The differend is the unstable state and instant of language
> wherein something which must be able to be put into phrases
> cannot yet be.... In the differend, something 'asks' to be put
> into phrases, and suffers from the wrong of not being able to be
> put into phrases right away.
>
> (*LD*: 13)

The differend, to take up our earlier example, is when the aboriginal
witness appears 'Mute', yet when there is an accompanying affect
that marks something which is trying to be said, but cannot be said. It
is impossible that the phrases of the aborigine be linked to those of the
court: the task of philosophy is to find a 'new idiom' which might
perform that linkage without suppressing one or other of the language
games. The differend does not demand a re-trial, but an as yet
unthinkable tribunal, a justice the nature of which has yet to be
decided. The responsibility of philosophy is to testify to this absolute
heterogeneity, to respect the irrepresentable differend suppressed by
any representable law. We don't pass judgment on a differend
(simply say that the aborigines are right – by whose law?), rather we
seek to make an indeterminate judgment that will testify to the
incommensurability of the claims of the aborigines and the mining
company (leave the differend open – judge so as not to *answer* or close
down the question 'what is happening?'). In all its strangeness,
Herzog's film is such a linkage, in which two languages are impossibly
co-present.[25] Such a judgment must seek to do justice to the affect
hidden in the silence of the 'Mute' victim, or the speech of the victim
forced to reduce a differend into a litigation (the Auschwitz survivor
whose testimony reduces the absolute terror of the Holocaust to a

cognitive experience among others in history). The name to which the differend is attached marks the breakdown of cognition, a necessity of judging what phrase to link accompanied by the loss of criteria by which to judge.

The idea of justice

I must now make an important clarification: there is a distinction between indeterminate judgment and a relativist refusal to judge, a pluralist insistence that all judgments are equally valid. The singularity of the event, the incommensurability of the differend, demand a judgment without criteria. As Lyotard puts it in *Just Gaming*:

> ... the thinker I am closest to in this regard is Aristotle, insofar as he recognizes ... that a judge worthy of the name has no true model to guide his judgments, and that the true nature of the judge is to pronounce judgments, and therefore prescriptions, just so, without criteria. This is, after all, what Aristotle calls prudence. It consists in dispersing justice without models.
>
> (*JG*: 25–6)[26]

The absence of criteria in indeterminate or reflective judgment is not a commitment to relativism, in which everything goes. Justice is not a representable law; it is an *idea*, emphatically not an object of cognition. To recognize the non-representability of law is to refuse undifferentiated relativism, which is the insistence upon the plural representability of law (the law is anything you say it is). Judgment is the linking of phrases: it is necessary, but it is indeterminate. Phrases are linked in respect of the idea of justice, an idea which can never be literally represented, turned into a norm. In this sense, justice remains always in the future, yet to be determined. The condition of a just judgment would thus be that it respects the indeterminacy of justice: in the language of *Just Gaming*, that it does not seek to justify its claim to justice by means of a descriptive. The just judgment leaves the question of what justice might be open to discussion; it does not allow justice to become a determinant concept (*JG*: 47). The multiplicity of justices evoked by the heterogeneity of language games is thus not a mere relativism, since it is regulated by a justice of multiplicity. This judgment is not an undifferentiated pluralism, rather it is based in the most rigorous respect for difference. This is a respect for differences *among* things, not relativism's respect *for* things, which ultimately erases difference by making all things worthy of respect. In contradistinction, pluralism represents the idea of justice as merely the totality of all things said about it, and retains the hegemony of the cognitive genre in presuming that if the law cannot be represented, then there is nothing to be said about justice. That is to say, pluralism or relativism represent the law as nothingness. They say that since we can't represent the law, we don't need to seek the just: we are not obligated to justice since nothing can be determined about it. Against pluralism, Lyotard is arguing that we are obligated to an idea of justice, although that idea is always to be determined. There are not 'all sorts of justice': there is a necessity that we keep discussion as to the nature of the just open.

The judge is obligated to the idea of justice that he or she can never master, which preserves Lyotard's argument from being a sceptical solipsism, a relativist defence of 'individual conscience'. Judgments are not made from a position of transcendent subjectivity which *precedes* or stands outside the judgments it makes.[27] Judgments, in that they are made without criteria, presuppose their own judgment. The justice of a judgment can only be judged, again, without determinate criteria. Thus the just person, the judge, does not make judgments, but is made *by* them, is continually judged by and in terms of the judgments which the judge makes. Since those judgments are also made without criteria, the process is continual, the judge can never be finally judged as just (and therefore justified, described as just), since the process of judging can never reach the point where an account could be given of it which would be final. We cannot make the good judgment, the 'right' linkage; we must link. Our only criterion is the indeterminate idea of justice, the search for the linkage that can testify to the differend, to the irrepresentable.

We are now at the point where we can understand what is at stake in the differend by referring back to our discussion of the immemorial as a figure. The historical differend arises as the sense that an event has taken place, and that the occurrence of the event is lost for representation. Something happens that disrupts the frame of reference by which it might be understood. As we have seen, Auschwitz is not presentable under the rules of knowledge that govern historical representation. The cognitive idiom can only betray the singularity of the event by reducing it to a moment: one atrocity among others. The singular eventhood of Auschwitz is surrounded by a silence, a silence which signals the inability to phrase and which is accompanied by the feeling that there is nevertheless a wrong that must be phrased. This affect is not a subjective state of mind, 'it is the sign that something remains to be phrased which is not, something which is not deter-mined' (*LD*: 57).

The affect appears as a *figure* for cognition, the incommensurable presence of the absolutely unspeakable in and against speech. Not an ambiguity but a heterogeneity, a differend: something which cannot be phrased. And yet this phrase must be linked onto. There must be another phrase, even if it is a silence. The problem of judgment, then, is that of finding the linkage which will testify to the differend con-tained in the phrase, which will not wrong the differend, silence it by prejudging it. And it is our problem. What are we to say, after Auschwitz? Nothing in the nature of the event provides us with criteria for judging this question, since the event consists in the extermination of not only human beings but of the means to under-stand that extermination (*LD*: 56). If we continue to understand the political as a set of criteria for judgment, then the political will produce injustice, will function as a metalanguage. What would it mean, however, to try to think of politics as Lyotard does, as 'the threat of the differend' (*LD*: 138), as the struggle over what the next phrase will have been? Politics insists on raising the differend, on refusing to let the hegemony of one genre of phrases determine the nature of linkage or resolve the crisis of judgment which linking demands. Specifically, *The Differend* sketches a political resistance to capitalism in terms of phrases. If capitalism is the hegemony of the economic genre, the rule of exchange, then political resistance con-sists of evoking the inexchangeable, the differend present to the economic linking of phrases as exchangeable. And since capitalism presumes that all objects are exchangeable because they speak a common language, as it were, the language of labour-time, resistance lies in the evocation of an unaccountable time: the time of the event, the 'it happens'. In short, the politics of the differend is a reading of the event's incommensurability with capitalism's claim to make all time accountable and exchangeable.

(D) THE TIME OF POLITICS

Reading the event

In this section I want to situate Lyotard's interest in indeterminate judgment (in *Just Gaming* and *The Differend*) as something which is made possible by a shift *from space to time* when thinking the political. The organic body, the theatre of representation, and the libidinal band that displaces them all share a predominantly spatial meta-phorics, even if the libidinal band is the explicit erasure of recog-nizable space. The shift that gets Lyotard out of the problems of the libidinal band is an explicit turn towards temporality, a turn parallel to the one I traced in the shift between our first two chapters from figural form to postmodern eventhood. I also want to introduce *reading*, a term which Lyotard doesn't use much except in the negative sense assigned to it in *Discours, figure*. He tends to talk about 'rewriting' in order to emphasize the status of attention to texts as an *act* with a temporality, rather than as pure (re)cognition of their meaning.

My interest in saving the word 'reading' and so distorting Lyo-tard's analysis proceeds from a desire to develop the literary-critical implication of deconstruction as an *ethics* of reading rather than a theoretical *method*.[28] The title of Hillis Miller's *The Ethics of Reading* marks out exactly the direction in which deconstruction pushes liter-ary criticism or literary theory; the exacerbation of textual difference is not a hermeneutic method but a way of insisting on reading as a crisis of judgment.

Deconstruction doesn't find what is 'in' texts, it pushes texts to the point at which they become events, happenings which disrupt any previously existing criteria by which they might have been 'under-stood', recognized, assigned a meaning. This means that deconstruc-tion's ethical turn is not a matter of drawing moral lessons. It is a recognition that doing justice to texts is not a matter of fidelity to their content but of listening to the points at which they are torn apart by a difference that they cannot express, yet must express. The gaps that deconstruction opens up in texts are not contradictions or failures; if they are lapses they are lapses in a Freudian sense, they arise at the site of radically heterogeneous libidinal investments, at points of incommensurability, at 'differends'. Deconstruction insists that to do justice to a text is to seek to activate these differends, to testify to the differend, to the clash between radically heterogeneous language games or orders of phrasing. The ethical implication of deconstruc-tion, after Lyotard, is thus that in reading we encounter the event, where we must judge but have no criteria by which to judge. Decon-structive reading cannot tell us how to judge, yet it can make us aware of the ethical necessity of judgment at points where the apparatus of conceptual representation seeks to bury the conflict, to reduce differ-ence. In concluding this argument I want to examine how reading may function to evoke the temporality of the event as a resistance to cultural representation. In terms of my last chapter, one might say that I want to use Lyotard to phrase reading as an activity of post-modern aesthetic experimentation, rather than any hermeneutics. The interpreter is always an *'interprêtre'* (*prêtre* = priest), priestly, even if she or he claims the radicality of Marxism, semiotics or cultural critique.[29]

Capitalism and time

Let me invoke our mobile supplement, 'work', in order to sketch the difference that a turn to temporality might make. A certain suspicion of the concept of labour, and a contrary insistence on the effect, trace, or sign of work, seem appropriate to our postmodern condition. If we allow, for brevity's sake, a recognition that this is an age of late monopoly capital, it is clear that work no longer occupies the same place that it did in the late nineteenth century. To play the sociologist for a moment, massive expansions in salaried as opposed to wage labour and concomitant steep rises in unemployment have resulted in a severe diminution of the proletariat in the West. The failure of organized labour to resist the expansion of capital doesn't simply invalidate the predictive status of Marxism; it suggests that the concept of labour as formulated in Marxism simply doesn't work. Labour isn't working, because it is understood as a concept, as a meaning. Time and motion men will organize a discourse of labour so as best to reveal that meaning in the product, Marxists will organize a discourse of the history of labour so as best to reveal that meaning in the destiny of the proletariat. In each case, work seems to be disappearing. Capitalism does not in its essence recognize labour, since capitalism is founded by the concept of exchange-value, by which labour as concept is progressively subsumed.

The function of the *concept* of labour is to reduce everything under the heading of the exchangeable. The time of modernism is that of a sequence or succession of moments, the time of the new, organized as a project of universalization, whether of humanity or of race. The ground of this possibility is the opening of moments to being thought in terms of universal concepts. Modernism is the moment of capitalism in that the rule of the market is the rule of universal exchange-ability; modernism's project of universal history parallels capitalism's drive towards a world market. And as Lyotard points out, the currency or universal language of the capitalist market is *time*:

> It is the time spent on professional qualifications, in making a profit from capital investments, the time of the succession of

demographic generations. We can say that such time is money. Money is presumably nothing else but the abstract reserve of time in general, be it spent on production, circulation, or the use of goods and services, insofar as it is computed in terms of the unit of mean social time presumed necessary to produce, circulate and use anything in the contemporary context.

(Peregrinations: 23)

Production is valued as labour time, whilst capital is stocked or stored labour time, according to Lyotard's reading of Marx as it appears in *Le Postmoderne expliqué aux enfants*. Indeed, Taylorism gives rise to 'time and motion' study rather than 'labour study'. Smith's remarks on the division of labour in Chapter 1 of *The Wealth of Nations* likewise insist upon its threefold benefit as an abridgement of time: (i) Increased dexterity reduces the time of the task; (ii) No time is 'lost' in the passage between tasks; (iii) Machines may 'save' time. This would allow us to understand why the service industry is capitalized as *'fast food'*. Capitalism's contradiction is thus the simultaneous drive to 'gain time' whilst understanding time as value: the ambiguity of 'saving time' as read by Lewis Carroll (*Alice, Sylvie and Bruno*: where does time go when it's been 'saved'?).[30] The system is driven by this contradiction in the sense that time must be saved but can't be spent (*PMEAE*: 94).[31] That is, time is 'gained' when capital accrues surplus-value. Time can only be 'stored' as more capital. To store time as capital, however, doesn't balance things, but *speeds them up more*. Put another way, capital is not stored labour so much as stored time, the application of which results in exponential acceleration.

The Differend transposes this analysis of capitalist commodification as primarily temporal into the terms of its 'phrase analysis' so as to show both the spread of capitalist relations in culture and the stakes in resistance to capitalism. In *The Differend*, Lyotard understands capitalism as the giving of hegemony over all other phrase-regimes to the *economic* genre of exchange. Capitalism as the rule of commodification and exchange becomes capitalism as the determinant rule of the economic genre over the linking of phrases. That is to say, in capitalism, all phrases are treated as if their linkage were *economic*, a matter of the exchange of values.

The movement of capitalist expansion is the reduction of labour to labour time, the subordination of work to the economic genre of exchange. And this is an ordering of phrases and the matter of a differend. Values are not the meanings of objects which are then

130

exchanged, exchange determines the meanings of objects as their value in the exchange (*LD*: 173). This is the differend of labour:

> A case of differend between two parties takes place when the 'regulation' of the conflict that opposes them is done in the idiom of one of the parties while the wrong suffered by the other is not signified in that idiom. For example, contracts and agreements between economic partners do not prevent – on the contrary they presuppose – that the laborer or his or her representative has had to and will have to speak of his or her work as though it were the temporary cession of a commodity, the 'service,' which he or she putatively owns.... By what well formed phrase and by means of what establishment procedure can the worker affirm before the labor arbitrator that what one yields to one's boss for so many hours per week in exchange for a salary is *not* a commodity?.... If the laborer evokes his or her essence (labor-power) he or she cannot be heard by this tribunal, which is not competent. The differend is signalled by this inability to prove.
>
> (*LD*: 9–10)

Alienation is here being rewritten: it is not the theft of a reality (the experience of labour) and its replacement by an abstraction, as Marx has it. Rather, it is the affect that signals a differend between the idiom of the boss (the economic genre in which labour is a quantifiable amount of time to be exchanged) and the idiom of the worker (the productive genre in which a day of work is an activity of transformation).[32] The rule of capital gives hegemony to the economic genre of the boss, the exchange of wages (abstract time) for labour (real time) is presumed to be equitable. Yet there is an absolute disymmetry between them. The boss exchanges money (stored time) for labour, the profit being a gain in time. The worker exchanges real time for stored time (money) but cannot recover the real time, in another life as it were (except by becoming a boss, and ceasing to be a wage-labourer). Thus, the boss gains time, the worker loses it. Lyotard summarizes the situation when he writes:

> There is an insoluble differend between working and gaining time. The feelings (sadness, anger, hatred, alienation, frustration, humiliation) that accompany the said working conditions are born from the differend and signal it. The subordination of work to exchange is also called wage-earning.
>
> (*LD*: 176–7)

Capitalism drives to gain time, arousing a differend with work. Matter becomes information (e.g. electric money, 'sound bites') as it is reduced to the most minimal temporal elements, a succession of pulses (on/off, 1/0). Computer technology is the organization of energy as pure temporal switching: the best computer is the one which works fastest. Capitalism, according to Lyotard, should thus be defined as the drive to *accountable time*:

> Anything at all may be exchanged, on the condition that the time contained by the referent and the time required for the exchange are countable.
>
> (*LD*: 177)

At the same time, as Lyotard reminds us, this account can never be closed, since market efficiency demands the quicker circulation of commodities and the effective erasure of time. Marx saw war as a response to crises of overproduction; in the nuclear age we understand war as the vanishing point of pure velocity. The market-place offers the imperative that we speed up, save time. Time is money. At the same time, capitalism can only preserve itself from speeds at which the masses might become critical by explaining the final utility of preserved time as the quickest route to total oblivion.

What then, would resistance to capitalism be? Anti-capitalist modernism, named romanticism, is an attempt to direct the temporal project towards the alternative end of an organic society: it has tended to produce an ultimate complicity with the extension of capitalism. On the other hand, merely to perform a reactionary Luddite resistance, to delay by introducing static, whether in machine breaking or through computer viruses, is merely a romantic negation which doesn't really challenge the system. Such resistant delays would in fact merely create more room for profit by opening new spaces in which time could be saved (the task of the computer-expert, until someone develops a machine to combat viruses, etc., etc.).

On the contrary, Lyotard contends that a resistance to the hegemony of the economic genre in the linking of phrases, a resistance to capitalism, would have to introduce a *temporal alterity*, an *unaccountable time*:

> In a universe where success is the gaining of time, thought has one incorrigible fault – making time be lost.
>
> (*PMEAE*: 63)

It is important to insist that Lyotard is not advocating simply an oppositional wasting of time; rather he proposes an opening of historical or sociological (modernist) time to a temporal *otherness* that displaces its accounting, that is untameable, irreconcilable:[33]

> The economic genre with its mode of necessary linkage from one phrase to the next ... dismisses the occurrence, the event, the marvel, the anticipation of a community of feelings. 'You'd never be done' taking into consideration the incommensurability of the stakes and the void this incommensurability opens between one phrase and the next.
>
> (*LD*: 178)

In the philosophical work of Lyotard, this is the time of the *event*; for textual studies, this is the time of *reading* (as opposed to all hermeneutic devices for extracting meaning in the shortest time possible); for the social sphere, it demands a turn towards the temporality of ethics rather than of political organization. The time of reading that refuses to 'gain time' is of course the time demanded by the prefatory 'Reading Dossier' to *The Differend*, which I discussed in the introduction to this book. In *Peregrinations*, Lyotard identifies an open, aporetic, temporality as disruptive of all claims to hermeneutic certainty, to total knowledge, drawing on Kant's account of reflective judgment:

> As postponement itself, time does not allow the full synthesis of the moments or positions the mind crossed through in approaching a cloud of thoughts or, *a fortiori*, the sky. Time is what blows a cloud away after we believed it was correctly known and compels thinking to start again on a new inquiry, which includes the anamnesis of former elucidations. Being the opposite of the Hegelian notion that time is a concept, time for Kant is the challenge that thinking had to take up; it is its self-deferring, its '*différer*'.
>
> (*P*: 7)

It is in these terms, as *The Differend* puts it, that 'Time is not what is lacking to consciousness. Time makes consciousness lack itself' (*LD*: 77). In considering what it might mean to open thinking to this temporality that disrupts the synthesis of sense-impressions into knowledge by means of concepts, I want to focus on the term reading: reading not as a Luddite resistance to the world, but an insistence on the literary event as irreducible to exchangeable moment. Reading would thus take on the quality of the experimental (the Latin word '*invenire*' means both to fabricate and to find out by reading) as delineated by Lyotard in *Peregrinations*: 'to start on [the] way without the goal of resolving or concluding . . . experiences, but rather with the intention of being unencumbered enough to meet events' (*P*: 25). This would be that reading of which Paul de Man gave us so many literary-critical examples; a reading that doesn't aim at speed, a thought of literature as that which always demands to be read once more, which isn't exhausted as information or knowledge. As Lyotard says of philosophical reading:

> It is an exercise of disconcerting with regard to the text, an exercise of patience. The long course of philosophical reading does not only teach that one must read, but that one can never finish reading, that one only begins, that one has not read what one has read. It is an exercise of hearing.
>
> (*PMEAE*: 158)

Thus, by virtue of the turn to reading, the consideration of capitalism in terms of time doesn't simply mean the eradication of the material in a whirlwind of speed (the succession of simulacra experienced by Baudrillard on the freeways of LA), but a recognition that materiality is not a property of objects which exist in time.[34] Rather, materiality is the capacity for the insertion of resistant or unaccountable time into the system, materiality is the raw temporality that capitalism seeks to reduce to accountable succession:

> But the occurrence doesn't make a story, does it? – Indeed, it's not a sign. But it is to be judged, all the way through to its incomparability. You can't make a political 'program' with it, but you can bear witness to it.
>
> (*LD*: 181)

Reading thus introduces materiality, as a temporal aporia, to the textual commodity.[35] We will not have read the texts that we have read.

De Man: the space of modernity

At this point, my distortion of Lyotard towards the term 'reading' is beginning to sound like a conscious evocation of the de Manian project of reading. I want to focus briefly on a parallel between Lyotard's rewriting of the event as political differend and de Man's literary deconstructions, so as to give the reader a sense of how Lyotard's work intervenes in the reading of culture. There are import

134

ant affiliations to be made to the way in which de Man understands modernity as a temporal predicament that is constitutive of the reading of literature. As de Man puts it, reading Nietzsche in 'Literary History and Literary Modernity', 'modernity invests its trust in the power of the present moment as an origin, but discovers that, in severing itself from the past, it has at the same time severed itself from the present' (de Man 1983: 149).[36]

The paradoxical predicament of modernity outlined here can be linked to Lyotard's work in that it renders the question of what it is to do justice to history in reading (the question that is posed to politics after Auschwitz); a matter that cannot be a matter of truth, of mimetic adequacy, but is a question of ethical judgment. This seems to me to be the importance of deconstruction, and what distinguishes it from epistemological critique or speculative negation without faith in dialectical sublation. And this seems to me to be also what is at issue for de Man in the term 'reading', the term addressed by de Man to the two predicaments in which literature is caught: the temporal relation of literary modernity to literary history and the epistemological relation of literature to criticism. 'Reading' names for de Man the ethical situation of attention at the point where literature both acknowledges and denies its referential claims to historicity and to knowledge.

De Man's reading of literature as modern is a reading of literature against modernism, but also a reading of modernity against any assumed privilege for literature as an instance. He insists upon the difficulty of the time of writing, the irreducibility of the event of writing to the modernist writing (description) of the event within the framework of a single history. For de Man, literature becomes the impossible act of self-reflection. Literature is both the representation of an action (writing of an event) and an action (an event of writing). The predicament of modernity is the impossibility of overcoming the temporal aporia imposed by this self-division. Literature cannot become itself, its modernity lies in the impossibility that it ever become modern, its specificity is its inability to be consistent to its own specificity. Literature is the moment at which modernity faces its constitutive inability to be modern. The distinctive characteristic of literature is thus to manifest inability to escape from a condition which is unbearable for literature. We might add politics to traditional literary history in the list of modes of understanding which have sought to ignore this predicament and to effect that escape, at the price of ignoring literature.

The parallel between de Man and Lyotard lies in reading directed towards an event that cannot be a matter of cognition. In a letter to Wlad Godzich, de Man discusses the pitfalls of the term 'Irony', 'Irony is a dangerous term, because people think they know what the term means and this forecloses all understanding. "Reading" is much better . . .' (de Man 1989: lxxiii). The upholding of the term 'reading' seems to me to be a crucial move in de Man's work. It comes at the end of 'Literary History and Literary Modernity', where the opposition of literary history to literary interpretation is dissolved into a general economy of reading: 'what we call literary interpretation – provided only that it is good interpretation – is in fact literary history' (de Man 1983: 165). The power of reading (good interpretation) is that it does not 'truncate literature by putting us misleadingly *into* or *outside* it' (ibid.: 164). Note that this temporal problematic has been experienced as a specifically spatial difficulty, a matter of the division of inside from outside in the consideration of literature. The work of reading that de Man performs is limited by this consistent reduction of the question of temporality. De Man does think the temporal problematic of reading, but he thinks it in resolutely spatial terms: and it is to this, rather than any mystical privileging of literature, that we owe the sense of literature as blockage that has left political critics unhappy with de Man's work.

At this point I must mark how my reading of Lyotard leads to a crucial revision of the de Manian project. The problem with de Man's work lies in the fashion in which its delicate tracing of conceptual aporias within literary work is conceived in spatial terms, even when he treats of time. In place of resistance, the recognition of aporia thus produces the conceptual awareness of undecidability, to which de Man responds by implicitly stepping back from the text in order to note it. This step back is the constitution of the aporia as the spatially constructed object of a gaze.[37]

As an institutional move, this can be recognized as fulfilling the conditions of the worship of the literary object, not as mystifying privilege, but as what Stephen Melville speaks of in *Philosophy Beside Itself* as the way in which 'the temporal predicament of literature ends in epistemology – literature ends as that which gives itself as both mystifying and demystified' (Melville 1986: 134). I would say that, once the attitudinizing gaze returns in this spatialization of metaphor, irony becomes, for all the wrong reasons, a better term than reading. History may not be inhabitable, but it has become all too visible as blindness. Lyotard is to be distinguished from de Man in that he does not stand and gaze ironically at the temporal impasse of modernity. For Lyotard, the event is not a property of the literary object which can be spatialized within the ambit of a gaze. Lyotard's reading is directed towards the event as a temporal condition which remains; remains as a resistance to the temporality that commodifies the text as the packaging of conceptual knowledge (even the knowledge of un-decidability). It is thus that reading is the site of a politics.

At this point, the politics of reading in the deconstructive sense become clearer. De Man's turn to a reading both within and against modernity may be understood in the language of Lyotard's account of the postmodern. Insofar as it is a new modernity (the same old modernity), a 'look', the 'latest [quickest] news', postmodernism is the greatest opportunity for capitalization yet (cf. use of the term in *New York Times* advertisements and the academic institution as a synonym for 'contemporary'). Insofar as it is the rigorously thought temporality of the future anterior ('it will have been'), it opens the possibility of just such an unaccountable time. The taking place of the event has to be thought as incommensurable to the commodification of the event as moment. Thus the event 'happens' *in excess* of 'what happens'. 'It happens', but the happening can only be represented later (*post*). Thus we can't say 'what is happening', only that it 'will have happened'. The determination of 'what has happened' is merely the recuperation of the event (the 'it happens') as a moment in the development of a structure or system. The distinction of the event from moment is that it cannot be commodified in this sense (repre-sented by means of a determinate concept): it is *unaccountable* as such. Reading evokes the sense that something is happening to which we cannot apply a cognitive concept. We have returned to the question of what it would be to read, after Auschwitz.

Anamnesis: the time of reading

This evocation of Auschwitz is not merely the effect of de Man's wartime guilt. The resistant and deconstructive temporality of read-ing is analogous to the figural temporality of the Immemorial that I discussed with regard to the Holocaust in Chapter 1. The radical force of a reading that always remains to be done is characterized by Lyotard's account of *anamnesis*, a not-forgetting that is yet different from remembering:

anamnesis: the search for that which remains unthought although it already has been thought . . . and the resistance that one finds in the work of hearing [reading] and anamnesis is of another kind to that which might simply oppose itself to the transmission of knowledges.

(*PMEAE*: 158)

This resistance which is yet not simply opposition, not merely static, lies in paying attention to the singularity of the event as it, belatedly, 'opens a wound in sensibility' (*PMEAE*: 142), never for the first or last time. It opens a wound in knowledge by introducing a temporal alterity to the time of historicity, of sociology, of cognitive understanding. It is in this sense, to return to the language of Chapter 2, that the work of postmodernity for Lyotard is anamnesic, the elaboration of the postmodern temporality that modernity forgets in order to begin. The postmodern is not a period, but the refusal, *from within modernity*, to forget what cannot be remembered in modernity:

> The 'post' of 'postmodern' does not signify a movement ... of repetition but a process of the order of '*ana-*', of analysis, of anamnesis, of anagogy, of anamorphosis, which works through an 'initial forgetting'.
>
> (*PMEAE*: 126)

Lyotard thus rejects the radical claim of the modernist avant-garde to critical breaks, revolutions in consciousness, ever newer modernities. However, as I pointed out in Chapter 2, this is by no means a blanket rejection of experimentalism. The work of the avant-garde is redescribed by Lyotard as the intellectual task of 'permanent anamnesis' (*PMEAE*: 114), of reading the event of modernity, a rewriting of modernity which in no sense prefigures a new universality.

Reading as anamnesis is a work of mourning, a refusal to forget the past either by consigning it to oblivion or by making it present (believing that we can fully remember). This is the condition imposed on literary reading by canonicity, by the fact that texts appear to us as having been read before and yet still requiring to be read, the fact that texts are always to be read, yet once more. The literary canon has been betrayed into essentialism (and racism and sexism thereby) by humanists who have believed that it might be remembered, by the understanding of the canon as a container of value. It seems to me that the importance of Lyotard's work when transposed into the literary-critical sphere is to produce a *pagan* account of the canon, which refuses to locate the canon as either the repository of value or merely an ideological trick.[38] As Lyotard points out in *Just Gaming*, the

138

tradition is in fact pagan insofar as the tradition marks the encounter of each individual act of reading with a tradition of reading that eludes its grasp; insofar as each act of reading cannot produce the metalanguage that will entirely account for the past. Each act of reading the canon would thus be like the retelling of stories by the Cashinahua, a matter of experimentation rather than of preservation, in which it is the event of telling rather than the object that is narrated that is the canonical or traditional stake (*JG*: 33–4). The paganism of the canon, its resistance to the metalinguistic function of telling the story of universal cultural values for which it has been variously appropriated and attacked, lies in the fact that canonicity marks texts as unable to be remembered or to be forgotten – what cannot be remembered cannot be left behind. Canonicity identifies texts as in some sense demanding to be read again, so that their reading is both necessary and impossible (cannot be brought to an end). In a pagan understanding of the canon as a figure for reading, the canonical texts do not have original authority or identify a universal cultural heritage. The fact that in the West the canon is constituted by *written* texts marks the impossible and necessary dependence of cultural representations upon an original instance (the 'speech' of God, Nature, Tradition) that is radically heterogeneous to cultural representation.

Lyotard's identification of the task of reading as anamnesis points the way towards an understanding of criticism as the experimental rewriting of the canon, rather than of authoritative (canonical) reading. Canon, that is, marks the irrepresentability of origin, condemns our readings to an irrevocable, unbridgeable belatedness. The canon should not stand as a concept of value but as the figure for the encounter of all reading with an immemorial past, an encounter that may give reading itself the status of an event, an experiment. Not a pure innovation, a new modernity, but a paralogical re-writing. To return to the Latin '*invenire*', to find out by reading is to perform an act, an act of both rendition and ingenious fabrication. The canon stands as law in this account, but an indeterminate law which we can never satisfy exhaustively, by which we are constrained to act without determinate rules to guide us. We are answerable, but we can never have the last word. It is in this sense that deconstruction moves reading towards an ethics. The radical or resistant force of the act of reading lies in its ethical indeterminacy rather than in political determination. Canonicity marks literary-critical reading as an ethical act, an encounter with an indeterminate law, a law that appears to reading as 'yet-to-be-determined'.

Mobile supplement II: work

Now that the book is over, one should begin to drift away from Lyotard. The mobile supplements, as I previously hinted, can be read alongside any of the three chapters; this one attempts to read work in some Blake poems in order to work over the question of where reading Lyotard leaves us, the question of what it might mean to read, after Lyotard. Placed between Chapters 1 and 2, work is a figure for an event that cannot be reduced to a concept; placed between Chapters 2 and 3, work is a differend, the site of a struggle between the incommensurable idioms of worker and capitalist. The two readings arise; we might characterize them respectively as the aesthetic judgment of forms and the political judgment of cases. One doesn't supply a rule for the other, the seam between them is not a bridge or a passage. All we can say, and we have hardly begun to say it, is that art and politics require to be read once more, that we will never have done with them. This reading of Blake traces the extent to which art and politics are always at work in the 'and' that links art *and* politics; it refuses to make either art the answer to politics, or politics the answer to art.

That 'work' should occur as a name for the '*nachträglich*', as rigid designator of a temporal and conceptual supplement in Lyotard's writing, is somewhat improper. It seems to hark back to a period before the writings considered in this book (which begins in 1971, with *Discours, figure*).[1] The use of the term 'work' persists on the fringes of *Discours, figure* and is evident in the earlier essays collected in *Dérive à partir de Marx et Freud* in 1973. Then the term seems to disappear. However, it returns, explicitly belated, *nachträglich, après coup*, in the introduction to *L'Inhumain* in 1988. Work, that is, doesn't go away. A characteristic Lyotardian switch of terms prevents its irreducible, unaccountable, transformative alterity to the concept from hardening into a deconstructive terminology, into a counter-tool, a determinant *anti-concept.* In this supplement, then, work works belatedly and too soon for this book as for the Lyotardian *œuvre* that it seeks to respect, to judge without criteria, to judge without prejudging.

To make labour the object of a conceptual representation is always to reify or commodify work. Which is not to say that sociology is simply another alienation of the lived experience of labour, since to consider work as the perceived experience of a subject is still to claim work as properly the object of subjective representation. Whether subjective or objective, both the sociology of labour and the theory of alienation rely upon an understanding of labour as a concept. Sociology seeks to extract the objective concept of labour from a network of interested subjective perceptions. Thus for example, Taylorism insists upon the organization of work in terms of the achieved product, eliminating any resistant subjective investments. Continuity of subjective contribution to the objective product is insistently minimized so that workers become machines. The theory of alienation insists upon the subjective experience of work as the meaning of labour, which capitalism seeks to minimize even as it defines subjects in terms of their position in relation to the means of production. What is at stake is not the concept of labour but the position from which it is described: that of the product (and ultimately the capitalist system) or that of the worker. The understanding of labour may be as an experience referred to the perception of a subject (what's it's like, to work) or as a commodity referred to the existence of an object (what it is that work has produced), but it remains squarely within an order of representation. In each case there is a reification or abstraction, from material process to either experience or commodity.

In this supplement I want to propose a *poetics of work* that is in no sense an aestheticization of labour (which I take to be a futurist, and ultimately an Italian Fascist project). My contention is that work as a transformative process resists being made the object of a sociological description in terms of content or meaning, and that in this sense it is analogous to the force of figurative as opposed to literal language. The truth of work cannot be spoken, cannot be made the object of a closed discourse of either achievement (Taylor) or of loss (Marx), not because work is irrational or inchoate but because any such representation of labour would ignore or suppress the labour of representation. The most rigorous language of labour must be a language that does not seek to exchange the work of discourse for the meaning that discourse assigns to work.

Lyotard would argue that such a language would resist the hegemony of the economic and of the cognitive genres in the linking of phrases. Work can only resist the expansion of capital and the suppression, exclusion or total misrecognition of labour that accompanies that expansion, insofar as it ceases to claim to have a meaning or an exchange-value, and insists upon the particularity of work-effects. Work must become resistant to exchange in the same sense that poetry is resistant to translation. If labour is thought as a concept, then it will vanish, lose any specificity, disappear into the Baudrillardian nightmare of an economy of exchange and consumption rather than one of production and exchange.

How might work be thought without a concept, as a trace or effect of resistance to representation (and thence of exchange)? In order to develop this possibility, I want to look at two poems by Blake, defences of labour and the proletariat in the face of emergent rather than dominant capitalism. These poems are usually read as claims for work as a lived or artisanal experience against the imposition of the enslaving 'Satanic mills' of capitalist relations of production. Such a reading is often supported by reference to Blake's own printing establishment. His single-handed authorship, illustration and printing of his texts is claimed by such as Thompson as a precursor of William Morris's attempts to return to artisanal production as a radical humane alternative to the alienating effect of the industrial organization of labour. This reading seems to me to betray the work that actually takes place in the poems, which is neither a matter of industrial production nor pre-capitalist subjective experience. Work in the text of Blake is not a matter of representation. How, then, can we read work against the theatre of representation without falling into mysticism?

London

I wander through each chartered street
Near where the chartered Thames does flow,
And mark in every face I meet
Marks of weakness, marks of woe.

In every cry of every man,
In every infant's cry of fear,
In every voice, in every ban,
The mind-forged manacles I hear –

How the chimney-sweeper's cry
Every blackening church appalls,

And the hapless soldier's sigh
Runs in blood down palace walls:

But most through midnight streets I hear
How the youthful harlot's curse
Blasts the new-born infant's tear
And blights with plagues the marriage hearse.

Blake's poem *London* seems to offer itself as a manifesto of the literary expression of alienation and ideology: a reading evident in both E. P. Thompson's use of Blake in *The Making of the English Working Class* (1968) and David Erdman's *Blake: Prophet against Empire* (1977). 'The mind-forged manacles' seem like an exemplary pre-Marxian account of ideology, establishing the rule of oppression in the domains of religion (the blackened sepulchre of the church), politics (the hapless cry of the soldier) and sexuality (the venereal curse that is the product of the economization of sexual desire in the face of the repressive institution of marriage). Repressive institutions of church, marriage and state (palace) exert an implacable ideological domination. Marriage in the capital city is brought under the rule of capital, and the disease of exchange appears as sexually transmitted disease, the syphilitic plague that attacks the eyes of new-born children. Ideology is here a 'false-consciousness' which keeps people in their place, and causes them to accept the facts of alienation as real (the work of capital in transforming relationships between people into relations between things).

At this point we might share with E. P. Thompson in applauding Blake's prophetic prefiguration of Marx's analysis of the dehumanizing work of capital. Others might issue an Althusserian corrective to the traces of psychological humanism. As with the young Marx, Blake's humanism leads him to produce an account of ideology as 'false consciousness' which implies the possibility of pre- or post-ideological cultural relations, failing to recognize that the subjects involved are themselves constructed as such by the mind-forged manacles. Blake simply hasn't made an epistemological break: a textual problematic of individual unhappiness rather than class struggle is the blinded symptom of an understanding of social relations as between individuals rather than classes. In *London*, as far as the Marxist is concerned, Blake fails to become Brecht. On the one hand, we appeal to 'real relations', to work as a pre-discursive reality. On the other, we insist that the only reality is that of discourse, the scientific discourse that analyses ideological effects.

143

However, there are severe problems with Althusser's simultaneous assertions that ideology has no history (and hence no end or beyond) and that an epistemological break into the scientific critique of ideology via historical materialism is possible. Althusserian Marxism teaches humanism that ideology is not a matter of bias and distortion in the content of representations, because the 'real relations' to which humanism appeals are themselves ideological constructs. The form of representation itself is ideological. Furthermore, that ideology is relatively autonomous of the last, economic, instance: the real is not hidden by ideology but is withdrawn from the prevailing conditions of representation. The real cannot appear as such, but can only be read in the symptomatic contradictions of the attempt to present any cultural construct as natural. Only science is free from ideology, and science is constituted as the self-knowledge of ideology, a *critical* rather than positive or direct access to the real. There is no position exterior to ideology other than ideology's self-awareness as science. Science can speak the truth insofar as it produces or displays the contradictions of its ideological moment in a way that breaks with the culture from which it comes. The problem of this critical reading is that the epistemological break that founds its critical distance from the ideological *naïveté* of empiricism cannot be accounted for.

Althusser derives an epistemology from *Capital* and then corroborates the status of historical materialism as a science with the aid of that same epistemology. Marx is read to produce a scientific Marx, which is confirmed by re-reading Marx symptomatically in terms of that 'scientific Marx'. What remains unspoken is the status of that first reading of Marx, by means of which a critical epistemology was extracted: by some miraculous birth the phoenix of ideology critique arose out of the ashes of a reading performed without the help of its scientific principles (and thus hopelessly prey to the ideological load of the supposedly empirical). The epistemological break which founds science as the critical self-knowledge of ideology is thus hopelessly flawed. It reproduces in its structure the very ideological myth of the originary autonomous subject (in this case science is ideology become self-conscious) that it claims to refute.

Against Althusserianism, a Foucauldian reading would give up the scientific pretensions of Marxism, whether direct or critical. Such a reaching might analyse Blake's text as an instance of the discourse of the urban. It would find the effects of power instanced to be intertwined with the kind of knowledge that cities impose, the discourse of surveillance inherent in the grid of town-planning. It's hard not to hear an echo of 'charted' in 'chartered', an echo that would link up with Blake's citation of various institutions (church, palace, marriage hearse) to phrase this text as exemplary of the discourse of the city as an apparatus for centralizing effects of power and knowledge.

Leaving aside the matter of my poor or partial ventriloquism, we may tease out the following concerns as particular to each of our three instances of the analysis of the discourse of culture. The first, human-ist-Marxist, reading is concerned with *alienation* as the effect of dehu-manization consequent upon the exchange of the lived relations that are our birthright for a mess of ideological pottage. Work under capitalism is no more than a discourse masquerading as a practice, a false representation. The second, Althusserian, reading is controlled by an understanding of *ideology* as actual rather than false, the necess-ary albumen of existence which is nonetheless imaginary in that it cites the individual as the centre of social relations. Ideology is no longer a trap that befalls individuals, it is the trap of subjectivity. Work is always and only a false representation, and the truth of labour can only be found indirectly, through a critical discourse that can speak labour as an exemplary representation of the contradic-tions of capitalism. The third reading, following Foucault, replaces ideology with *discourse* in order to leave no perspective open that might claim to escape the domination-effect that links claims of knowledge to assumptions of power. Work is merely a signifying element in the discourse of labour which, as a discourse, orders and disposes work in the name of a discipline parallel to that which the market-place imposes upon the workplace: the organization of labour into ex-changeable commodities. Not for nothing was Taylorism elaborated in the testing-ground of penitential forced-labour.

And that, of course, was also the site at which so much of Foucault's replacement of ideology with discourse took place. Reading Foucault, we give up the understanding of power and knowledge as inherently neutral tools to be seized from the ideological stranglehold of the ruling class and the clerisy.[2] In 'modern' post-Enlightenment society, power is exercised as the knowledge, rather than the simple repres-sion or domination, of subjects. There is thus a major difficulty with any discourse that claims to offer a knowledge of work that might counteract effects of power. Any sociological discourse of labour (from right- or left-wing positions) is formally complicit with Taylo-rism in its reduction of work to a more or less systematic structure of components which can be exhaustively studied from a perspective of knowledge.

Foucault, that is, refuses what he calls 'the Satanic no' of simple opposition, calling for a discursive transgression that can evade merely confirming the force it negates. The pitting of labour against capital is also the recognition of capital by labour as the power which it seeks to appropriate. Labour is placed in the position of seeking to be more properly capital than capital itself. Thus, in the Soviet Union, the capturing of capital by the proletariat merely causes a bureaucratic instance, the state, to function analogously to capital. The oppositional terms of the struggle force labour to express its liberation as a capacity for self-oppression. The up/down model of oppressor and oppressed is thus replaced by an understanding of political struggle as a matter of the organization of competing discourses in terms of margin and centre. The power accorded the bureaucratic state in late capitalism, and the vanguard party in Communism, is thus analysed as a matter of discursive organization, rather than being referred to directly conflicting economic instances. In each case, a hegemonic centre seeks to organize and dominate a discursive field, marginalizing other discourses, such as those of labour, women, gays and ethnic minorities. The important factor here is the extent to which margin and centre cannot be rotated through ninety degrees to reproduce the old vertical model of oppression. Power is now the problem, not the solution for labour. Instead, a series of transgressive moves must fracture the discursive field, dispersing the counter-centre of labour. The idea of labour is split into a patchwork of multiple discursive practices.

The problem with this is the condition of all those minoritarian discourses of labour, which still remain discourses, although at a second order. The Empire has fragmented, but it has broken up into a multiplicity of nation states. Specific practices of labour are still the objects of multiple minoritarian discourses. The transgression of totalitarian discourses is still carried out at the level of a second order of discourse. Our objects may have changed, but we are still speaking the same language – another discourse, not an other to discourse. The Foucauldian model of transgression is not heterogeneous to the discourse of power, although it resists the easy complicity of opposition. The play of margin and centre is thus finally unable to resist transposition into a more complex, yet still oppositional, model. Uphold the margin against the centre. The problem is clear: if knowledge is itself an effect of power, and vice versa, how can we say anything that is not complicit with a domination or an exploitation? This paradox is more or less where contemporary Foucauldianism is stuck, producing analyses of representation as coded by race, class and gender, whilst recognizing race, class and gender as structured by representation. Discourses may be transgressed, but that transgression is a second-order discourse. The transgression of the language of power has become merely its dispersal, with the concomitant hope that mere dispersal can keep power at bay. Thus, even a Foucauldian sociology of labour, however widely dispersed its localization of discourses, is ultimately complicit with the rule of prison and of time and motion management: the attempt to analyse labour in the name of a discipline, to make it the object of an ordered and orderly representation. However radically micrological the perspective of the sociologist, the structure of vision itself is necessarily Panoptical. The sociology of labour, however rarefied its notion of discourse, rests upon the understanding of labour as a concept. In the case of Foucault labour is no longer one concept. Yet however dispersed, discourses operate as the formation and disposition of objects by means of concepts. And since capitalism is the moment of possibility of the concept, as Lyotard says in *Dérive à partir de Marx et Freud*, such discourse analysis is always complicit with the aims of capitalism, is just one more attempt to capitalize upon labour, this time in the interests of intellectual capital.

Marx's distinction of labour from labour-power is the crucial point of his analysis of capitalism. Capitalism is grounded in the understanding of work or labour as a concept, as labour-power. The concept of labour (which is not the same thing as work, but is the representation of labour by means of a concept) is necessarily capitalist. Blake is thus not so much writing at the point of emergent capitalism, but at the point of emergence of the concept of labour as such. And the work of his poetry is not a representation of labour as experience (a concept for a subject) in simple opposition to industrial alienation (the effect of understanding labour as objective concept). Blake's poetry sets labour to work as a figural trace or effect, radically heterogeneous to the understanding of labour as concept. This is anti-capitalist in the sense that capitalism is precisely the understanding of work in terms of a universal concept of labour (labour-power) which is what allows all work to be the subject of exchange. The universal concept of labour (labour-power) is what makes one commodity translatable into another. Labour-power as exchange value guarantees the understanding of objects as commodities (in terms of exchange value) and hence the rule of the market-place over people and things. For Foucault, we may replay the same analysis, inscribing a cultural rather than an economic conceptualization of the power of

147

labour, of labour-power. Thus, in Foucauldian analysis, a multiplicity of discourses are not finally incommensurable, however discontinuous their chronologies may be, in that as discourses they repose upon the possibility of conceptual organization. If, for Foucault, oppression is combatted by dispersal, power is finally ovecome by being shared amongst discourses.

I don't want to dismiss this as Utopian, merely to state that all these discourses leave power *in place* as the universal language that all discourses speak in the same way that capitalism proposes exchange as a universal language. What is required is the development of a language that is radically *untranslatable* into the discourse of power: my proposal is that such a requirement is the evocation of a *poetics*. Such a poetics demands a sense that there is something radically irrepresentable to its object, something that prevents the object from being exhaustively represented in discourse by means of a concept, something that would, in Kantian terms, suspend the possibility of determinate judgment. We would then find ourselves in the ethical or aesthetic domains, barred from the cognitive, which would become the possibility of the domination of our object, labour, by means of knowledge.

The problem which our poetics confronts is the understanding of work as exhaustively representable by means of a concept (labour-power). That is what guarantees both the rule of the market and the discourse of labour. What if work were not representable (and hence translatable or exchangeable in this way)? What if work were precisely what is lost in translation, like poetry? What if work were the resistance to the translatability of discourses, the sign of their incommensurability? Work would be a process of making, *poiein*, that was irreducible either to the exchange-value of labour-power, the micrology of discourses, or to the meaning of a poem. The materiality of work as process or object in industrial, agricultural and literary labour would be recognized as in excess of any concept by which work could be represented to a subject.

In the light of the preceding three chapters, we can investigate the possibility of the non-discursive force of work as a figure, as the evocation of the event, as a differend. This, it should be clear, is not to make a naïve empirical claim that work participates in any pre-linguistic reality, or that it is a 'lived experience'. Rather, work inhabits discourse as a radical alterity to the language of meaning (signification). The force of work, its resistance to power, lies in its evocation of the irrepresentable event or affect which is constitutive of representation itself. Work takes place in excess of any discursive meaning that can be assigned to it, any representation that can be made of it. As a transformative praxis, work appears for discourse as a deconstructive figure, a *difference* which cannot be recuperated and signified by the *oppositions* between terms that constitute language (after Saussure). To return to Blake, let us trace the figural force of work as a working over of language, even as it seeks to represent work discursively and linguistically, by means of a series of opposed elements, whether concepts or linguistic units. Both the discursive understanding and the language of work are themselves worked over by the figural poetics of work. This figural difference is the work of discourse that undermines and transforms the discourse of work that has historically sought to survey, determine and dispose labour in the interests of capital.

The work of discourse can be paralleled to Lyotard's evocation of the dream-work in *Discours, figure*. The dream-work transgresses the orders of language in a manner which is radically incommensurable with its discursive functioning. Lyotard, for example, analogizes the effect of condensation upon the discursive organization of language as a schema of differential elements as the crumpling of the paper on which a text is written, moving the two-dimensional space of the conceptual network into three dimensions. The transparent virtual space of the concept is shifted into the opaque actual space of objects. The dream-work appeals to that in the object (here, the work of words) which resists reduction to the concept. The poetic work of Blake's poem is an analogous working-over of language to the point at which words become things, things that appear in discourse as figures *in excess* of any conceptualization. As such, the work of poetry is deconstructive.

In Blake's poem, this resistance appears as an irreducibility of language to the visual. Words, that is, exceed the virtual or conceptual space of which the tradition of Albertian Renaissance perspective imposes upon the visible world. There is an incommensurability between the perceived world and the work of language that marks words as more than just signs of the concepts of things. Blake vs. Locke. The work of poetry cannot be reduced to a discursive *representation* of work. Instead, a poetic working-over of language makes words into things.

In the interests of space, I'll be somewhat brief in indicating this problematic in Blake's *London*. Let us note first the way in which the poem opens by describing the false liberty of London in terms of

149

written charters. The order of writing as guarantor of liberty is ironically displaced by the undertones of charting, of map-making, that seem at odds with the possibility of 'flow'. One might want to note the heavy stress on 'does flow' as itself indicating that this flowing is far from free, but takes place only within ordained channels, analogous to the grid of streets. And the repeated emphasis on 'marks' identifies the extent to which the sufferings of the downtrodden are a function of their reduction to mere marks or elements in the text of the city. The workers are oppressed by the city as an order of textuality. Blake's own use of 'mark' further emphasizes the problems of writing: to represent the oppression of writing in writing is only further to inscribe it: the poet is under the threat of himself reinforcing oppression, himself engraving the marks of oppression upon the faces of the dispossessed. He courts this risk insofar as an order of poetic textuality mirrors the discursive articulation of space at work in both the visual order of the city and the linguistic order of its texts or charters. Chartered textuality and the city stand as the discursivization of space (the organization of space by means of a system of signs or marks representing a network of concepts) in the linguistic and the visual fields respectively.

The city, that is, is itself a model of the discursive articulation of space, the grid of streets, which the poem resists. The city and the charter are themselves the problem to which the poem opposes itself: the problem of representation as writing by concepts. Writing is figured by Blake as the reduction of the object to its concept within the discursive network of power and exchange. The object is determined by its concept as given by the discursive network, so that the individual face becomes merely the virtual mark of the concept behind it, much as in *The Chimney Sweeper* the little chimney sweep can only name his misery by naming himself in terms of the discourse of labour, 'crying, 'weep, 'weep, in notes of woe'. And yet, in the very cry that marks the sublimation of the experience of work by the discourse upon work, the pure model of either alienation or oppression by discourse, the rule of discourse, the domination of the concept, is only achieved at the expense of a certain disfigurement. There is a certain work performed upon the material of language, which Blake's editor Stephenson is concerned to dismiss as a 'pathetic pun': the hypogrammatic reduction of 'sweep' to 'weep'.[3]

To return to 'London', the work of the poem similarly resists the dominance of the concept, and the discursivization of work as labour. Against the virtual space of the visual and of the charted text, a cry is raised. And that cry does not owe its force to the expression of individual subjective experience, since it is insistently collective, 'every cry of every man'. The capacity of the cry to resist 'mind-forged manacles' (which by now you will realize I want to read as something like 'concepts', or at least 'mental representations') is not an appeal to a real or lived individual experience. The cry as pure noise, inexpressive of any individual state of mind, devoid of any objective referent, disrupts the understanding of language as exhaustively cognitive. The cry cannot be reduced to a subjective or an objective representation, an expression of feeling or a description. To put it another way, the effects of this cry have a material operation incommensurable with any meaning that might be assigned to it. Reading after Lyotard does not permit us to apply a new technique by which to decode or interpret the poem, rather it allows us to confront the extent to which, in the poem, an *unreadable* cry gets heard. That cry witnesses to a differend, we feel that something is trying to be said which cannot be phrased. The task of criticism is to seek the phrase that can link onto this cry.

And the cry in each case is the evocation of work. For the sweep it is what 'appalls' (literally, 'whitens') that which is blackened. For the soldier, the cry 'runs in blood'. For the harlot, the curse is the mark of venereal disease. The cry returns from the misery of work, not as expression of that misery, but as a figural *displacement* of the language of work away from representation toward something which has the force of an operation that stains or disfigures the orders of discourse. There is a scattering of syllables, as 'cry' and 'sigh' become 'curse', 'hear' and 'curse' become 'hearse'. And if we cannot easily assign a meaning to this dissemination of marks, of the letters inscribing weakness and woe, it is because the dissemination is both effect of, and unaccountable for, the chartered rule of meaning. The dissemination of the cry allows the cry to be *hear*d in *'hear*se', resists its negation within monumental institutions of meaning, without being an oppositional description or expression. We are not finding a material truth of language, but a materiality that cannot be reduced to a meaning or truth, a materiality that resists being accounted for. The untying and recombination of marks or characters performs a work of transformation, issues a demand of transformation that experiments, that asks what impotence can do.

In the synaesthetic transgression which makes a cry something that 'stains', the cry lets us hear the hearing of the concept as hearse. The impotence or inaudibility of the cry of the miserable can become its strength insofar as it evokes a work beyond representation, an irrepresentable work, which would be the whitening of the church, the revolutionary overthrow of the palace, the interment of the institution of marriage. Insofar as it transgresses the order of representation or expression by concepts, the order of discourse, the poetics of work displaces the cry from expression of misery to appeal to the transformative power of the irrepresentable: a Utopics of the literally inconceivable is to put in play. And the transgression of the order of the concept offers the possibility of a language of labour that cannot be appropriated by the dominant order, translated back into the language of power or of capitalist exchange. The figure of work thus evokes the irrepresentable, the possibility of a justice that is not just an effect of power, an aesthetics that cannot be commodified, a thought that is not merely the rationalization of conceptual knowledge. The ultimately uncommodifiable and inexchangeable cry of labour in Blake's poetry appears as an event, the happening of the 'hapless' that cannot be systematized within the order of discourse. The work of the event, as that which cannot be accounted for by the structure or system to which it occurs, demands a poetics of the indescribable, not a description in terms of alienation, ideology or discourse.

If post-structuralism insists that the materiality of labour is thus textual, this must not be taken as implying that work is a pure fact of discourse. Its figural force is always to transform and undermine the attempt to negate work by putting it to rest as an achieved meaning, the signification of a discourse or the expression of a subjective experience. An attention to the work of discourse, a poetics of labour which traces language as transformative work, offers the possibility of forging a radical politcs of labour that escapes the patrician or patriarchal attempt to speak the truth of labour from a discursive position which does not allow itself to be worked upon.

Art

From this point of view theory, aesthetic theory, would seem, would have seemed to be, the ploy by which the spirit sought to do away with words, of the matter which they are, of matter *tout court*. Luckily, this ploy has no chance of success. One does not do away with the Thing. Always forgotten, it is unforgettable.

(*LI*: 155)

Politics

Politics, however, is the threat of the differend. It is not a genre, it is

152

the multiplicity of genres, the diversity of ends, and *par excellence* the question of linkage. It plunges into the emptiness where 'it happens that ...'. It is, if you will, the state of language, but it is not *a* language. Politics consists in the fact that language is not a language, but phrases, or that Being is not Being but *There is*'s.

(LD: 138)

Notes

INTRODUCTION

1 The reader may wish to turn to the discussion of the postmodern to assess the impact of this displacement of the modernist idea of the Book and the Academy.

2 'Signature Event Context' in Derrida 1982.

3 Bennington 1988: 4. Bennington's strategy produces a work that is satisfyingly hard to categorize or pigeonhole. It is certainly a thoughtful book, one that demands too much attention to language for me to dismiss it here as either wrongheaded or dealing with a different aspect of Lyotard's writing. However, the reading of Lyotard that takes place in these pages differs in some crucial respects. Bennington's aping of Lyotard seems to me unfaithful precisely to the extent that it is overly mimetic.

Bennington presents a Lyotard standing firmly in the domain of philosophy in order to mark Lyotard's revision of the question of philosophy. The mixture of paraphrase and critique that Bennington's work offers seems to me exemplary in its intelligence. However, Bennington's typographical interpolations and collated aphorisms (when they are not merely 'writerly' attempts to capture Lyotard's disruption of the place of theory within a stylistics) don't directly confront the difference Lyotard's writings must make to theory. Second, Bennington's work of description and exposition rarely marks the conditions of his own reading, his difference. His reading remains perhaps too masterly, too much that of the good disciple, to testify to the difference Lyotard makes. Bluntly, reading Bennington is at times too much like reading Lyotard. I do not think that my book in any sense surpasses Bennington's in accuracy or intelligence. It's simply a different book, a more passionate one perhaps, one that tries to foreground what is at stake in reading Lyotard more directly.

4 There is another significant introductory study of Lyotard in David Carroll's *Paraesthetics*, which offers a great deal of lucid and intelligent paraphrase, especially as regards *The Differend*. Carroll tells a persuasive story about Foucault, Lyotard and Derrida's negotiations of the relation between art and politics in the wake of Nietzsche's displacement of the rule of theory. Carroll's stress on Nietzsche perhaps locates a difference from this book: I'm inclined to see Nietzschean vitalism, specifically a

Nietzschean reading of psychoanalysis which stresses the unconscious drives (Eros and Thanatos) as a lure or trap by which Lyotard is at times seduced.

5 The stakes in this distinction between the genre of phrasing called 'introducing' and the cognitive genre of descriptive phrases are elaborated in the discussion of *The Differend* in Chapter 3.

6 In 'Little Libidinal Economy of Narrative Apparatus: The Renault Corporation Narrates the Murder of Pierre Overney', Lyotard explicitly links the temporality and narrative pragmatics of the summary to the functioning of capitalism as the reduction of events to the homogeneity of a process of accumulation which may be organized and profited from, just as labour is capitalized upon in the factory (*DP*: 190).

7 For Stuart Sim in 'Lyotard and the Politics of Antifoundationalism', Lyotard's insistence that epistemological discourse cannot be finally isolated from the figural condition is reduced to a 'hermeneutical turn' (Sim 1986: 12) with 'ideologically suspect motives' (ibid.: 13). This attack is so misguided as to imply an almost total failure to read Lyotard's work, which has been a consistently rigorous examination of the intersection of theory, politics, and ethical/aesthetic judgment.

MOBILE SUPPLEMENT I

1 See, for example, Lyotard's reading of Butor's *Mobile* in *Discours, figure*.
2 See, for instance, Lyotard's analysis of the differend of class practice in 'A Memorial for Marxism', appended to *Peregrinations*.

1 FIGURE

1 Disputing the rule of truth and reason does not mean that Lyotard embraces lying and madness: to do so would merely be to inhabit the rule of opposed concepts (true/not-true), to confirm the rule of discursive truth by playing the role of pure negation. Thus, the figural attack on the rule of objective truth in accurate description or subjective truth in effective communication does not produce either a sophistic scepticism in matters of cognition or the replacement of intersubjective community by the violent clash of isolated subjective wills. Within traditional discursive understandings, objectivity is opposed to relativism, or the capacity of intentional subjects to communicate is opposed to a stark landscape of solipsism in which the strongest will imposes its own understanding on others. Deconstruction is often accused of either relativism or solipsism by virtue of its stance against objectivity and intentionality. To question the assurance of objective meaning and subjective intention is dismissed as leaving the questioner unable to 'mean what s/he says'. This is incorrect, especially in light of Lyotard's work, insofar as deconstruction is not simply opposition to truth and reason, but a worrying at and displacing of the binary oppositions truth/falsehood or reason/irrationalism. Thus, Lyotard will use the word 'truth', but in the sense that the truth of figurality can never be simply made the object of a conceptual, discursive, representation. To put it another way, Lyotard refuses to think irrationality and desire in reference to the will of a conscious subject.

2 This example is perhaps insufficiently radical. The singularity of objects is more properly their absolute difference, their resistance to being thought under a logic of identity. Derrida's reading of Heidegger has thus insisted, as it were, that the statement 'A is A' already betrays A's difference from itself in the non-coincidence of the 'same' term in two places.

3 The latter claim produces the vicious hermeneutic circle that character-izes much contemporary critical practice, perhaps most evident in the 'New Historicism' clustered around journals such as *Representations*. On the one hand representations are culturally constructed: class, race, gender, etc. are shown to be cultural constructs. On the other hand, culture itself (since we admit no conspiracy theories) is merely made up of representations of class, race, gender, etc. Our radical claim to find that culture is made up of representations is vitiated by the accompanying admission that representations are culturally constructed.

4 Derrida 1976: 158. In saying 'a mistranslation', I do not mean Gayatri Spivak's (she marks the phrase as problematic). Rather, I am referring to a reading of the phrase as meaning something like 'everything is just a representation'. I will not dwell on correcting this error – see Derrida 1986, and Gasché 1986: 278-80. Since '*hors-texte*' may mean an 'inset' in a book (a graphic plate for example), the point is not that we are always inside the text, but that nothing is ever wholly external *or internal* to effects of textuality.

5 'One should be able to establish a correlation between the actual handling of the plastic support [in political posters] and the desired handling of social space. We make the following hypothesis: underneath the articu-lated signification or iconic meaning that are immediately offered, the plasticity of the poster works autonomously as the symptom of a political unconscious. Following this hypothesis, it is legitimate to try to localize this symptom with the help of Freudian categories. Working along these lines one is trying to develop an ideology-critique' (*DPMF*: 276–7). The crude analogies for which Lyotard leaps have already been left behind by the time that the book is published. Nonetheless, it is important to note Lyotard's insistence on the value of a more or less *formalist* analysis of the political. There is an insistence that the space of political representation is not the neutral vessel of a political content, that politics is not simply a matter of 'real meanings', that will drive Lyotard's continuing investi-gation of what may be said that is political. It is precisely this critique of the understanding of politics as merely a matter for representation that will lead Lyotard to accuse Marxism of betraying just that materiality that it claims to uphold, betraying materiality by making it a matter of meaning – thinking matter as the *meaning* of historical representation.

6 This concern with the point of co-existence of the incommensurable is a guiding strand in Lyotard's work, leading towards his rediscovery of Kant's *Third Critique* in *Just Gaming* and *Le Différend*, his account of the paralogism that characterizes postmodernity, his insistence on the aes-thetics of the sublime and the immemorial. Lyotard describes himself as a Kantian 'of the Third Critique' (*IP*: 36), interested in Kant's identifi-cation of the faculty of the judgment of the sublime as intervening when

the cognitive faculty is exhausted – when judgment is both necessary and impossible by virtue of the fact that no determinate criteria exist for judgment. Indeterminate judgment intervenes at the point when rational criteria reach a point of incommensurability, as in the sublime, where the object exceeds cognitive comprehension. A 'differend', as we shall see, is a dispute between two incommensurable systems of representation, where no determinate criteria exist for resolution of the conflict that do not prejudge the case by suppressing one or both of the languages of the parties. To make a claim which it will be the work of this book to explain, one may say that Lyotard's work is nothing less than the attempt to produce an aesthetics, philosophy and politics/ethics of the incommensurable.

7 The notion of the *langue* as a totality is crucial in determining the fusion of structural linguistics with Marxism in French thought. As Ducrot and Todorov put it, 'what all the Saussurians retain in common, however, is that the linguistic unit, through its phonic and semantic aspects, always refers back to all the other units and that it is impossible either to hear or to comprehend a sign without entering into the global play of the language.' (Ducrot and Todorov, 1979: 19). The fact that the linguistic element is always confronted with the totality is picked up in the two main trends of post-war Marxist thought in France: Goldmann's genetic structuralism and Althusser's relational account of the working of ideology. For Goldmann's sociology, the historical 'fact' gains significance only in relation to the totality of historical and social relations (the Lukacsian 'world view' functions as the '*langue*'). Thus, 'it is when he replaces the work in a historical evolution which he studies as a whole, and when he relates it to the social life of the time at which it was written – which he also looks upon as a whole – that the enquirer can bring out a work's objective meaning' (Goldmann 1964: 8). Likewise, the influence of structural linguistics (transmitted via Lacan) allows Althusser to rethink the base-superstructure model of the determination of ideology as the differential relation of each ideological instance to social totality of instances. Instead of the economic base determining everything else (politics, art, etc.), each instance is determined in relation to all the others, as each historical moment is determined in relation to the concept of history which it is the historian's task to elaborate.

8 For an example of the strong claims for cultural relativism proceeding from Saussurean linguistics, see Catherine Belsey 1980.

9 Barthes 1972. See Coward and Ellis 1977 for an overt theorization of the special relationship between Marxism and structural linguistics.

10 Lyotard is not entirely alone in this respect. Derrida's 'Structure, Sign and Play' famously demonstrates that, in Lévi-Strauss's exemplary application of structural linguistics to anthropology, the position of the observer remains as a structural flaw. In order for the system or *langue* of a culture to be comprehended as a series of oppositions, the exteriority of the observer must be inscribed within the system, at its centre. To put it another way, structuralism can account for culture as a system, but not for how it might be possible to grasp that system as a system. This perhaps offers an explanation of the irony by which Saussure, prophet of system-

atic linguistics, was unable himself to put together his book, leaving it to be assembled posthumously from lecture notes.

11 See Saussure 1966: 105.
12 See Merleau-Ponty, *The Primacy of Perception* (1964), *The Visible and the Invisible* (1968), and 'Cézanne's Doubt' in *Sense and Non-Sense* (1964).
13 See 'The Intertwining – The Chiasm' in Merleau-Ponty 1968: 130–55.
14 As Merleau-Ponty points out, Descartes's is an optics of blindness, an account of vision modelled by analogy with a blind man's perception by touch, 'the breviary of a thought that wants no longer to abide in the visible and so decides to construct the visible according to a model-in-thought' ('Eye and Mind', in *The Primacy of Perception* 1964: 169).
15 Merleau-Ponty quotes Cézanne in 'Cézanne's Doubt', 'the landscape thinks itself in me' (*Sense and Non-Sense* 1964: 18). Painting is thus not the recording of an objective given, but the celebration of 'the enigma of visibility ... voracious vision, reaching beyond the "visual givens" opens upon a texture of Being of which the discrete sensorial messages are only the punctuations or the caesurae. The eye lives in this texture as man lives in his house.' ('Eye and Mind', in *The Primacy of Perception* 1964: 166).
16 This insistence on an anti-conceptual 'depth' of the visible is drawn from Merleau-Ponty's 'Eye and Mind', especially pp. 174–5 (*The Primacy of Perception*).
17 Where Derrida attacks Saussure for 'phonocentrism' in his privileging of spoken over written language (Derrida 1976), Lyotard is here pointing out that Derrida remains within the phonocentric insofar as he privileges the textual mark over the visible figure, reading/hearing/decoding (however infinitely deferred) over viewing. Derrida's *Dissemination* (1981), especially in its work on Mallarmé, seems to me to avoid this implication of Derrida's insistence on a general textual economy.
18 That is, Lyotard is not counterposing a sensible real to the abstraction and artificiality of the alphabet or the *langue*.
19 See for example MacCabe 1978: 80:

> What we can read in this passage is the interplay of letters and words as material. Far from attempting to efface the process by which meaning is produced, Joyce is concerned to show how the mechanism of writing works. The first two pages, in which phrases without context litter the text, refuse all possible meaning.

The silliness of the claim that Joyce's text can 'refuse all possible meaning' reveals the degree to which MacCabe's is merely an inverted metaphysics, the bad conscience of logocentrism.
20 Thus for example MacCabe reads Joyce's *Ulysses* 'as the material of language becomes the concern of the text' in order to conclude that 'this deconstruction has definite political effects as it demonstrates a contradiction between writing and nationalism' (MacCabe 1978: 79).
21 'The pertinent opposition here is not between the spoken word and the speaking word, the first belonging to the *langue*, the second to gesture, to movement. ... [T]he work of the poet, the writer, the dream, puts the figural into the abstract, the "real" into the "arbitrary", and gives to discourse almost the same fleshliness as that of the sensible. This work ...

makes it apparent that the relevant opposition is solely that between variant and invariant, between mobile and rigid negations.... But the relation between these two negations is *not dialectical*; one is not the moment of the other.... Invariance and variance, that is to say secondary and primary processes, are at once always given together and yet absolutely unable to form a unity' (*DF*: 58–9).

22 The relation of this to the work of Paul de Man is discussed at length in Chapter 3.

23 As we shall see, the figure is the clash of incommensurable spaces of representation; the postmodern is the clash of incommensurable temporalities; the differend is the clash of incommensurable language games.

24 Lyotard's treatment of anamorphosis is distinct from that of Lacan in Seminar XI (Lacan 1977). For Lyotard, Lacan's account remains within the domain of the representational apparatus – an argument that is discussed in Chapter 3 of this book.

25 As we shall see in Chapter 3, by the time Lyotard writes *The Differend* this responsibility has been passed on: it has become the task of thought itself, of philosophy as the 'genre in search of its rules'.

26 On 'tensional criticism' see 'Horses of Wrath: Recent Critical Lessons' in Wimsatt 1966.

27 It is in this sense that Lyotard's later work, specifically his interest in the postmodern, can best be understood as an attempt to reconceive the figural in primarily *temporal* terms.

28 Lyotard also uses Butor as an example, lest we think that the poetic is being essentialized. Butor's 'novels' rely on the fragmentation of phrases: in one 'Mobile' the text is composed entirely of units to be recombined. In Butor's texts, which are concerned with the relation of word and image (one of Butor's critical works is *Les Mots dans la peinture* [Butor, 1969]), writing exceeds the application of a cut-up technique to texts to become a figural writing which shows a condition of the line that is heterogeneous to that of the letter. His fragments appear discontinuously, cannot be linked, and yet do not erase each other in their discontinuous appearance. In this quasi-anamorphic mode they evoke an incommensurable compossibility of motivated and unmotivated signifiers: language is invaded by a space which is not its own, so that gaps in the text do not have the function of intervals of opposition between linguistic units, but of interstices of difference.

29 The terms in which Lyotard has sought to evoke the figural have shifted through his work. *Discours, figure* insists upon the motivated quality of plastic as opposed to textual space and upon the unconscious as the site in which words are treated plastically, as things rather than as signifiers of concepts. *Economie libidinale* opposes the radically singular force of affects to the understanding of emotions in terms of the calculation of their meaning for a subjective consciousness or an organic body. *Rudiments païens* and *Instructions païennes* introduce an analysis of narrative as figure which will form the basis of Chapter 2. In Lyotard's later works, there is a crucial shift to a consideration of the figural in terms of *temporality*: the figural eventhood of the event, the singularity of an occurrence that is

ignored by the claim to account for the event by understanding its meaning, the 'it happens' that cannot be reduced to 'what happened'.

30 Lyotard provides a detailed critique of Todorov's structuralist tabulation of the effects of distortion due to figural language, *DF*: 311–6.

31 This insistence on the opening of a radical heterogeneity to the literal order of meaning by the figural is closely parallel to Derrida's distinction between the effect of *dissemination* opened by the trace in which meaning both multiplies (re-seeds itself) and is radically dispersed (recedes) and the *polysemy* or simple accumulation of literal meanings in rhetorical language that is the object of traditional formalist criticism.

32 Barthes 1977.

33 Barthes 1977: 34: 'its *signified* [my italics] is Italy or rather *Italianicity*'.

34 Thus, de Man retains the rule of a semanticizing tendency that reduces the performativity of rhetoric to a signification that is 'semantically controlled' along rhetorical rather than grammatical lines, as *failed* intention. Accordingly, the figural remains for de Man a swerve away from literal meaning, even if it takes place proleptically so as to forestall literal meaning. He stays close to Rousseau in thinking the relation of figure to discourse in terms of deviation and propriety, even if deviation *precedes* propriety. As Rousseau puts it in the *Essay on the Origin of Language*, 'Figurative language was the first to be born. Proper meaning was discovered last' (Rousseau 1986:12). De Man differs from Rousseau in pointing out that the precedence of figural deviation means that we will never quite get to proper meaning. In this sense, *Allegories of Reading* stays within the terms of the critique of Derrida's *Of Grammatology* that de Man makes in *Blindness and Insight*.

35 Lyotard will later call this a differend, as we shall see in Chapter 3.

36 Lacan echoes Jakobson's dissociation, but claims pre-eminence for the 'metonymic'; *Discours, figure* devotes several pages to showing that what Lacan calls 'metonymic' is in fact Jakobsonian metaphor.

37 Lyotard draws our attention to Breton's theorization of the Surrealist image in the first Surrealist Manifesto, which I quote at length:

> The innumerable types of surrealist images would give rise to a classification that, for now, I do not propose to attempt. To group them according to their particular affinities would take too long; I want to note, essentially, their common quality. For me, the strongest is the one which offers the highest degree of arbitrariness, the one which it takes longest to translate into practical language, whether because it contains an enormous level of apparent contradiction, or because one of its terms is peculiarly hidden, or because in claiming to be sensational it seems to add up to very little. . . .
> (Breton 1979: 52)

38 See the distinction that the Mad Hatter and the March Hare draw at the Mad Hatter's Tea-Party in *Alice in Wonderland*:

> 'Then you should say what you mean,' the March Hare went on. 'I do,' Alice hastily replied; 'at least – at least I mean what I say – that's the same thing, you know.' 'Not the same thing a bit!' said the Hatter. 'Why, you might just as well say that "I see what I eat" is the same thing as "I eat what I see"!' 'You might just as well say,'

added the March Hare, 'that "I like what I get" is the same thing as
"I get what I like."!'

(Carroll 1965: 68–9)

39 For a more detailed analysis of Lyotard's differences with Althusser see
'Mobile supplement II: work'.

40 Chomsky's addition of generativism to structuralism in linguistics is a
further reinforcement of a *positivity* to opposition in the divisions of a
system, in the distinction of the grammatical from the ungrammatical
(*DF*: 143).

41 For more on earthquakes, see Lyotard's experimental fiction *Récits Tremblants* (Lyotard 1977).

42 See Bennington 1988: 80–91, and Dews 1984 for detailed summaries of the
argument between Lyotard and Lacan.

2 POSTMODERNITY AND NARRATIVE

1 The latter is a collection of short essays, purporting to be missives of
various kinds, one of which ('Answering the Question: What is Postmodernism?') is printed with the English version of *The Postmodern Condition: A Report on Knowledge*.

2 Linda Hutcheon's *A Poetics of Postmodernism: History, Theory, Fiction* is an
exemplary account of formal elements which might characterize cultural
activities named postmodern. According to Hutcheon, postmodernism is
thus a not-quite-new style, which takes up the past in a way that neither
simply reiterates it (classicism) nor rejects it (modernism). Postmodernism's rejection of these alternatives refuses the binary straight-
jacket of the modernist understanding of history as simple diachronic
succession offered to a subject who is its point of synthesis.

As Lyotard puts it, modernism is not an epoch, but a mode of thought
about time, which rests upon two elements: time as succession and an
ultimately atemporal subject. The discourse of history is thus structured
as a narrative sequence around an 'I' dedicated to the possession and
control of both nature and itself through the organization of time as a
sequential series of phrases. The first person is thus the position of the
mastery of speech and meaning in modernism (*Le Postmoderne expliqué aux
enfants*: 46–8).

Lyotard's version of the postmodern rejection of modernist temporal
choices is thus not the break with modernism that Hutcheon claims, if it
remains only a matter of style, or an *attitude* towards history, which
appears as a style. For Hutcheon, however, style reveals the attitude of the
postmodern subject as ironic, playful, irreverent and contradictory or
anachronistic. Hutcheon's survey boils down the postmodern at every
turn to an ultramontane modernist *attitude*, a consciousness of the finitude
of self-consciousness. According to Hutcheon, postmodernism is not a
simple rupture, not a 'new paradigm' because 'it is contradictory and
works within the very systems it attempts to subvert' (Hutcheon 1988: 4).
The irreverences of postmodernism are directed at history, and are found
in the practices of anachronistic *bricolage*. This has two consequences.
First, modernism's striving for the new and the original is rejected.

Second, incongruous citation of elements from various historical styles and practices lends the postmodern the appearance of a historical self-contradiction. In each case, practices of parody ironically undermine the understanding of history as progress. What Hutcheon shares with Jencks's stylistic description of postmodernism as 'the continuation of Modernism and its transcendence' (Jencks 1987: 10), is an insistence that the 'presence of the past' is understandable as an attitude of irony, critique or playful dialogue, situating the postmodern as a combination of negation and negotiation. This attitude is then given meaning by an appeal to the 'political'. To put it another way, it is assumed that the ultimate meaning of all attitudes is political, so that postmodernism may be securely evaluated, even ultimately legitimated, in relation to the eventual success of its project of subversion (for Jencks, the socio-political meaning of the postmodern attitude is not a matter of subversion but a transcendence of modernist aesthetic purism, a shift from élitism into the social field of public communication).

3 Thus in the 1979 preface to *Des Dispositifs pulsionnels* Lyotard notes that 1968 in France can be described in modernist terms, as a moment in the grand narrative of emancipation. Such a description would, he claims, reduce the experimentation around the events of 1968 to the innovative developments of new commodities for the future, a kind of intellectual retooling of capitalism. On the other hand, a postmodernist description of 1968 would see it as an event of experimentation in politics and art whose force resides in the capacity to evade any such grand narratives.

4 'The Question of Postmodernism' in Hassan 1980, see also Hassan 1987, where postmodernism remains, as in Chapter 4, very much a concept; Hutcheon 1985; Jencks 1987; Baudrillard, *America* (1988). I think that Baudrillard's writings on symbolic exchange should have warned him against the attitude of the *flâneur* or tourist, denotative of modernism since Baudelaire. Quotations around 'Bakhtin' indicate that I am referring to the *mélange* of Bakhtin with American ego-psychology current in the literary critical academy. Apparently, the problem with modernism was that 'we never really talked'.

5 Kroker and Cook 1986.

6 The desire to fix a politics of the postmodern, to pin down an inherent subversiveness, guides the animadversions of Fredric Jameson's 'Postmodernism and Consumer Society' (in Foster 1983) and Hal Foster's *Recodings* (Foster 1985). Foster convincingly identifies both a 'neoconservative' and a 'post-structuralist' 'position' on postmodernism (ibid.: 7).

7 David Carroll's *Paraesthetics* (1987) provides a very detailed and authoritative account of the philosophical problematic of the aesthetics of experimentation.

8 We follow Lyotard (*LD*: *passim*) in the use of 'phrase' as the term for the minimal element of language.

9 Derrida's 'Signature Event Context' (in Derrida 1982) provides the basis of a general account of language in terms of an economy of 'iteration' or repetition-as-different. He points out that the founding condition of the linguistic mark is its capacity to be *cited*, or repeated in a different context. That difference of context will alter its meaning, leaving it as no longer the

'same' mark. Structured by the possibility of repetition in another context, the linguistic mark is thus constitutively different from itself. Likewise this capacity to be cited elsewhere disrupts the terms in which the
linguistic mark might be said to inhabit or be determined by any one
context. It is this sense that there is no original identity or finally deter-
minable context that might pin down the functioning of linguistic marks
(and not any epistemological timidity) that leads postmodernists to use
quotation marks to such a degree. Our language, like our architecture, is
haunted by citation, by a sense of meaning or form become uncanny.
Context and history speak with an otherness that cannot be kept in its
place.

10 See, for one example, 'Freud and the Scene of Writing' in Derrida's
reading of the functioning of belatedness (*Nachträglichkeit*) as constitutive
of the functioning of the unconscious (Derrida 1978: 211–12):

> The call of the supplement is primary, here, and it hollows out that
> which will be reconstituted by deferral as the present. The supple-
> ment, which seems to be added as a plenitude to a plenitude, is
> equally that which compensates for a lack. '*Suppléer*: 1. To add what
> is missing, to supply a necessary surplus', says Littré, respecting,
> like a sleepwalker, the strange logic of that word.... That the
> present in general is not primal but, rather, reconstituted, that it is
> not the absolute, wholly living form which constitutes experience,
> that there is no purity of the living present – such is the theme,
> formidable for metaphysics, which Freud, in a conceptual scheme
> unequal to the thing itself, would have us pursue. This pursuit is
> doubtless the only one which is exhausted neither within meta-
> physics nor within science.

11 A fuller description of the analogy between the immemorial in history and
the belated action of the unconscious affect can be found in *Heidegger et 'les
Juifs'*, 21–37:

> The first act strikes the psychic apparatus without perceptible
> internal effect, without affect. A shock without affect. In the second
> act an affect takes place without shock: I buy clothes in a shop,
> anguish strikes me, I flee, but nothing had really happened. The
> energy dispersed in the affective cloud condenses, organizes itself,
> forces an action, orders a flight without 'real' motive. And it is this
> flight, with the affect that accompanies it, that teaches conscious-
> ness *that* there is something there, without consciousness being able
> to tell *what* it is. A warning of the *quod*, but not of the *quid*. It is the
> essence of the event that *there is* 'before' *what* there is.
>
> (*HJ*: 34–5)

12 The postmodern is not the age of psychoanalysis in that its disruption is
not the revelation of the unconscious speaking as a Nature (the unconscious become conscious). There is no simple translation of the repressed of history here.

13 See Lyotard, 'Rewriting Modernity', in *SubStance* 54.

14 See Lyotard, 'The Sign of History' in Bennington, Attridge and Young
(eds) 1986. On history as affect, see Lyotard's *L'Enthousiasme: la critique
Kantienne de l'histoire* (1986).

15 The epistemological condition of the postmodern is the major concern of *The Postmodern Condition* proper. The English edition appends 'Answering the Question: What is Postmodernism?', an extract from *Le Postmoderne expliqué aux enfants*, a text in which Lyotard addresses more directly the aesthetic and historical implications of the postmodern.

16 Briefly, no more speculative or rational history after Auschwitz (which is both real and irrational), no more historical materialism after Prague 1968 (which pits workers against the party), no more parliamentary liberalism after Paris 1968 (when the people rise up against the representative institution), no more economic liberalism after the crises of 1911, 1929 and 1974–9 (when market forces no longer give rise to general increase of wealth) (*PMEAE*: 53–5).

17 See *L'Assassinat de l'expérience par la peinture: Monory*, on subjective experience as a figure of modernity, opposed to the objectivity of a world. The postmodern would be the name of the non-coincidence of the two, of consciousness with self-consciousness, the predicament of modernity:

> Experience is a modern figure. It requires first a subject, the instance of an I, someone who speaks in the first person. It requires a temporal disposition like that of Augustine in *Confessions XI* (a modern work if ever there was one), where a perspective on the past, the present and the future is always taken from the point of view of an actual ungraspable consciousness.
>
> (*AEP*: 7)

18 In *The Postmodern Condition*, Lyotard takes a less productive route in confronting classicism with the narrativity it denies, a route that spills into the simplistic relativism of 'everything is narrative'. In *The Postmodern Condition*, Lyotard points out that traditional science (reposing on the classical claim to objective description) in fact has recourse to the very narrative it scorns (the epic of discovery) in order to legitimate the knowledge it offers (*PMC*: 27–8). This account of the narrativity of knowledge remains within narratology, producing a cultural sociology of knowledge at best (another way of putting this would be that this is a modernist rather than a postmodern displacement of classicism).

19 *Just Gaming* instances Judaism as a complementary instance of the privileging of the addressee, obligated by a deity whose position as sender s/he can never occupy (*JG*: 33, 38). Judaism is brought forward as a displacement of the modernist privileging of the sender by virtue of its insistence on the subject as always already addressed by an other. However, the fact that the sender's pole is always absolutely elided in Judaism differentiates Judaism from paganism by requiring a piety with regard to the inaccessible position of the divine sender (*JG*: 39).

20 The paradox of the man who says 'All Cretans are liars and I am from Crete' was 'resolved' by Russell as a distinction between a statement and a metastatement. As Lyotard points out in *Rudiments païens*, the humour of the paradox (something which philosophers are inclined to ignore) comes precisely from the fact that no metalanguage can ever be authoritatively established, can ever be preserved against being read as a first-order statement (*RP*: 143).

21 Theory is a subset of metanarratives: that kind of metanarrative which claims to put an end to time and achieve omnitemporality. Theory is the claim to speak an atemporal metalanguage. All theories are metanarratives, but not all metanarratives are theories.

22 For more on the case of Freud, see 'The Freudian Novel' in de Certeau 1986.

23 As Cohan and Shires put it in *Telling Stories*, the assumption of narratology is that 'stories structure the meanings by which a culture lives' (Cohan and Shires 1988: 1). Those 'meanings' are themselves considered as the presentation of signs for a subject. Narrative is the site governing the cultural manufacture and situation of both meaningful signs and a subjectivity capable of consuming them. Narratology is thus the positive critical knowledge of the form and content of the construction of cultural meaning. It ultimately dissolves all narratives into the nexus of social relations (issues of gender, race, class, etc.) from which they arise.

24 This point has been misunderstood by such critics as Frederic Jameson, who sees Lyotard's emphasis on invention as indistinguishable from the Poundian modernist drive to 'make it new':

> Lyotard's own aesthetic retains much of this protopolitical thrust; his commitment to cultural and formal innovation still valorizes culture and its powers in much the same spirit in which the Western avant-garde has done so since the *fin de siècle*.
> (Jameson's 'Foreword' to *The Postmodern Condition*, Lyotard 1984: xvi)

Likewise, Victor Burgin calls Lyotard an aesthetic modernist, though a political and cultural postmodernist (Burgin 1986: 176). The error proceeds from a misunderstanding of the distinction of invention, as Lyotard characterizes it, from that of innovation.

25 David Carroll deals with this point in *Paraesthetics* (Carroll 1987).

26 Lyotard's account of modernism here shares a common ground with Heidegger's description of the 'Age of the World Picture'. I shall discuss the nature of this community in Chapter 3.

27 Translation modified. I prefer 'it is not *one* genre' to 'it is not *a* genre' since what is at stake is Lyotard's refusal to accord to the political the status of a master narrative, the status of the genre in terms of which all other phrases may be understood, the genre in which all cows are black (or red). The use of 'a genre' risks lending the political just the wrong kind of 'special status'.

28 This would tend to be Fredric Jameson's argument about the postmodern.

29 I will deal with the reinscription of psychophysiological topology in terms of the 'great ephemeral skin' or libidinal band in *Economie libidinale* in Chapter 3.

30 Here we should remember Lyotard's caveat from *The Differend*, 'Politics is not everything, though, if by that one believes it to be the genre that contains all the genres' (*LD*: 139).

31 This parallels Derrida's insistence in 'White Mythology' (Derrida 1982) that there can be no metaphor of metaphor that would not itself be a

metaphor. The analogy perhaps helps to clarify the extent to which Lyotard's insistence on the 'little narrative' is more than simply a resentment of totality on the 'small is beautiful' model. The point is that there is no narrative of narrative, nor any governing concept of narrative, there are only narratives.

32 The same applies to Hayden White's account of narrative as structured by founding tropes (White 1975), insofar as those tropes, whilst they may structure the discourse of history, are themselves understood as second order connotations of an authorial *Weltanschauung*.

33 Lyotard has moved from speaking of narrative pragmatics and language games to the term 'phrase analysis' in order to avoid misunderstanding on this point.

34 Mieke Bal 1985. For a general study of narratology, more concerned to draw out the cultural implications of narrative constructions, see Cohan and Shires 1988.

35 Barthes's 'third meaning' is precisely an attempt to evade this functioning of semiotic analysis, to depart from his earlier account of the 'Rhetoric of the Image'. This is an attempt that leads him towards analysing film in terms of an 'obtuse' deconstructive trace. The obtuse meaning disturbs the assurance of critical metalanguage. This is because it is the signifier *for which there is no signified*, which cannot be reduced to its meaning (signification). It is the metonymy (the angle of a beard) which cannot be lent a metaphorical significance in the work of the critic, but which works over meaning nonetheless. This trace is not a supplementary meaning or connotation, but an awareness of a *signifiance*, the excessive work of the signifier which subverts meaning even as it constitutes it ('Rhetoric of the Image' and 'The Third Meaning' in Barthes 1977).

36 Thus, despite his scorn for the term 'postmodernism', I share Geoffrey Bennington's understanding of Lyotard as 'writing the event' (Bennington 1988).

37 An example of this insistence on a metonymic function irreducible to metaphor is the way in which the unconscious treats words as rebuses (not signifiers, *pace* Lacan) in dreams, discussed in Chapter 1.

3 POLITICS AND ETHICS

1 'The Work of Art in the Age of Mechanical Reproduction', in Benjamin 1970.

2 This parallels the shift that we noted from the spatial forms considered in *Discours, figure* to the temporal figure of the event in the reading of the postmodern by Lyotard.

3 Lyotard often spells capital this way, to indicate a usage derived from Marx's description.

4 Here is the description of the 'great ephemeral skin' of the libidinal band with which *Economie libidinale* opens:

> Open the supposed body and lay out all its surfaces: not only the skin with each of its folds, wrinkles, scars, with its great velvety spaces, attached to it the scalp and its mop of hair, the tender pubic fur, the nipples, the nails, the transparent corns under the heel, the

light fripperies, grafted with lashes, with eyelids, but also open and pin down, reveal, the great labia, the lesser labia with their blue mucous covered network, dilate the diaphragm of the anal sphincter, cut the black tunnel of the rectum and flatten it, then the colon, then the caecum, henceforth a ribbon with a tattered and shit-spattered surface, with your dressmaker's scissors opening the leg of an old trouser, go on, bring to the light of day the supposed interior of the small intestine, of the jejeunum, of the ileum, of the duodenum, or maybe from the other end slit into the mouth at the corners, dig out the tongue at its deepest root and split it, pin out the wings of the bats of the palate and its damp basements, open the trachea and make of it the skin of a hull under construction; armed with lancets and the finest pincers, take apart and set down the bundles and the bodies of the encephalon; and then the entire circulatory system intact flat on a great mattress, and the lymphatic system, and disassemble and place end to end all the fine bony pieces of the wrist, of the ankle, with all the layers of nervous tissue that surround the aqueous humour and the cavernous body of the penis, extract the great muscles, the great dorsal networks, spread them out like smooth sleeping dolphins. Do the work that the sun does when you sunbathe, the job that pot does.

And that is not all, not at all: attached to these lips we need a second mouth, a third, a great number of other mouths, one, many, vulvas, nipples ... [and so on]

(*EL*: 9–10)

American insurance laws probably make it advisable for me to dissuade the credulous from trying this at home. See the section on 'The Libidinal Band and the Organic Body' for further discussion.

5 In 'Matter and Time', Lyotard calls this an 'immaterialist materialism', which draws on contemporary physics to detach matter from any teleology, making matter the succession of singularities by chance and necessity (*LI*: 54).

6 This essay is a study of how the singular, intense, event of a striking worker's death is framed and neutralized by the discourse of historical representation in the accounts of it released to the press by the Renault company.

7 See Heath 1981.

8 This scorn for the organic body and the *Gestalt* marks the extent of Lyotard's divergence from Merleau-Ponty's phenomenology.

9 I haven't discussed the debt to Nietzsche for the thought of the singularity of the event which Lyotard shares with Deleuze and Guattari among others. I am wary of the temptation of grand philosophical narratives (for an example of their damaging effects see the preface to this book).

10 This analysis has affinities with Heidegger's argument in 'The Age of the World Picture' (Heidegger 1977). Where Lyotard writes 'Kapital', Heidegger writes 'modern man'. In the modern world, everything is conceived and grasped as picture, as representation (ibid: 126–7). According to Heidegger, the characteristic of modern science is to understand the

knowledge of nature as *research*. The modern 'thing' is thus different from the 'thing' from which Aristotelean empiricism argues, because nature and history become the objects of a representation that explains and existence is granted only to that which becomes object in this way. Science proceeds by comparison between such objects, so as to exclude the unique 'thing'. The total predominance of the methodology of research over any object of study indifferently reduces things to the status of becoming-objects-of-research.

11 This is perhaps most shocking in the chapter of *Economie libidinale* entitled 'The Desire named Marx'. Here, Lyotard parodies Althusser's division of Marx into a foolish young humanist and a later scientific historical materialist by reading Marx in terms of a tension between a foolish young woman Marx who desires, and an old lawyer Marx who prosecutes desire. In the course of the narrative desire goes wild as the old critical Marx begins to take a rather fetishistic interest in the young woman. The chapter is working over the ambivalent relation of fascination and condemnation that Marx has towards the 'perversion' of commodity fetishism that he condemns in capitalism.

12 '*Acéphale*', literally 'headless', was the name of a group and the title of a review largely run by Georges Bataille from 1936–9. Acephalic man renames the Nietzschean superman so as to distinguish it from Fascism: this figure of the eternal recurrence is not a new head for society but the absence of head. Without political or religious leadership, devoid of cognitive regimes of understanding, man is opened to the 'ecstatic time' or 'time-explosion' of the event, 'a world like a bleeding wound, endlessly creating and destroying particular finite beings' (Bataille 1985: 199–201).

13 Bennington 1988: 9.

14 David Carroll's *Paraesthetics* provides an excellent detailed summary of Lyotard's negotiation with Kant (Carroll 1987: 173–84).

15 Let us be clear that this issuing of a prescriptive is what distinguishes conservative politics (the demand for a reactionary transformation of society back to its former glory) from the absence of politics.

16 This account of the incommensurability of prescription and description is extremely important for *Just Gaming*, which tends to attack the conflation of prescription and description on the basis of certain exemplary historical terrors. The problem that might arise here, were it not for the distinction between reflective and cognitive judgment, is that an argument about the impossibility of historico-political grounds for judgment is being validated on historico-political grounds.

17 'The problem is indeed one of translation and translatability ... language games are not translatable because, if they were, they would not be language games. It is as if one wanted to translate the rules and strategies of chess into those of checkers' (*JG*: 53).

18 The book is arranged in numbered sections, with longer 'notices' interspersed. Since it is available in translation, I have used page number references throughout, doing a certain injustice to its organization, which is that of the genre of the philosophical note- or sketchbook.

19 This is an expansion of the pragmatic instances of narrative discussed in

Chapter 2. Meaning is no longer opposed to the pragmatic, but is a component of it, distinct from the referent.

20 As Lyotard puts it later on, in section No. 102:

> For there to be no phrase is impossible, for there to be *And a phrase* is necessary. It is necessary to make a linkage. This is not an obligation, a *Sollen* [an ought to], but a necessity, a *Müssen* [a must]. To link is necessary, but how to link is not (*LD*: 66).

21 One instance of a play being linked to a revolution is the Earl of Essex's staging of Shakespeare's *Richard II* on the eve of an abortive coup attempt against Elizabeth I.

22 '[I]n the absence of a phrase regimen or of a genre of discourse that enjoys a universal authority to decide ... the linkage (whichever one it is) necessarily wrong[s] the regimens or genres whose possible phrases remain unactualized' (*LD*: xii).

23 Lyotard is particularly concerned to use Adorno's reading of Auschwitz to mark that with which the Hegelian speculative discourse of experience cannot deal, which cannot be 'known', even by dialectical sublation (*LD*: 86–91).

24 *Just Gaming*'s account of the totalitarian derivation of prescriptives from descriptives is transposed into the rule of the *normative* genre in the linking of phrases by *The Differend*. In the normative genre, a prescription is made the object of a description:

> *You ought to carry out such and such an action* formulates the prescription. The normative adds: *It is a norm decreed by x or y* (No. 155). It puts the prescriptive phrase in quotation marks.
>
> (*LD*: 142)

This 'citation' makes the law representable, an object of cognition, rather than the indeterminate 'Idea' or irrepresentable law that is the object of the prescriptive language game. The difference between an obligation to 'be just' and a norm of 'Be American' is that the one imposes a respect for the indeterminacy of the event; one must seek to be just without knowing in advance what it means to be just. In case of the norm, what it is to be American is not a matter for experiment; 'America' is not an idea, but an object of cognition, defined by the normative laws issued by 'we Americans'. The authority of the norm, or represented law, depends upon its suppression of all idiolects, any language which is not that of the 'we'. The instance of the speaker ('we Americans') functions in the normative genre as a universal subject capable of determining the one right linkage at any point. The effect of the norm is that the phrase-event by which the addressee is obligated without knowing the exact nature of the obligation, 'this threat, this marvel, and this anxiety, namely the nothingness of a "what-is-to-be-linked"' are thus normalized' (*LD*: 143).

25 The aborigines have a strange habit of stopping elevators, the mining company's earth-movers trace a mysterious writing on the landscape, the aborigines come to an agreement with Western technology by taking a green transport plane and flying it over the horizon in an allegory of the green ants, Kinski shows entomology as madness, a suburban woman

waits indefinitely for her lost dog at a mine entrance. These are not so
much resolutions as insistences on an alterity at work within and against a
discourse that might seek to resolve the conflict. A new filmic idiom
demands a new idiom for thinking the clash of the universal (imperial
progress) and the local (tribal), of the modern and the archaic, recognizes
that any rush to a 'progressive solution' would pre-judge the case, against
the aborigines.

26 An everyday example of this is the way in which we talk about soccer
referees. The judgment we pass on a referee's performance is not simply a
question of whether all his or her decisions were correct but also a
question of whether he or she did a good job, allowed a good game.

27 '... he who states the just is himself as caught in the very sphere of
language as those who will be the recipients of his prescriptions, and may
eventually be judged by the judge. The judge is in the same sphere of
language, which means that he will be considered just only by his actions,
if it can be seen that he judges well, that he is really just ... And his actions
can be judged to be just only when one adds up all the accounts. But in
matters of opinion there is no adding up of accounts, no balance sheet'
(*JG*: 28).

28 In talking about 'reading' I hope to be 'sav[ing] the honour of the name'
(*PMC*: 82), as it were.

29 The pun is Derrida's, at least.

30 Lewis Carroll's writings are consistently obsessed with temporal paradoxes: we remember the Red Queen in *Through the Looking Glass* who has to
run extremely fast in order to stay in one place (Lewis Carroll 1965: 135).
In 'A Hemispherical Problem' and 'Where Does the Day Begin?' in
Original Games and Puzzles, consideration of the international date line
produces an absolutely unaccountable time (ibid.: 1054–6). Gilles Deleuze's *Logique du sens* (1969) provides a brilliant account of the paradoxes
of the time of the event in Carroll's writings.

31 As Baudrillard points out in *Simulations*, capitalism doesn't have contradictions, it *is* contradiction; contradiction drives rather than flaws the
capitalist system:

> Capital in fact has never been linked by a contract to the society it
> dominates. It is a sorcery of the social relation, it is a *challenge to
> society* and should be responded to as such. It is not a scandal to be
> denounced according to moral and economic rationality, but a
> challenge to take up according to symbolic law. (Baudrillard 1983:
> 29–30).

32 As Lyotard phrases it in 'A Memorial for Marxism: for Pierre Souyri' in
Peregrinations:

> If *Capital* had been the critique, or a critique, of political economy,
> it was because it had forced the *differend* to be heard where it lay,
> hidden beneath the harmony, or at least beneath the universal.
> Marx had shown that there were at least two idioms or two genres
> hidden in the universal language of capital: the MCM [Money-
> Commodity-Money] spoken by the capitalist, and the CMC
> spoken by the wage earner ... there was between them a difference

which operated in such a way that in the transcription of a certain
situation, experience or referent expressed by one in the idiom of
the other, this referent became unrecognizable for the first one, and
the result of the transcription became incommensurable with the
initial expression. The 'same' thing, a day of work, said in the two
genres, became two things, just as the 'same' affective situation
which is tragic for one of the protagonists can be a melodrama for
the other.

(P: 60–1)

33 This marks Lyotard's differend with Paul Virilio's Speed and Politics: An
Essay on Dromology, where reading is merely delay posed against the speed
of the propaganda politics of fascism:

> 'Propaganda must be made directly by words and images, not by
> writing' states Goebbels, who was himself a great promoter of
> audiovisuals in Germany. Reading implies time for reflection, a
> slowing-down that destroys the mass's dynamic efficiency.

(Virilio 1986: 5)

As the reader will have gathered, Lyotard's sense of the 'reflection'
involved in reading is far more complex, disruptive and Kantian than
Virilio's 'slowing-down'. The problem is that for Virilio, speed is the pure
language of all temporality, to which reading as delay is merely opposed as
absence of temporality. According to Virilio time is a unified quality,
subject merely to quantitative accelerations. Thus, time is utterly commensurable, and is introduced in terms in which despair masks itself as 'facing
reality' in a manner reminiscent of the Dukakis electoral campaign of
1988:

> The time has come, it seems, to face the facts: revolution is move-
> ment but movement is not a revolution. Politics is only a gear-shift,
> and revolution only its overdrive ... in the same way, 'political
> socialism', by its political nature (polis) usually fails when the accel-
> eration of civil war towards urban collision stops, itself being
> nothing other than ... [sic].

(ibid.: 18–19)

34 Lyotard decisively distances himself from Baudrillard over the latter's
privileging of the situationist concept of 'spectacle', preferring to concentrate on capitalism's technological relation to time and space ('Towards
an Architecture of Exile', conversation with Giovanna Borradori in Diani
and Ingraham (eds) 1989: 15–16).

35 Reading might be paralleled in this sense to Lyotard's remarks on
Cézanne's use of colour as 'a strategy of being receptive to the matter of
sensations, to the existence rather than the essence of the painted subject'
(P: 19–20). Here 'sensations' stand for the irreducibility of the seen to the
understood, the singularity of affects paralleling the temporality of the
event. As Lyotard puts it, in looking at a Cézanne, 'we have to make our
condition that of a suspicious, exacting receiver, with reception focused on
the unmistakable, uncanny "fact" that "there is" something hidden here
and now, regardless of what it is' (P: 19).

171

36 In the light of the furore over de Man's juvenile Fascist writings,we may make an observation here. The significance of this version of the predicament or paradox of modernity for de Man may be grasped from the violence of his reading of Nietzsche. De Man seems to be setting Nietzsche up as too much of a straw man when he contrasts a commitment to modernity of which there cannot be 'any doubt' to a 'shrill grandiloquence of tone' (de Man 1983: 148). The effect of this is to make the suspicion of modernity that de Man then traces in Nietzsche into *de Man's own* suspicion, something for which de Man's reading is necessary. This curious relapse into the position of the critic as purveyor of latent meaning marks a desire. It's the more curious given that it is precisely what 'The Rhetoric of Blindness' accuses Derrida of doing to Rousseau. De Man, it seems to me, doesn't do justice to Nietzsche because he must make sure that it is he who has learnt the lesson of history, the lesson that modernism is impossible, because the past is irrevocable and unforgettable. De Man wants to make the lesson of the impossibility of modernity his own, and he misreads Nietzsche in order to do it. De Man's writing evades his past, as it evades the necessity of its own errors, but this amounts to refusing in the first place the delusion of auto-critique, of the negative appropriation of subjective identity. De Man refuses to forget the past by making it the object of a cognitive representation that will no longer haunt us. Nor does he simply consign the past to oblivion, but evokes its necessity and irrecoverability as a counter to the positive appropriation of identity in the present. De Man's writing is haunted by a sense of the past that it will not delude itself it can come to terms with. And furthermore, de Man resists the turn to a personal past which, we can now see, could have been used to provide, not a way of inhabiting history, but a way of inhabiting the necessity and impossibility of inhabiting history.

37 Thus, the problematic of literary temporality finishes up as a matter of inside/outside oppositions, a topology of knowledge. So, in the reading of Baudelaire on Guys in *Blindness and Insight*, temporal difference opens in the instant, not as an affirmation of the displacement of the event, but as a 'perspective of distance' (de Man 1983: 157), remaining within the calculation of space by ratios. This difference is that of writing, writing as 'a sequence of geometric figures' (ibid.: 160). What I want to point out is that this becomes a kind of metaphysics of writing: since time is merely the alternation between geometric figures, 'a successive movement that involves at least two distinct moments' (ibid.: 161). This understanding of time as alternation, opposition, would precisely permit the consideration of the relationship between two geometrical figures as itself a *geometrical relation*. Nothing escapes the rational consciousness, not even its own inescapability. The unaccountability of time is accounted for as writing's experience of itself in literature.

38 I have tried to develop this argument in a reading of Freud's *Moses and Monotheism* entitled 'Canon and On: From Concept to Figure' in Readings 1989.

MOBILE SUPPLEMENT II: WORK

1 After beginning with an introduction to phenomenology in one of those series of introductory studies which we are wont to denigrate as facile (*La Phénoménologie, 'Que Sais-Je?'* 625, 1954), Lyotard wrote more or less anonymously for *Pouvoir Ouvrier* and *Socialisme ou Barbarie*, Marxist journals.

2 'Clerisy' is Coleridge's term for a general priestly ruling class charged with governing the culture and morals of the nation. It would not be restricted to clergy, but would comprise teachers, bureaucrats and other professionals insofar as the authority that they exercise is quasi-priestly. The term can be found in *On the Constitution of the Church and State According to Idea of Each.*

3 Blake 1971: 218n. The text of the poem is:

The Chimney Sweeper

A little black thing among the snow
Crying *'weep, 'weep* in notes of woe!
Where are thy father and mother, say?
'They are both gone up to the church to pray.

'Because I was happy upon the heath
And smiled among the winter's snow,
They clothed me in the clothes of death
And taught me to sing the notes of woe.

'And because I am happy and dance and sing,
They think they have done me no injury –
And are gone to praise God and his priest and king,
Who make up a Heaven of our misery.'

Bibliography

An extensive authorized bibliography of works by and about Lyotard, compiled by Eddie Yeghiayan, is appended to *Peregrinations*. References are to English language translations, where available. Works are listed in order of first publication.

Adorno, Theodor (1973) *Negative Dialectics*, New York: Continuum. 1st edn 1966.

Adorno, Theodor and Horkheimer, Max (1979) *Dialectic of Enlightenment*, trans. Cumming, London: Verso. 1st edn 1944.

Althusser, Louis (1971) *Lenin and Philosophy*, trans. Ben Brewster, London: NLB.

(1977) *For Marx*, trans. Ben Brewster, London: NLB.

Althusser, Louis and Etienne Balibar (1970) *Reading Capital*, trans. Ben Brewster, London: NLB.

Austin, J. L. (1962) *How to do Things with Words*, Oxford: Oxford University Press.

Balibar, Etienne (see Althusser, Louis).

Bal, Mieke (1985) *Narratology: Introduction to the Theory of Narrative*, trans. van Boheemen, Toronto: Toronto University Press.

Barthes, Roland (1972) *Mythologies*, trans. Annette Lavers, London: Jonathan Cape.

(1977) *Image Music Text*, ed. and trans. Stephen Heath, London: Collins/Fontana.

Bataille, Georges (1985) *Visions of Excess*, trans. Stoekl, Manchester: Manchester University Press.

Baudrillard, Jean (1983) *Simulations*, trans. Foss, Patton and Beitchman, New York: Semiotext(e).

(1988) *The Ecstasy of Communication*, trans. B. and C. Schutze, ed. Lotringer, New York: Semiotext(e).

(1988) *America*, trans. Chris Turner, London: Verso.

Belsey, Catherine (1980) *Critical Practice*, London: Methuen.

Benjamin, Walter (1970) *Illuminations*, London: Jonathan Cape.

Bennington, Geoffrey (1986) ed. with Attridge and Young, *Post-Structuralism and the Question of History*, Cambridge: Cambridge University Press.

(1988) *Lyotard: Writing the Event*, Manchester: Manchester University Press.

Blake, William (1971) *Blake: The Complete Poems*, eds Stephenson and Erdman, London: Longman.

Breton, André (1979) *Manifestes du surréalisme*, Paris: Gallimard.

Burgin, Victor (1986) *The End of Art Theory*, Atlantic Highlands: Humanities Press.

Butor, Michel (1969) *Les Mots dans la peinture*, Geneva: Skira.

Carroll, David (1987) *Paraesthetics: Foucault, Lyotard, Derrida*, London: Routledge.

Carroll, Lewis (1965) *Works*, London: Spring Books (Hamlyn).

Cohan, Steven and Shires, Linda (1988) *Telling Stories: A Theoretical Analysis of Narrative Fiction*, London: Routledge.

Coleridge, Samuel Taylor (1972) *On the Constitution of the Church and State According to the Idea of Each*, ed. John Barrell, London: J. M. Dent and Sons. 1st edn 1830.

Coward, Rosalind and Ellis, John (1977) *Language and Materialism*, London: Routledge & Kegan Paul.

de Certeau, Michel (1986) *Heterologies*, trans. B. Massumi, Minneapolis: Minnesota University Press.

Deleuze, Gilles (1969) *Logique du sens*, Paris: Minuit.

de Man, Paul (1983) *Blindness and Insight*, 2nd edn, London: Methuen. 1st edn 1971.

(1979) *Allegories of Reading*, New Haven: Yale University Press.

(1989) *Critical Writings, 1953–1978*, ed. Lindsay Waters, Minneapolis, University of Minnesota Press.

Derrida, Jacques (1976) *Of Grammatology*, trans. Gayatri Spivak, Baltimore: Johns Hopkins University Press. 1st edn 1967.

(1978) *Writing and Difference*, trans. Alan Bass, London: Routledge & Kegan Paul. 1st edn 1967.

(1981) *Dissemination*, trans. Barbara Johnson, London: Athlone Press. 1st edn 1972.

(1982) *Margins of Philosophy*, trans. Alan Bass, Chicago: University of Chicago Press. 1st edn 1972.

(1986) 'But Beyond...', *Critical Inquiry 13 no. 1* (Fall).

Dews, Peter (1984) 'The Letter and the Line', *Diacritics* vol. 14 no. 1 (Fall).

Diani, Marco and Ingraham, Catherine, eds (1989) *Restructuring Architectural Theory*, Evanston: Northwestern University Press.

Ducrot, Oswald and Todorov, Tzvetan (1979) *Encyclopedic Dictionary of the Sciences of Language*, trans. C. Porter, Oxford: Blackwell.

Eagleton, Terry (1987) Review of Lyotard in *Times Literary Supplement* (February 20).

Ellis, John (see Coward, Rosalind).

Erdman, David (1977) *Blake: Prophet against Empire*, Princeton, N.J.: Princeton University Press.

Foster, Hal (1983) ed., *The Anti-Aesthetic*, San Francisco: Bay Press.

(1985) *Recodings*, San Francisco: Bay Press.

Foucault, Michel (1965) *Madness and Civilization: A History of Insanity in the Age of Reason*, trans. Richard Howard, New York: Random House.

(1979) *Discipline and Punish: The Birth of the Prison*, trans. Alan Sheridan, London: Peregrine Books.

Freud, Sigmund (1966), *Standard Edition of the Complete Psychological Works of Sigmund Freud*, ed. & trans. James Strachey, London: Hogarth Press.

Gasché, Rodolphe (1986) *The Tain of the Mirror*, Cambridge, Mass.: Harvard University Press.

Goldmann, Lucien (1964) *The Hidden God*, trans. P. Thody, London: Routledge & Kegan Paul.

Hassan, Ihab (1980) *Romanticism, Modernism, Postmodernism*, Lewisburg: Bucknell University Press.

(1987) *The Postmodern Turn*, Columbus: Ohio State University Press.

Heath, Stephen (1981) *Questions of Cinema*, Bloomington: Indiana University Press.

Hegel, Georg Wilhelm Friedrich (1977), *Phenomenology of Spirit*, trans. A. V. Miller, Oxford: Clarendon Press.

Heidegger, Martin (1977) *The Question Concerning Technology & Other Essays*, trans. Lovitt, New York: Harper Colophon.

Horkheimer, Max (see Adorno, Theodor).

Hutcheon, Linda (1985) *A Theory of Parody: The Teachings of Twentieth Century Art Forms*, London: Methuen.

(1988) *A Poetics of Postmodernism: History, Theory, Fiction*, London: Routledge.

Ingraham, Catherine (see Diani, Marco).

Jakobson, Roman (1971) *Selected Writings II*, The Hague: Mouton.

Jencks, Charles (1987) *What is Post-Modernism?*, New York: Academy Editions/St. Martin's Press.

Kant, Immanuel (1980) *The Critique of Judgement*, trans. J. C. Meredith, Oxford: Clarendon Press.

Kroker, Arthur and Cook, David (1986) *The Postmodern Scene*, New York: St Martin's Press.

Lacan, Jacques (1977) *The Four Fundamental Concepts of Psychoanalysis*, ed. J.-A. Miller, trans. A. Sheridan, London: Penguin Books. 1st edn 1973.

Lyotard, Jean-François (1954) *La Phénoménologie*, 'Que Sais-Je?' no. 625, Paris: Presses Universitaire de France.

(1971) *Discours, figure*, Paris: Klincksieck.

(1973) *Dérive à partir de Marx et Freud*, Paris: Union Générale d'Editions 10/18.

(1983) *Des Dispositifs pulsionnels*, 2nd edn, Paris: Christian Bourgeois. 1st edn 1973.

(1974) *Economie libidinale*, Paris: Minuit.

(1977) *Instructions païennes*, Paris: Galilée.

(1977) *Rudiments païens: genre dissertatif*, Paris: Union Générale d'Editions 10/18.

(1977), *Les Transformateurs Duchamp*, Paris: Galilée.

(1977) *Récits tremblants*, Paris: Galilée.

(1979) *Le Mur du pacifique*, Paris: Galilée.

(1984) *The Postmodern Condition*, trans. Bennington and Massumi, Minneapolis: University of Minnesota Press. 1st edn 1979.

(1980) *Sur la constitution du temps par la couleur dans les oeuvres récentes d'Albert Ayme*, Paris: Editions Traversière.

(1988) *The Differend: Phrases in Dispute*, trans. G. Van den Abbeele, Minneapolis: University of Minnesota Press. 1st edn. 1983.

(1983) 'The Dream-Work does not Think', trans. Mary Lydon, Oxford Literary Review vol. 6 no. 1.

(1984) *L'Assassinat de l'expérience par la peinture: Monory*, Paris: Castor Astral.

(1984) *Tombeau de l'intellectuel et autres papiers*, Paris: Galilée.

(1984) *Driftworks*, trans. R. McKeon *et al.*, New York: Semiotext(e).

(1984) 'Interview' with Georges van den Abbeele, *Diacritics 14 no. 3* (Fall).

(1985) ed., *La Faculté de juger*, Paris: Minuit.

(1986) *Le Postmoderne expliqué aux enfants*, Paris: Galilée.

(1986) *L'Enthousiasme: la critique Kantienne de l'histoire*, Paris: Galilée.

(1987) *Que Peindre? Adami Arakawa Buren* (2 vols), Paris: Editions de la Différence.

(1987) 'Rewriting Modernity', *SubStance no. 54*.

(1988) *Peregrinations: Law, Form, Event*, New York: Columbia University Press.

(1988) *Heidegger et 'les juifs'*, Paris: Galilée.

(1988) *L'Inhumain: causeries sur le temps*, Paris: Galilée.

(1985) and Chaput, Thierry, eds, *Les Immatériaux*, Paris: Editions du Centre Georges Pompidou.

Lyotard, Jean-François and Jean-Loup Thébaud (1985) *Just Gaming*, trans. Godzich, Minneapolis: University of Minnesota Press. 1st edn 1979.

MacCabe, Colin (1978) *James Joyce and the Revolution of the Word*, London: Macmillan.

Melville, Stephen (1986) *Philosophy Beside Itself: On Deconstruction and Modernism*, Minneapolis: University of Minnesota Press.

Merleau-Ponty, Maurice (1964) *The Primacy of Perception*, ed. and trans. Edie *et al.*, Evanston: Northwestern University Press.

(1964) *Sense and Non-Sense*, trans. H. L. and P. A. Dreyfus, Evanston: Northwestern University Press.

(1968) *The Visible and the Invisible*, ed. Lefort, trans. Lingis, Evanston: Northwestern University Press.

Miller, J. Hillis (1987) *The Ethics of Reading*, New York: Columbia University Press.

Readings, Bill (1989) 'Canon and On: from Concept to Figure', *Journal of the American Academy of Religion* 57 no. 1.

Rousseau, Jean-Jacques and Herder (1986), *On the Origin of Language: Two Essays*, trans. Moran and Gode, Chicago: Chicago University Press.

Saussure, Ferdinand de (1966) *Course in General Linguistics*, trans. Wade Baskin, New York: McGraw-Hill.

Shires, Linda (see Cohan, Steven).

Sim, Stuart (1986) 'Lyotard and the Politics of Antifoundationalism', *Radical Philosophy* (Autumn).

Smith, Adam (1979) *The Wealth of Nations*, London: Pelican Books, 1st. edn 1776.

Thompson, Edward P. (1968) *The Making of the English Working Class*, London: Penguin.

Todorov, Tzvetan (see Ducrot, Oswald).

Virilio, Paul (1986) *Speed and Politics: An Essay on Dromology*, trans. Polizzotti, New York: Semiotext(e).

White, Hayden (1975) *Metahistories*, Baltimore: Johns Hopkins University Press.

Wimsatt, William K. (1966) *Hateful Contraries*, Lexington: University of Kentucky Press.

Index

Adorno, Theodor 87, 89, 103; and Auschwitz 22, 169 n23; *Dialectic of Enlightenment* 93
aesthetics: of sublime xx; and singularity xxii, 23–8; postmodern and modern 53–6, 72–4; and politics 79–109; and experimentation 129; *see also* judgment, invention, postmodernism
affect 101, 127; *see also* resistance
Althusser, Louis 40, 69, 78, 143–4; and linguistic totality 157 n7
anamnesis: defined in glossary xxix: xxviii, 58, 62, 104, 137–9; *see also* immemorial
aneconomic 73; *see also* resistance
Aristotle 167 n10
Augustine: *Confessions* and modernity 164 n17
Auschwitz: 22, 121–2, 124–7, 137, 164 n16, 169 n23; *see also* immemorial
Austin, J. L. xviii; *see* performance.

Bakhtin, Mikhail: inverted commas around 162 n4
Bal, Mieke 81; *Narratology: Introduction to the Theory of Narrative* 166 n34
Barthes, Roland 157 n9, 87; and third meaning 166 n35; and rhetoric 32; *Image, Music, Text* 160 n32, 160 n33; *Mythologies* 157 n9

Bataille, Georges: *Visions of Excess* 168 n12
Baudrillard, Jean 55, 134, 142; *America* 162 n4; *Simulations* 169 n31
Belsey, Catherine: *Critical Practice* 157 n8
Benjamin, Walter 87; *Illuminations* 166 n1
Bennington, Geoffrey xxi, 105, 154 n3, 161 n42, 166 n42, 166 n36; *Lyotard: Writing the Event* xx, 154 n3, 161 n42, 168 n13
Blake, William 31, 140, 142–5, 149–53; 'London' text of 142–3; discussion of 149–52; 'The Chimney Sweeper' text of 150, 173 n3
blocking together: defined in glossary xxx, 20, 25, 50, 58; *see also* incommensurable, figure, rebus
Brecht, Bertolt 95, 143
Breton, André: *Manifestes du surréalisme* 160 n37
Burgin, Victor: *The End of Art Theory* 165 n24
Butor, Michel: *Les Mots dans la peinture* 159 n28; *Mobile* 155 n1

Caesar, Julius 120
capitalism 77, 147; and contradiction 170 n31: and desire 47; and the incommensurable 101–5; resistance to 87–93; and

178

Erdman, David: *Blake: Prophet
Against Empire* 143
ethics: defined in glossary xxxi; and
reading xix; vs. politics xx, xxiv,
37, 87, 105; *see also* judgment,
invention, deconstruction
event: defined in glossary xxxi, 43,
56, 57, 97, 126–7; vs. moment 55,
57; and figure 55; and judgment
of 80–5, 106; and resistance to
capitalism 127; *see also* differend,
ethics, immemorial, singularity,
history, figure, narrative
exchange: law of 102, 129–32; and
work 142–7; *see also* capitalism,
commodification, Marxism
experiment or invention: defined in
glossary xxxi

Faurisson, Robert 122
figure: defined in glossary xxxi;
terms to evoke 159 n28; as
pointing 15; in Mallarmé 28; and
psychoanalysis 43–52; as trope
3–52, 103; and narrative 58–62,
69–72, 80–5; as temporal figure
17–23, 53, 56; as resistance xix,
88–93; vs. text 3; vs. discourse
xix, 70; and singularity xxiii,
126–7; *see also* blocking together,
incommensurability
Foster, Hal: *The Anti-Aesthetic* 162
n6; *Recodings* 162 n6
Foucault, Michel: and Derrida
60–1, 78; and Althusser on Blake
144–8; *Madness and Civilization: A
History of Insanity in the Age of
Reason* 60; *Discipline and Punish* 61
Frankfurt School *see* Habermas,
Jürgen and Adorno, Theodor
Freud, Sigmund 44, 103, 165 n22;
Lyotard's interest in xxix; and
indeterminate judgment 51;
Lyotard's drift away from 52;
and *Nachträglichkeit* 59; and
resistance to theory 70; *Beyond the
Pleasure Principle* 71; *Moses and
Monotheism* 172 n38
futurism 141

Gasche, Rodolphe 156 n4

generative grammar *see* Noam
Chomsky
Genesis 81–2
genres 116–17; *see also* linkage,
phrase
Godzich, Wlad 136
Goldmann, Lucien: *The Hidden God*
157 n7
Guattari, Felix: and debt to
Nietzsche 167 n9; and capitalism
77

Habermas, Jürgen xxi, 119–20
Hassan, Ihab 55; *Romanticism,
Modernism, Postmodernism* 162 n4
Heath, Stephen 98; *Questions of
Cinema* 167 n7
Hegel, Georg Wilhelm Friedrich
65, 74; *Phenomenology of Spirit*
15–16
Heidegger, Martin: Derrida's
reading of 156 n2; and the thing
167 n10: 'Age of the World
Picture' 165 n26, 167 n10
Herzog, Werner: *Where Green Ants
Dream* 169 n25, 118, 124
historical materialism: 110; *see also*
Marxism
history: 53–63, 74; and the event
100–4; and narrative 76–97; has
a stutter xiv, 99; *see also*
modernism, postmodernism,
narrative, the event
Hitler, Adolf 79, 109
Holbein, Hans: *Ambassadors* 26
Horkheimer, Max: *Dialectic of
Enlightenment* 93
humanism 86, 99, 138, 143
Hutcheon, Linda: *A Poetics of
Postmodernism: History, Theory,
Fiction* 161 n2; *A Theory of Parody:
The Teachings of 20th Century Art
Form* 55

idea 109–10; *see also* judgment
ideology: and deconstruction 39–40,
89; and narrative 74–80
ideology critique 92, 95; *see also*
commodification, Althusser,
Marxism, capitalism

narratology: and classicism 164
n18; assumptions of 165 n23;
impossibility of 63, 71–2, 80–5;
and ideology critique 78; and
history 97; *see also* theory,
narrative
New Criticism 25
New Historicism 60–1, 156 n3
Nietzsche, Friedrich: vitalism 154
n4; and the singularity of the
event 167 n9; de Man's reading
of 135, 172 n36
Nixon, Richard 120–1

organic body vs. libidinal band 93,
97–101

pagan: defined in glossary xxxiii,
66, 69, 138–9; *see also* resistance
paradox: of Cretan liar 164 n20; in
Lewis Carroll 169 n30; of
modernity, for de Man 172 n36
paralogism vs. innovation *see*
invention
paraphrase: attacks of xx; problems
of xxi–xxvi; ruled out xxiv
performance: of introductions xxi,
xxii, 38–9, 77, 80–5; of theatre of
representation 94; and language
games 107; *see also* Austin,
narrative
perspective: 3, 25, 149; *see also* text
philosophy: 123–5
phonocentrism: Derrida's attack on
Saussure 158 n17
phrase 65, 113–19; and reading
xviii; phrase analysis 77; and
language games 107; and names
119–20; and political resistance
127, 132–3; *see also* differend,
event, linkage, language game,
genre
Picasso, Pablo 73
Plato xxiii, xxvii, 38, 96, 105, 111
politics xxvii; a matter of judgment
xxiii, 105–13, 127; isn't
everything 165 n30; and
narrative 74–80; vs. ethics xxiv,
37, 87, 105; deconstructed 88–93,
101; of representation 86–8;

space of 95; and totalitarianism
109–10; *see also* rhetoric,
Marxism, deconstruction, theory,
aesthetics
positivism *see* epistemology
postmodernism: as defined in
glossary xxxiv; xxvii; and
narrative 64–9, 80–5; and history
58–65; and aesthetics 72–4; and
politics 74–80
Pouvoir Ouvrier 173 n1
psychoanalysis: desire and the
figural 44–52, 97; *see also* the
unconscious

reading: as resistance xix, xx, 52,
88; as event xix, 133; and
paraphrase xxv; and literary
criticism xxv; vs. seeing 17–23,
50; and textual reduction 50, 52;
and theory 71; and ethics of 106,
127–9, 133–4; and anamnesis
137–9; and linkage 116; and de
Man 134–7
rebus: and figure 49, 166 n37; and
incommensurability 48, 50–2; *see
also* vision, blocking together
relativism *see also* epistemology,
indifference
representation: and introductions
xxii; and judgment 125; and
work 141–2; politics of xxvii,
86–8, 110–13; space of 88–93,
theatre of 92–9, 103–4, 109; and
figure 20; and the unconscious
44; and postmodernity 56; vs.
presentation via phrase 114–16;
and differend 122; *see also* text,
vision, politics, commodification,
totalitarianism
resistance xviii, 66; to concept xix;
of figure against text 4, 5; to
politics 88, 101; to capitalism
127; and anamnesis 138; and
work 148–9; *see also* figure,
theory, pagan, differend,
aneconomic, work, paralogism,
event, affect, incommen-
surability, tensor
rhetoric: and politics 86; and